Synchronizing the Body in Ancient Medicine and Philosophy

CHRONOI

Zeit, Zeitempfinden, Zeitordnungen

Time, Time Awareness, Time Management

Edited by
Eva Cancik-Kirschbaum, Christoph Markschies
and Hermann Parzinger

on behalf of the Einstein Center Chronoi

Volume 22

Synchronizing the Body in Ancient Medicine and Philosophy

Edited by
Giouli Korobili, Kassandra J. Miller and Philip J. van der Eijk

DE GRUYTER

ISSN 2701-1453
ISBN 978-3-11-223568-3
ISBN 978-3-11-223569-0 (PDF)
ISBN 978-3-11-223570-6 (EPUB)
DOI https://doi.org/10.1515/9783112235690

Library of Congress Control Number: 2026934784

Bibliographic information published by the Deutsche Nationalbibliothek
The Deutsche Nationalbibliothek lists this publication in the Deutsche Nationalbibliografie; detailed bibliographic data are available on the Internet at http://dnb.dnb.de.

De Gruyter and Walter de Gruyter GmbH are part of De Gruyter Brill.
www.degruyterbrill.com

Questions about General Product Safety Regulation:
productsafety@degruyterbrill.com

Contents

Giouli Korobili, Kassandra J. Miller and Philip J. van der Eijk

Introduction

Time is of the essence in medicine, and Greek and Roman doctors were acutely aware of this. The famous first Hippocratic *Aphorism*, which sums up what medicine is all about, contains three references to time: the brevity of human life in comparison to the length of time and experience it takes to master the art of medicine; the fleeting nature of "opportunity" (*kairos*), the right time for medical intervention; and the difficulty of the doctor's "judgement" (*krisis*), often to be made under great time pressure in the face of the rapidly changing condition of the patient.

Many ancient medical texts confirm the impression that time, timing and time management were a constant concern for Greek and Roman physicians: symptoms had to be observed at the right time, or at the right moment between time intervals (the so-called "critical days"), or over the right period of time, in order to cast a correct and accurate prognosis; treatment had to be applied at the right, critical moment, or for the correct length of time. But what counted as right or correct, and how this should be determined, was subject to difference of opinion among the experts.

Comparable concerns about the right moment, measure, and judgement are found in philosophical texts, from Presocratic reflections on cosmic cycles to Aristotle's analyses of motion and change. Heraclitus spoke of cosmic processes which are governed by measures, cycles of time and the balance of opposites (22 B30; cf. 22 B94 DK), while Stoic writers would later link timely action to living in accordance with cosmic order (Cleanthes, *Hymn to Zeus* [*SVF* I 537]; Seneca, *On the Shortness of Life* 10).

In medicine, diseases were divided into acute ("fast", *oxus, celer*) and chronic ("slow", *chronios, tardus*) diseases, the former requiring rapid action resulting in immediate success or failure, the latter calling for patient, long term monitoring and care with uncertain outcome. But, again, there was debate among ancient medical writers about the classification of some diseases, and about the criteria for distinguishing acute from chronic disease.

Note: We are grateful to the Directors and the staff of the Einstein Center Chronoi for their support of the project "Synchronizing the Body in Ancient Medicine and Philosophy". We gratefully acknowledge the financial support of the Einstein Foundation Berlin for the Chronoi Fellowships of Annette Heinrich, Giouli Korobili and Kassandra Miller, for teaching relief for Philip van der Eijk and for the workshop from which this volume has arisen.

The human body and its functioning was believed to be subject to specific time cycles, intervals and rhythms, such as the pulse; and irregularities in these rhythms were believed to provide significant clues for diagnosis and prognosis, though opinions differed as to the precise interpretation of these variations and the underlying physiological mechanisms. Many pathological phenomena were believed to manifest themselves in fixed time sequences, such as the periodic fevers mentioned in the case histories of the Hippocratic *Epidemics*, or symptoms occurring on particular "critical days" in the course of a disease; yet here, too, irregularities and ambiguities gave rise to debate and controversy about the determination and classification of phenomena.

Similarly, natural philosophers treated the cosmos itself as governed by recurring cycles, within which the body was thought to participate as a microcosm. For the Pythagoreans, the harmony of the spheres and the recurrence of cosmic periods reflected a mathematical order that extended into the rhythms of bodily life. This idea of correspondence between cosmic and corporeal cycles was later developed by Plato in the *Timaeus*, where the human organism is explicitly constructed as a reflection of the ordered motions of the heavens. Aristotle, though critical of Pythagorean number mysticism, nonetheless maintained that natural beings move and change according to temporal cycles, so that growth, decay, and disease could be situated within broader patterns of motion. The Stoics systematized these notions under the doctrine of *sympatheia*, positing that all things are interconnected and subject to recurring cosmic conflagrations and renewals. Within this framework, the body was not an isolated entity but a miniature cosmos, whose health and stability depended upon its capacity to remain in harmony with the larger periodicities of nature and the universe.

The relevant ancient texts show a rich and fascinating discourse on time, timing and time management in Greco-Roman medicine and philosophy, which was characterized by diversity, debate and competition between rival thinkers and schools. They also provide evidence of development and change in theory and practice over time, e.g. in pulse theory, diagnostic methods or disease classification, and in methods and instruments of time-management and time-keeping. Taken together with philosophical discussions of time, motion, and cycles, these writings illustrate a shared Greco-Roman effort to situate human life within broader temporal frameworks.

1 Synchronizing the Body in Ancient Medicine and Philosophy

Greco-Roman physicians and philosophers were interested in considering these temporal modes not only in isolation, but also in relationship to one another. They were particularly curious about when and how to assign meaning to the temporal co-incidence of (medically) relevant events. Today, we often call such significant co-occurences "synchronicities", a term which, despite its ancient Greek roots (σύν, "together with" + χρόνος, "time"), was actually coined by Carl Jung in the mid-20th century.[1] Despite the absence of this or an equivalent term in extant Greek and Roman texts, we use "synchronicity" in this volume as a shorthand to refer to the many ways, explored by the volume's contributing authors, that ancient Greeks and Romans assigned social, cultural, philosophical, and medical significance to coeval phenomena.

Another concept central to this volume is "synchronization", which designates a process aimed at establishing (or reestablishing) synchronicity between multiple temporal cycles. Though this term has a longer history than "synchronicity" does,[2] it, too, is a neologism that lacks a direct equivalent in ancient Greek or Latin. We employ it here, like "synchronicity", as an umbrella term to unite the wide range of strategies that Greco-Roman authors propose for restoring synchronicities between bodily and environmental or social rhythms, for example, or between disease patterns and treatment regimens.

Perhaps because our extant Greek and Roman authors do not have specific equivalents for the terms "synchronicity" and "synchronization", the importance of the underlying concepts—meaningful temporal co-incidence and efforts to manufacture such co-incidence—has hitherto been underappreciated in modern scholarship on ancient medical and philosophical understandings of the body.[3] These concepts are often implied or surface glancingly, in scholarship on other temporal constructs like the Greek *krisis* (a "medical turning or decision point") and *kairos* (the "right or opportune time").[4] A previous Einstein Center Fellow Research Group (2019–2020) explored the understandings of and interactions between *kairos, krisis,* and *rhythmos* ("regularly recurring motion") within Greco-

1 Jung 1960.
2 According to the Oxford English Dictionary, the verbal form "synchronize" is attested as early as the 17th century CE.
3 In contrast, e.g., to scholarship on ancient historiography, such as Feeney 2007.
4 On *krisis* and schemes of critical days, see Lloyd 1979: 154–168; Langholf 1990: 78–127; Cooper 2013; Longhi 2020; Singer 2022: 102–122; Miller 2023: 115–134. On *kairos*, see Eskin 2002; Sipiora 2002; Miller 2023: 156–179; Ecca 2017.

Roman writings on the pulse, critical days, and periodic fevers.[5] Though synchronicity and synchronization were not explicit themes within this project, the concepts proved to be intimately entangled with its findings. For example, many ancient authors state that the *kairos* for performing a therapeutic action is indicated by the co-occurrence of another phenomenon, such as the appearance of a particular symptom or *krisis* point, the movement of a celestial body to a certain position in the sky, or the transition from one season to another.[6] Notions of synchrony and synchronization are also entangled with a wide range of other philosophical and medical concepts that have bearing on Greco-Roman understandings of the body, such as *sympatheia* (often translated as "sympathy") and the idea of the body as a microcosm of the larger cosmos.[7]

The present volume builds upon such prior work, but is the first to make bodily synchronicities and synchronizations the central focus of its inquiry. It emerged from an Einstein CHRONOI Fellow Research Group in 2023–2024 titled "Synchronizing the Body in Ancient Medicine and Philosophy",[8] which concluded with a conference in Berlin featuring talks by both Fellows and invited scholars. This volume's chapters, which are revised versions of those papers, highlight the many and varied ways in which authors from the Hippocratics to Aristotle, from Juvenal to Dorotheus used concepts analogous to synchronicity in order to structure and evaluate the temporal relationships involved in health care and how they developed a range of methods intended to fix, through synchronization, asynchronies that were coded as abnormal, unhealthy, and/ or socially unacceptable. The contributions speak to synchronicity's (and synchronization's) relationship with three different kinds of bodies: the healthy body, the gendered body, and the sick body.

5 The group, entitled "Kairos, Krisis, Rhythmos", consisted of Glen Cooper, Sean Coughlin, Orly Lewis, Christine Salazar, Peter Singer (Fellows) and Philip van der Eijk (Co-ordinator); see https://www.ec-chronoi.de/Fellows (last accessed on December 18, 2025). For some of the publications arising from this group see Singer 2022; Lewis 2022 and 2024; Cooper 2020 and forthcoming; Coughlin 2020 and 2024; Salazar 2024; Salazar and Singer forthcoming; van der Eijk forthcoming.

6 Such movements and transitions could be determined by direct observation or by the use of a tool such as a sundial, water clock, parapegma, or astrological calendar.

7 On the Stoic concept of sympathy and its application within medical contexts, see especially Holmes 2019; 2020.

8 The group consisted of Annette Heinrich, Giouli Korobili, Kassandra Miller (Fellows) and Philip van der Eijk (Co-ordinator); see https://www.ec-chronoi.de/Fellows (last accessed on December 18, 2025). For other publications arising from the project see Miller 2023; 2024; 2025; Korobili 2025 and forthcoming; Heinrich 2022; 2024 and forthcoming.

2 Synchronicity and the Healthy Body

In ancient medicine and natural philosophy, living bodies and their functioning were believed to be subject to specific time cycles, intervals and rhythms, which were related to similar time patterns in the external world surrounding them. From the fifth century BCE onwards, early Greek philosophers and medical writers developed cosmological and biological theories according to which processes and time sequences in the macrocosmos of the universe and in the microcosmos of human and animal bodies were closely related in ways that went further than just parallelism or analogy. Philosophers such as Aristotle tried to spell out the causal mechanisms underlying this synchronous relationship. And medical writers such as the authors of *Airs, Waters, Places* and *On Regimen* argued that health and well-being are constituted and enhanced by synchronicity between the body and the universe. They drew the consequences of this for medical theory and practice by stressing the importance of "living according to the seasons" for the preservation and enhancement of human health. Consequently, in medical dietetics, diagnosis and prognosis, great attention was paid to the study of cosmic cycles, weather phenomena, astronomy, meteorology and the environment in general. In the present volume, the chapters by Korobili and Sherbakova provide case studies of this theme: Korobili discusses a chapter from the Aristotelian *Natural Problems* devoted to meteorological processes leading to changes in winds and corresponding changes in human health, thus showing that health stability is maintained in synchrony with environmental stability, while any disruption of this synchrony negatively affects living bodies; and Sherbakova discusses the views of the author of the Hippocratic treatise *On Regimen* on the intricate relationship between the elemental cycle within the body and the way this is modelled on the course of the year, and how observation and management of this relationship forms the basis of medical, i.e. prophylactic and therapeutic practice.

3 Synchronicity and the Gendered Body

Within ancient medical and philosophical views about synchronicity between the body's time cycles and those of its surroundings, special attention was paid to differences between male and female bodies. Extensive discussion of the internal and external factors affecting the temporal aspects of menstruation, conception, pregnancy and menopause, and of attempts to influence these, can already be found in fifth and fourth century BCE gynaecological texts transmitted under the name of Hippocrates and also in Aristotle's biological works; in the Imperial period, the *Gynaecia* by the Methodist doctor Soranus provides an invaluable source of further information. While some of the ideas in these texts were based on observations of gender specific physical and physiological features, others had less clearly empirical justification and seem to reflect broader cultural attitudes and values embedded in Greek and Roman society. The interaction between medical ideas and such broader attitudes is discussed in this volume in Miller's chapter, which uses case studies from Athenaeus, Juvenal and Galen to show how elite male authors of the early Imperial period portray female clock users in their writings and how Roman-period women, in using or resisting "clock time" to exercise personal autonomy over their lives and bodies, created pointed synchronies or asynchronies with normative "clock time".

4 Synchronicity and the Sick Body

Disease, too, was believed to display natural patterns, rhythms and time cycles, whose analysis and understanding were the subject of intense medical and philosophical engagement and debate. The dynamics of disease processes presented major challenges to doctors and their patients: "chronic" diseases called for long term therapeutic planning, in which the co-operation of the patient was considered of vital importance for the success of the therapy. "Synchronizing" here meant adjusting the therapy to the disease's development during the treatment, which required careful time-keeping. In medical literature ranging from the Hippocratic writings in the fifth century BCE through Galen's therapeutic works in the second century CE to the late ancient Methodist author Caelius Aurelianus, we can see elaborate, meticulous therapeutic regimes being spelled out in which time factors, timing and time-keeping are explicitly considered in relation to the course of the disease during the treatment. In the present volume, Greenbaum's chapter on prognosis in astrological medicine takes up the theme of critical days. It begins with a discussion of the meanings of *chronos, kairos* and *krisis* and their use in the discourse on timing in ancient medicine, in particular their relationship with one another in determining the course of an illness or injury and its outcome. It further explores these concepts within two commonly used timing methods of medical astrology: decumbiture and critical days. Heinrich's chapter provides a case study of a Hippocratic medical doctor's ideas on time management in the treatment of a large variety of chronic diseases; using the specific example of a number of diseases referred to by the author of *Internal Affections* as variants of "typhus", she shows how the author closely monitors the course of the disease during treatment and synchronizes his therapeutic measures accordingly.

Finally, Ker's chapter on bereavement and its management adds the dimension of mental health and illness. Using Seneca's *Consolatio ad Marciam*, he shows how the philosophical consoler seeks to impose a clear temporal schedule for the subject's recovery from grief, thus using synchronization to transform the addressee's time experience, especially as this is encoded in her literal and metaphorical body.

5 Note on References to Primary Medical Texts

In references to writings attributed to Hippocrates, "L." refers to Émile Littré, *Œuvres complètes d'Hippocrate*, 10 Vols., Paris: J. P. Baillière, 1839–1861, each reference specifying the volume and page number in Littré's edition.

In references to writings attributed to Galen, "K." refers to the edition by Karl Gottlob Kühn, *Claudii Galeni opera omnia*, 22 Vols., Leipzig: Knobloch, 1821–1833 (repr. Hildesheim: Olms, 1964–1965), each reference specifying the volume and page number in Kühn's edition.

In addition, where relevant the volume and page number of the edition in the Corpus Medicorum Graecorum (CMG, De Gruyter) and/or the Loeb Classical Library (LCL, Harvard University Press) are given.

Bibliography

Primary Sources

Cooper, G. M. *Galen* On Crises. *Critical Edition of the Arabic Version with Translation and Notes*. Brill: Leiden, forthcoming.

Ecca, G. *Die hippokratische Schrift* Praecepta. *Kritische Edition, Übersetzung und Kommentar. (Mit Anhang: Ein Scholion zu* Praec. *1)* Wiesbaden: Reichert Verlag, 2017.

Heinrich, A. *Studien zu Hippokrates,* De internis affectionibus. Doct. Diss., Humboldt-Universität zu Berlin, 2022.

Salazar, C. F. and P. N. Singer. *Galen. Commentary on the Hippocratic* Prognostic. Cambridge: Cambridge University Press, forthcoming.

Secondary Literature

Cooper, G. M. "Approaches to the Critical Days in Late Medieval and Renaissance Thinkers". *Early Science and Medicine* 18.6, 2013: 536–565.

Cooper, G. M. "The Reception of an Empirical Medical Theory: Galen's Crisis Theory in the Arabic Commentaries on the Hippocratic *Aphorisms*". In *The First International Prof. Fuat Sezgin Symposium on History of Science in Islam*, ed. F. Başar, M. Kaçar, C. Kaya and A. Z. Furat. Istanbul: Istanbul University Press, 2020: 327–336.

Coughlin, S. "Cohesive Causes in Ancient Greek Philosophy and Medicine". In *Holism in Ancient Medicine and Its Reception*, ed. C. Thumiger. Leiden: Brill, 2020: 237–267.

Coughlin, S. "Galen's Hippocratism". In *The Oxford Handbook of Galen*, ed. P. N. Singer and R. M. Rosen. New York: Oxford University Press, 2024: 100–144.

Eskin, C. R. "Hippocrates, Kairos, and Writing in the Sciences". In *Rhetoric and Kairos: Essays in History, Theory, and Praxis*, ed. P. Sipiora and J. S. Baumlin. Albany, NY: State University of New York Press, 2002: 97–113.

Feeney, D. C. *Caesar's Calendar: Ancient Time and the Beginnings of History*. Berkeley, CA: University of California Press, 2007.

Heinrich, A. "Praktiken der Texttradition in spätantiken griechischen medizinischen Sammelwerken – Fallstudie Uroskopie". In *Logbuch Wissensgeschichte*, ed. M. Becker-Sawatzky, K. Wächter, H. Wendt, Ş. Dadaş, A. Eusterschulte, K. Hasselmann, A. James Johnston, F. Quenstedt, C. Reufer, H. Z. Trauer and C. Vogel. Wiesbaden: Harrassowitz Verlag, 2024: 409–420.

Heinrich, A. "Der Text *De internis affectionibus* als Zeugnis hippokratischer Medizin". In *XVIIth Colloque Hippocratique. Das Corpus Hippocraticum – Einheit in der Vielfalt?*, ed. M. Witt. Leiden: Brill, forthcoming.

Holmes, B. "On Stoic Sympathy: Cosmobiology and the Life of Nature". In *Antiquities Beyond Humanism*, ed. E. Bianchi, S. Brill and B. Holmes. Oxford: Oxford University Press, 2019: 239–270.

Holmes, B. "Holism, Sympathy, and the Living Being in Ancient Greek Medicine and Philosophy". In *Holism in Ancient Medicine and Its Reception*, ed. C. Thumiger. Leiden: Brill, 2020: 47–83.

Jung, C. G. *Synchronicity: An Acausal Connecting Principle*. New York: Bollingen Foundation, 1960.

Korobili, G. and S. M. Hoffmann. „Mahlzeit im Himmel. Ernährung der Himmelskörper bei Seneca und in der modernen Astrophysik". *Codices Manuscripti & Impressi*, Suppl. 22 (*Zeitkonzepte IV. Zeit, Leben und Lebensmittel*, ed. M. Niederkorn), 2025: 27–40.

Korobili, G. "The *Historia Animalium* on Synchronous Changes in Living Bodies and Natural Phenomena". In *Philosophical Essays on Aristotle's* Historia Animalium, ed. S. M. Connell. Philosophia Antiqua, Brill, forthcoming.

Langholf, V. *Medical Theories in Hippocrates: Early Texts and the 'Epidemics'*. Berlin: De Gruyter, 1990.

Lewis, O. "Galen against Archigenes on the Pulse and what it teaches us about Galen's Method of diairesis". In *Galen's Epistemology: Experience, Reason, and Method in Ancient Medicine*, ed. R. J. Hankinson and M. Havrda. Cambridge: Cambridge University Press, 2022: 190–217.

Lewis, O. "Galen on the Pulse: Theory and Method". In *The Oxford Handbook of Galen*, ed. P. N. Singer and R. M. Rosen. New York: Oxford University Press, 2024: 379–416.

Lloyd, G. E. R. *Magic, Reason, and Experience: Studies in the Origin and Development of Greek Science*. Cambridge: Cambridge University Press, 1979.

Longhi, V. Krisis *ou la décision génératrice: Épopée, médecine hippocratique, Platon*. Villeneuve d'Ascq: Presses universitaires du Septentrion, 2020.

Miller, K. J. *Time and Ancient Medicine: How Sundials and Water Clocks Changed Medical Science*. Oxford: Oxford University Press, 2023.
Miller, K. J. "Intentional Menstrual Suppression in Imperial Rome". *The Journal of Roman Studies* 114, 2024: 27–59.
Miller, K. J. "Resetting Her Biological Clock: Menstrual Induction in Imperial Rome". *Journal of the History of Medicine and Allied Sciences* 2025, jraf017. https://doi.org/10.1093/jhmas/jraf017.
Salazar, C. F. "Galen in the Late Imperial and Early Byzantine Periods". In *The Oxford Handbook of Galen*, ed. P. N. Singer and R. M. Rosen. New York: Oxford University Press, 2024: 477–492.
Singer, P. N. *Time for the Ancients: Measurement, Theory, Experience*. Chronoi 3. Berlin: De Gruyter, 2022. https://doi.org/10.1515/9783110752397.
Sipiora, P. "Introduction: The Ancient Concept of Kairos". In *Rhetoric and Kairos: Essays in History, Theory, and Praxis*, ed. P. Sipiora and J. S. Baumlin. Albany, NY: State University of New York Press, 2002: 1–22.
van der Eijk, P. J. *Aristotle, Aristotelianism and Ancient Medicine*. Cambridge: Cambridge University Press, in press.

Elisaveta Sherbakova

Time of the Essence: Cyclical Change and the Human Body in *Regimen* and *Nature of the Human Being*

Abstract: This paper examines the theory set out in the 'Hippocratic' medical work *Regimen* of the nature of the human body as a cycle of its changing components, fire and water. It compares this to the ideas in the near contemporary work *The Nature of the Human Being* (*Nat.Hom.*), which also describes the body as undergoing a regular alternation of its elemental components. Such cycles are typically framed through an analogy with cosmic rhythms, especially the course of the year and the sun's annual movement between the summer and winter solstices. They are understood not as static states but as dynamic processes. While *Nat.Hom.* uses the analogy to synchronise bodily processes with seasonal time, *Regimen* uses it to reveal a fundamental law of change, which also becomes the basis for medical intervention and for season-specific dietetic recommendations, ranging from food and exercise to baths and emetics. This universal law of the regular shift of opposites governs the cycle, that is the rhythm of heating and drying, cooling and moistening, that sustains both body and cosmos. Medicine in this sense is itself, as the author would say, an imitation of the universal law.

Keywords: cosmos, body, cycle, rhythm, elements, dietetics

1

This paper grew out of what first seemed a local exegetical difficulty. I set out to explain a thorny passage in *Regimen* (*Vict.*), which defines the nature of the human body as a cycle of its changing components.[1] How this cycle works has long been a puzzle: its structure is unclear, and the theory of change behind it appears contradictory.

This puzzle matters because *Regimen*'s entire therapeutic project hinges on its concept of *nature*: a doctor must know the *physis anthrōpou* in order to heal.[2]

1 *Vict.* I.3–I.4.

2 *Vict.* I.2.1 (= VI.468 L.) "I maintain that anyone who wishes to write accurately about the human regimen must first understand and discern the *nature of the human being* (φύσιν

© 2026 the author(s) | https://doi.org/10.1515/9783112235690-002

Yet the broader purpose of that project—whether it should be read as "environmental", "philosophical", or "cosmological" medicine—remains unsettled. By clarifying how *Regimen* understands *physis*, we may also get a better sense of what the text is ultimately trying to do.

To understand how this cycle works, we need to consider both a broader context and a broader question that goes beyond the merely exegetical—namely, why (and how) should we think of the body in cyclical terms at all? The best place to start is *The Nature of the Human Being* (*Nat.Hom.*), a near-contemporary of *Regimen* that also describes the body as undergoing a regular alternation of its elemental components. It shows, among other things, that such cycles are typically framed through an analogy with cosmic rhythms—especially the course of the year. This raises further questions: what kind of relationship between body and cosmos does this analogy establish, and what kind of physiological models does it produce?

It has often been interpreted through the "meteorological" or "environmental"[3] lense: the point, roughly, is to think of living things as rooted in their surroundings and dependent—for good or ill—on climate, season, and other external conditions. But I will argue that this interpretive model is not only too limited—it may be misleading, especially in the case of *Regimen*.

Discussions of "environmental" or "meteorological" medicine tend to focus on static correspondences—like between elements and seasons—as a kind of explanatory bridge between body and cosmos. But to understand why the analogy seemed useful and interesting to early medical writers, I suggest we need to focus on its processual and temporal aspects. After all, this is exactly what it picks out: body and cosmos are alike, first and foremost, *qua* regular, structured processes. And depending on how one thinks these processes relate to each other, one can

ἀνθρώπου) in general: to know from what it is originally composed (ἀπὸ τίνων συνέστηκεν ἐξ ἀρχῆς), and to discern what predominates (ὑπὸ τίνων . . . κεκράτηται)."—Unless otherwise noted, all translations are my own. This reliance on the concept of *physis* as the basis of medical techne places *Regimen* within a particular intellectual tradition, though its contents and boundaries remain debated (see van der Eijk 2008: 390–395; Schiefsky 2005: 9–10); more on this in the final sections of the paper.

3 The term "meteorological medicine" goes back to von Brunn 1946–1947, but the idea of a distinct meteorological approach in early Greek medicine is older; for an overview, see Liewert 2015: 1–5. "Meteorological" here renders *meteōrologia*, and encompasses everything from astronomy and atmospheric phenomena to climatology and hydrology (Le Blay 2005: 253–254). "Environmental medicine" is sometimes used as an alternative, though it is more specifically associated with climate and its effects on the body. The main texts in this context are *Airs, Waters, and Places* (*Aer.*), followed by *Nat.Hom.* (see Liewert 2015: 45–59), and, to some extent, the *Aphorisms.*

end up with quite different—and not necessarily meteorological—models of the body, and quite different conceptions of medical intervention.

The paper has three main parts. I begin with *Regimen* and the problem of its elemental cycle. I argue that the cycle only becomes intelligible once we see it as implicitly modelled on the course of the year. In the second part, I turn to *Nat.Hom.* and argue that its account of bodily change is much closer to *Regimen* than generally acknowledged. Both rely on the same underlying analogy between the body and the yearly cycle. In the final part, I ask what that analogy is doing in each case. I suggest that *Nat.Hom.* uses it to synchronise bodily processes with seasonal time, while *Regimen* uses it to reveal a fundamental law of change—one that becomes the basis for medical intervention. Finally, I consider how best to classify these accounts, and whether labels like "meteorological" or "cosmological" medicine are adequate to capture what they are doing.

1.1

Few passages in *Regimen*, a text famous for its obscurity,[4] have been as difficult to interpret as the one below:

> All animals, including the human being, are made up of two things, differing in their power but complementary in their usefulness: fire and water. Together, they are sufficient for themselves and for everything else; apart, each by itself is sufficient neither for itself nor for anything else. The power of each is as follows: fire has the power always to move all things, while water has the power always to nourish all things. In turn, each dominates and is dominated, from the greatest possible measure to the least. For neither can gain a complete victory, for the following reason: fire, when it advances to the uttermost limit of water, comes to lack nourishment, and so retreats to where it can be nourished. Water, as it advances to the uttermost limit of fire, comes to lack movement; it halts at that point, and as soon as it halts, it is no longer in power and is consumed as nourishment by fire that assails it. This is why neither can fully overcome the other. For if either one were ever to be defeated first, nothing that now exists would be as it is. But since things are as they are, they [scil. fire and water] will always remain the same, and neither, whether singly or to-

4 Especially in Book I, *Regimen* clearly imitates Heraclitus' oracular, asyndetic style—but why it does so has never been satisfactorily explained. The extent of Heraclitus' influence is also a matter of dispute: some see it as superficial and purely stylistic (Kirk 1954: 21; Joly in Joly and Byl 2003: 25–27), while others, like Lebedev (2014: 27–42), take Heraclitus to be a major inspiration and even treat *Regimen* as a source for reconstructing aspects of Heraclitus' doctrine. Yet even minimalist readings—including Joly's—struggle to account for the decision to imitate this style so closely, especially in an introductory book that lays out the text's foundations. It remains unclear why a manual intended to guide dietetic practice would open with something so deliberately obscure.

gether, will ever fail. Thus, as I said, fire and water are always sufficient for all things, whether in their greatest or smallest measure.

Each of these two [elements] has the following attributes: fire has the hot and the dry; water, the cold and the wet. Each also takes from the other one attribute: fire, from water, has wetness, for there is wetness in fire; and water, from fire, has dryness, for there is dryness also in water. (*Vict.* I.3.1–I.4.1 = CMG I 2,4, p. 126 (= VI.472–474 L.))

συνίσταται μὲν οὖν τὰ ζῶα τά τε ἄλλα πάντα καὶ ὁ ἄνθρωπος ἀπὸ δυοῖν, διαφόροιν μὲν τὴν δύναμιν, συμφόροιν δὲ τὴν χρῆσιν, πυρὸς καὶ ὕδατος. Ταῦτα δὲ συναμφότερα αὐτάρκεά ἐστι τοῖσί τε ἄλλοισι πᾶσι καὶ ἀλλήλοισιν, ἑκάτερον δὲ χωρὶς οὔτε αὐτὸ ἑωυτῷ οὔτε ἄλλῳ οὐδενί. Τὴν μὲν οὖν δύναμιν αὐτῶν ἑκάτερον ἔχει τοιήνδε· τὸ μὲν γὰρ πῦρ δύναται πάντα διὰ παντὸς κινῆσαι, τὸ δὲ ὕδωρ πάντα διὰ παντὸς θρέψαι· ἐν μέρει δὲ ἑκάτερον κρατεῖ καὶ κρατεῖται ἐς τὸ μήκιστον καὶ τὸ ἐλάχιστον ὡς ἀνυστόν. Οὐδέτερον γὰρ κρατῆσαι παντελῶς δύναται διὰ τόδε· τὸ μὲν πῦρ ἐπεξιὸν ἐπὶ τὸ ἔσχατον τοῦ ὕδατος, ἐπιλείπει ἡ τροφή, ἀποτρέπεται οὖν ὅθεν μέλλει τρέφεσθαι· τὸ δὲ ὕδωρ ἐπεξιὸν ἐπὶ τὸ ἔσχατον τοῦ πυρὸς, ἐπιλείπει ἡ κίνησις, ἵσταται οὖν ἐν τούτῳ, ὅταν δὲ στῇ, οὐκέτι ἐγκρατές ἐστιν, ἀλλ᾽ ἤδη τῷ ἐμπίπτοντι πυρὶ ἐς τὴν τροφὴν καταναλίσκεται. οὐδέτερον δὲ διὰ ταῦτα δύναται κρατῆσαι παντελῶς. εἰ δέ ποτε κρατηθείη καὶ ὁπότερον πρότερον, οὐδὲν ἂν εἴη τῶν νῦν ἐόντων ὥσπερ ἔχει νῦν· οὕτω δὲ ἐχόντων αἰεὶ ἔσται τὰ αὐτά, καὶ οὐδέτερα καὶ οὐδὲ ἅμα ἐπιλείψει. Τὸ μὲν οὖν πῦρ καὶ τὸ ὕδωρ, ὥσπερ εἴρηταί μοι, αὐτάρκεά ἐστι πᾶσι διὰ παντὸς ἐς τὸ μήκιστον καὶ τὸ ἐλάχιστον ὡσαύτως.

Τούτων δὲ προσκεῖται ἑκατέρῳ τάδε· τῷ μὲν πυρὶ τὸ θερμὸν καὶ τὸ ξηρὸν, τῷ δὲ ὕδατι τὸ ψυχρὸν καὶ τὸ ὑγρόν· ἔχει δὲ ἀπ᾽ ἀλλήλων τὸ μὲν πῦρ ἀπὸ τοῦ ὕδατος τὸ ὑγρόν· ἔνι γὰρ ἐν πυρὶ ὑγρότης· τὸ δὲ ὕδωρ ἀπὸ τοῦ πυρὸς τὸ ξηρόν· ἔνι γὰρ ἐν ὕδατι ξηρόν.

As I work through it, I'll try to untangle the main knots. So, all living things are made up of two basic stuffs: fire and water.[5] What exactly these "stuffs" are is a matter of debate. At first sight (though things quickly get more complicated), they seem much like Aristotelian elements: they are defined by two properties—fire is hot and dry, water cold and wet—and apparently change into one another in a regular way.[6] Although in this respect, they are perhaps closer to the two Empedoclean powers: they are locked in a perpetual cycle of gain and loss, with neither side ultimately prevailing—since any definitive triumph would bring the cycle to an end.

5 Bartoš (2015: 74) objects that *Regimen* is making a more limited claim—not that fire and water are constituents of the body, or cosmic elements to which everything can be reduced, but simply that the body contains them. He contrasts this with *Nat.Hom.* However, as Enache (2019: 194) observes, the examples he cites of other supposed 'elements' in *Regimen* are problematic: *pneuma*, which cannot be an element anyway, and *aēr* and *gē* are never clearly treated as basic stuffs, but if anything as cosmic masses. Moreover, the overall cosmological tone of the passage—with phrases like οὐδὲν ἂν εἴη τῶν νῦν ἐόντων ὥσπερ ἔχει νῦν (on which more below)—strains such a narrow reading.

6 Point made by Enache 2019: 181–184, although, as I suggest below (note 13), he may overstate the case. See also Bartoš 2015: 248, who draws attention to some of the key differences.

Exactly how this cycle works is not clear, and the author says many contradictory things about it. At first glance, it seems to be a straightforward process of mutual transformation[7] between two opposites—ἐξ ὑγρῶν ξηρὰ, ἐκ τῶν ξηρῶν ὑγρά—as he often repeats, likely echoing Heraclitus.[8] Yet the author never quite sticks to it: he mentions water turning into fire—at least, this is what fire feeding on water in *Vict.* I.3.1 (= VI.472 L.) appears to suggest—but never the reverse.

Instead, he frames the cycle as a kind of reciprocal movement of the two 'elements' between certain fixed limits.[9] And curiously these limits are cast in both spatial and quantitative terms; fire 'marches out' against water until it reaches its *furthermost* (ἔσχατον) point (note spatial implications!), at which water routs it and does the same. At the same time these furthermost points are also reciprocal *quantitative* maxima and minima: when fire reaches its *mēkiston*, water is at its lowest (*elachiston*), and *vice versa*.[10] We can tentatively diagram the cycle as follows (Fig. 1):

If the author simply means a cycle of mutual transformation, why all this talk of paths and movements? If "path" is meant as some kind of metaphorical model—and that's far from clear—it is inconsistent and raises serious conceptual issues. On the

7 For this interpretation, see, e.g., Schluderer 2018: 34–35.

8 *Vict.* I.22.2 (= VI.494 L.), I.17.1 (= VI.492 L.): the phrase occurs five times in the text without variation. It is reminiscent of Heraclitus B126 DK (τὰ ψυχρὰ θέρεται, θερμὸν ψύχεται, ὑγρὸν αὐαίνεται, καρφαλέον νοτίζεται), and given that the part of Book I in which it appears—a curious catalogue of various human crafts and how they 'imitate' human nature—is especially Heraclitean in style (as even Joly acknowledges, Joly and Byl 2003: 243), it may even preserve a lost authentic quote. Whether it is Heraclitean in substance is another question, and lies beyond the scope of this paper. Heraclitus certainly drew on technological examples to illustrate the unity-of-opposites principle (B59 DK, B58 DK). On Heraclitus' influence on the crafts-catalogue, see, e.g., Halliwell 2002: 15 (dismissive of the catalogue itself); a more sympathetic view in Lebedev 2014: 35–40; full discussion of the literature in Bartoš 2015: 119.

9 *Regimen* even compares the process to two carpenters sawing wood, where the saw moves up and down from a maximum to a minimum point. This image seems especially important in the text, where it appears repeatedly (*Vict.* I.6, I.7, I.16 = VI.478, 480, 490 L.). Peck calls it "the cosmic saw" (Peck 1928: xv) and suggests it serves as a tangible model for the cyclical process described in the text. Bartoš (2012; 2015: 145–152) has argued that there are, in fact, two related analogies at play: one involving sawing, the other drilling. All our principal manuscripts (M, θ, and the Latin translation P) support the reading τρυπῶσιν ("they are drilling") in chapters 7 and 16. However, it is not immediately clear how the sawing motion—characterised by ἄνω-κάτω movement—could also describe drilling. Peck interpreted τρυπῶσιν—ὁ μὲν ἕλκει, ὁ δὲ ὠθεῖ—as referring to a large bow-drill operated by two carpenters, functioning much like a saw. Bartoš prefers to see it as a two-man helical auger, but the rotary motion of such a tool would not naturally involve maximum and minimum points (μήκιστον/ ἐλάχιστον), which are clearly central to the analogy.

10 Apart from "greatest", μήκιστος commonly also means "farthest", as in Xenophon, *Cyropaedia* IV 5.28: τοὺς ἐχθροὺς μήκιστον ἀπελαύνοντες.

Fig. 1: Schematic cycle of fire (πῦρ) and water (ὕδωρ), showing their reciprocal advance to the furthermost limit (ἔσχατον) and corresponding quantitative extremes.

one hand, fire and water advance and retreat by turn (as shown in the diagram). On the other, the author seems to be thinking of a single path of fire; where it continually feeds on water, and so chases after it, and when it advances towards its limit and reaches its quantitative/ spatial maximum when it has consumed nearly all of it, it runs out of fuel and turns (*apotrepetai*) to feed elsewhere; as I have attempted to diagram (as much as it *is* diagrammable) in Fig. 2.

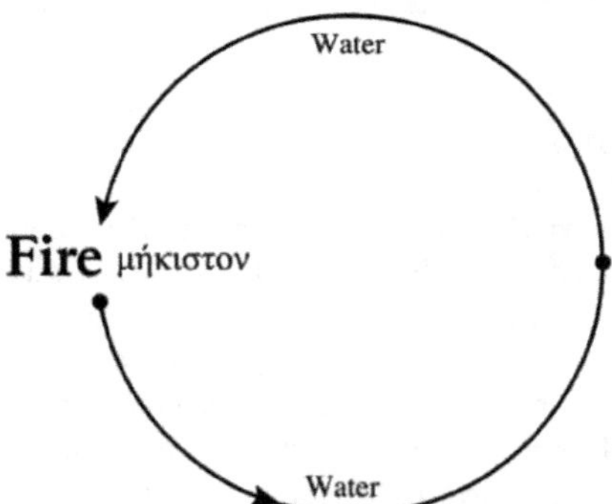

Fig. 2: Diagram of the author's "path" model of fire and water.

But this single-path of fire looking for lunch doesn't seem to fit with advance and retreat nor with mutual transformation. For one, when fire achieves its maximum by consuming all the water, where is it supposed to turn for more nourishment? This seems spatially incoherent unless a new source of water is introduced—something the author neither explains nor allows, since, in his words, the elements "suffice for each other". Moreover, what makes it turn in the first place, once it has exhausted its supply, instead of just dying out, and stopping the cycle for good?

My sense is that the author was clearly concerned with the problem of how a closed-loop system like this—where the 'elements' shift back and forth—could work and sustain itself. If it's by transformation (to restate my previous point) what accounts for them transforming *back and forth*, instead of completing the process once and for all? The author does stress that the elements dominate and are defeated only *epi to mēkiston* and *elachiston*—to the highest/ lowest degree possible, so by implication not completely. But that is precisely the *explanandum*.

And *Regimen*, I suggest, may offer an answer. With the help of some recent cosmological theories,[11] the author sketches a remarkably inventive solution. To save his transformation cycle, he does nothing less than shift to a different—Anaxagorean—type of ontology.

Regimen, at the outset, casts its supposed 'elements' as something closer to mixtures: they are defined by two properties of their own, but also take on one from the other. Fire is not just hot and dry, but also "has some moisture" in it, and *vice versa*.[12] The language of possession here is not accidental; *Regimen* seems to treat these qualities as true primitives, which themselves are immune to qualitative change. Otherwise, the moist would fall prey to the dry in the fire mixture.[13] What we seem to get here, then, is a reinterpretation of the Anaxagorean principle that everything contains a portion of everything, applied to a parsimonious ontology of just two elements.[14]

The author, in fact, makes his Anaxagorean commitments explicit when he says that "coming to be" and "perishing"—the kind of change that occurs when water turns into fire as fire feeds on it—are just words he uses for the sake of the general public (*Vict.* I.4.3 = VI.476 L.). In reality, he means separation and recom-

11 *Regimen*'s engagement with fifth century cosmology is a longstanding problem. It goes beyond the text itself and touches on the larger, vexed question of the relationship between early Greek medicine and early Greek philosophy (van der Eijk 2005: 10–21; Camden 2023). *Regimen*'s Heraclitism, in particular, has drawn sustained attention. The first study, Johann Matthias Gesner's *De animabus Heracliti et Hippocratis*, appeared as early as 1752. Scholarship has traditionally approached the issue from a source-critical angle—especially to assess whether *Regimen* can offer any evidential value for Heraclitus (on which opinions differ considerably). More broadly, it has often been unclear what *Regimen* actually wants from its sources, and the text has not always fared well in this respect. Barnes 1982: 49, for example, dismissed it as "a silly farrago of ill-digested Presocratic opinions". More recent work has moved toward a synchronic approach—especially Bartoš 2015—asking what *Regimen* (and other supposedly philosophically inclined texts) is trying to do on its own terms. This shift has helped rehabilitate *Regimen* as a serious and ambitious work. Still, the question remains: why does it make the references it does—above all to Heraclitus, Anaxagoras, and Empedocles? An answer, perhaps, will depend on an approach that integrates synchronic and diachronic perspectives.

12 *Vict.* I.4.1 (VI.474 L.).

13 On the *dry* (not fire!) feeding and its opposite, *Vict.* II.37 (= VI.528–530 L.). Enache 2011: 40 n. 4 insists that "hot" and "cold" must be understood as elemental qualities, but the Aristotelian framework he applies to *Regimen* (Enache 2019) seems ill-suited to accommodate an *element* with an opposite quality "in it". He does not acknowledge the reference to Anaxagoras or its implications for *Regimen*'s ontology—on which more below.

14 Anaxagoras B12 DK ἐν παντὶ γὰρ παντὸς μοῖρα ἔνεστιν. B6 DK ἀλλὰ πάντα παντὸς μοῖραν μετέχει.

bination: "Ὅ τι δ' ἂν διαλέγωμαι γενέσθαι ἢ ἀπολέσθαι, τῶν πολλῶν εἵνεκεν ἑρμηνεύω· ταῦτα δὲ συμμίσγεσθαι καὶ διακρίνεσθαι δηλώσω."[15] This is clearly an echo of Anaxagoras' B17 DK: "τὸ δὲ γίνεσθαι καὶ ἀπόλλυσθαι οὐκ ὀρθῶς νομίζουσιν οἱ Ἕλληνες· [. . .] ἀπὸ ἐόντων χρημάτων συμμίσγεταί τε καὶ διακρίνεται."[16] In other words, so-called coming-to-be and perishing are just changes in composition, not true origins or endings.

By reinterpreting his elements as mixtures, the author wants to make sure that—even when fire has consumed all the water—it doesn't die out from lack of fuel: some seed of water remains, letting it grow back, as it were. And *vice versa*—when fire is nearly drowned, some 'portion' of dryness still persists. Thus, by combining a transformation model he apparently got from Heraclitus with the more up-to-date rearrangement model from Anaxagoras and Empedocles,[17] he wants to explain

15 *Vict.* I.4.3 (= CMG I 2,4, p. 128 = VI.476 L.):—"When I speak of coming to be or perishing, it is for the sake of the many; but I will show that these are really mixing and separating." A related Anaxagorean quotation appears in *Vict.* I.4.1 (= VI.474 L.): Οὕτω δὲ τούτων ἐχόντων, πολλὰς καὶ παντοδαπὰς ἰδέας ἀποκρίνονται ἀπ' ἀλλήλων καὶ σπερμάτων καὶ ζώων, οὐδὲν ὁμοίων ἀλλήλοισιν οὔτε τὴν ὄψιν οὔτε τὴν δύναμιν.—"Things being as they are, they [fire and water] mutually separate from themselves many varied forms of seeds and living things, which resemble one another neither in appearance nor in power." Cf. Anaxagoras B4 DK: τούτων δὲ οὕτως ἐχόντων χρὴ δοκεῖν ἐνεῖναι πολλά τε καὶ παντοῖα ἐν πᾶσι τοῖς συγκρινομένοις καὶ σπέρματα πάντων χρημάτων καὶ ἰδέας παντοίας ἔχοντα καὶ χροιὰς καὶ ἡδονάς.—"These things being so, one must think that many things and of all kinds are present in all the aggregates and [or: i.e.] seeds of all things, possessing all kinds of shapes, colors, and flavors." (Trans. Laks and Most 2016: 61.)

16 Anaxagoras B17 DK: τὸ δὲ γίνεσθαι καὶ ἀπόλλυσθαι οὐκ ὀρθῶς νομίζουσιν οἱ Ἕλληνες· οὐδὲν γὰρ χρῆμα γίνεται οὐδὲ ἀπόλλυται, ἀλλ' ἀπὸ ἐόντων χρημάτων συμμίσγεταί τε καὶ διακρίνεται. καὶ οὕτως ἂν ὀρθῶς καλοῖεν τό τε γίνεσθαι συμμίσγεσθαι καὶ τὸ ἀπόλλυσθαι διακρίνεσθαι.—"The Greeks do not conceive correctly either what it is to come to be or what it is to be destroyed. For no thing comes to be or is destroyed; but rather, out of things that are, there is mixing and separation. And so, to speak correctly, they would have to call coming to be 'mixing' and being destroyed 'separating'". (Trans. Laks and Most 2016: 63.)

17 Already Fredrich 1899: 129–130 saw the two strands of thought woven together here—an Anaxagorean-Empedoclean and a Heraclitean one—but in the tradition of 19th-century *Textkritik*, he took this not as a sign of conceptual innovation but of compilation. He thought *Regimen* was patched together from a work by some 'Physiker' of the Anaxagorean-Empedoclean school (probably Archelaus) and an equally hypothetical "younger Heraclitean". Empedocles, of course, shares the rearrangement model (albeit with fewer primitives), and understands coming to be and perishing as mixis and diallaxis (B31 DK: φύσις οὐδενὸς ἔστιν ἁπάντων θνητῶν, οὐδέ τις οὐλομένου θανάτοιο τελευτή, ἀλλὰ μόνον μίξις τε διάλλαξίς τε μιγέντων ἔστι, φύσις δ' ἐπὶ τοῖς ὀνομάζεται ἀνθρώποισιν). *Regimen*'s wording and overall scheme is closer to Anaxagoras, but that doesn't rule out Empedocles' influence.

how the cycle keeps going—how the elements don't get destroyed, but both change and endure.[18]

If this is what he is doing, then the move is both ingenious and original. Still, for all its subtlety, the attempt to reconcile two types of change—transformation and rearrangement of unchangeable parts—doesn't quite hold together. For one, as the author himself admits, the whole point of rearrangement is to eliminate the kind of change that allows for perishing and coming to be;[19] if fire contains a portion of water and if transformation is an option, why doesn't fire just consume it? But if fire and water are really mixtures of immutable primitives, how can water turn into fire as it feeds, or both transform into each other at all? So, the author is essentially trying to have his cake and eat it too.

Second, a rearrangement model requires an influx (or loss) of additional particles to account for the increase and decrease of fire and water. But if, as the author insists, fire and water are balanced and "sufficient for each other," then this should be impossible—an increase would upset the balance.

To sum up the difficulties, as I see them: (1) it's unclear why the author describes what seems to be a cycle of transformation with alternating heating and cooling phases in terms of path(s) and turnings. He also seems unable to decide whether he's referring to a single path of fire or a periodic advance of both fire and water. (2) If the whole process relies on fire consuming (chasing after) water (a one-directional transformation), it's hard to see how the maximum points, which are also somehow turning-points of fire, that punctuate this cycle, fit into this story. (3) To account for a cycle of change from fire to water and back the author appears to have combined two incompatible theories of change.

---

18 *Regimen* is clearly concerned with denying primitive perishing. Peck 1928: xiv argued that this may be part of an effort to rescue Heraclitus from the charge of positing it, as he seems to do in his cyclical account in B36 DK (ψυχῇσιν θάνατος ὕδωρ γενέσθαι, ὕδατι δὲ θάνατος γῆν γενέσθαι, etc.). Indeed, *Regimen* appears to aim at a kind of Heraclitean–Anaxagorean synthesis when it states that "separation and recombination are one and the same, coming to be and perishing the same"—a version of *coincidentia oppositorum* in which what counts as separation (perishing) from one perspective is, from another, combination into a new thing (coming to be).

19 *Vict.* I.4.2 (= VI.474 L.): Ἀπόλλυται μὲν οὖν οὐδὲν ἁπάντων χρημάτων, οὐδὲ γίνεται ὅ τι μὴ καὶ πρόσθεν ἦν· συμμισγόμενα δὲ καὶ διακρινόμενα ἀλλοιοῦται.—"Thus, nothing perishes of all things, and nothing comes into being that did not already exist before; but through mixing and separating, everything changes." As Sider 2005: 156 points out, ἀλλοιοῦται here is used broadly and vaguely to mean "change" in general, not in the stricter later sense of qualitative change (cf. Aristotle, *De generatione et corruptione* I 1.314a13–15). Still, the terminology is clearly in the process of being developed. The passage's point is that what is here termed ἀλλοιοῦται is, in fact, to be understood as "coming together" and "separating".

1.2

For all these problems, we shouldn't lose sight of the fundamental—and, in a way, naïve—question: *why is this cycle like that?* Its most distinctive, and most perplexing, features are the maxima and minima—somehow both spatial and quantitative. They are clearly essential: the author insists this is simply how the cycle works. And yet, it's hard to say why they are there at all. Despite the author's considerable efforts, they remain theoretically difficult.

Attempts have been made to trace the scheme back to one or more suitable 'Presocratics'—where one might more naturally expect to find an elemental cycle.[20] But while sources matter, a single-minded *Quellenforschung* focus hasn't served *Regimen* particularly well,[21] and can't, on its own, explain what it's trying to do.

Regimen's model for the cycle, meanwhile, is fairly clear even without appealing to diachrony. The paths and turnings, the spatial and quantitative maxima, even fire feeding on water, make most sense when seen as modelled on the sun's annual movement between the summer and winter solstices.

During the year, the sun moves back and forth from north to south. At the summer solstice, it reaches both its northernmost point (after which it visibly reverses course—hence the name *tropai)*—and the point where daylight (it's the longest day of the year) and the hot, dry summer season peak. After that, both

20 There has been near-unanimous agreement, going back at least to Zeller 1892: 696 and Fredrich 1899: 129, that the cycle in *Regimen* draws—at least in part—on some strand of Presocratic cosmology. But there is no consensus on which one. Joly (Joly and Byl 2003: 32) leans towards Hippo, and possibly Archelaus, citing a couple of brief doxographic reports. Yet as far as the limited evidence shows, neither appears to describe a recurring fire–water cycle. Their accounts instead suggest one-off cosmogonic events in which fire triumphs over water. There are some verbal parallels with Empedocles (especially B31 DK ἐν δὲ μέρει κρατέουσι περιπλομένοιο χρόνοιο. Cf. *Vict.* I.3.1 = VI.472 L.: ἐν μέρει δὲ ἑκάτερον κρατεῖ καὶ κρατεῖται), and the structure of the *Regimen* cycle—alternating between watery and fiery phases—vaguely recalls the opposing phases of his cosmic sequence. But beyond the general idea of recurrence, the parallels are thin. Burnet 1920: 124 n. 66 had already pointed to Heraclitus, noting other Heraclitean references in *Regimen* and drawing on Diogenes Laertius's Peripatetic report (IX.9.5), which says that Heraclitus described periodic macrocosmic shifts from a dry/ bright to a moist/ dark state—an alternation framed as the rise of opposing forces: fire and water. Otherwise, we, of course, have elemental cycles in Heraclitus, but either three- or four-partite ones, as in B31 and B36 DK. The latter, about the mysterious πυρὸς τροπαί, seems to invoke a similar image—an elemental cycle marked by something like solstices—as in *Regimen*. Bartoš (2015: 125), with some reservations, accepts Heraclitus as at least one main source. My point here is not to trace sources—this is certainly not the place for a systematic account—but to highlight just a few necessary points.
21 Cf. note 10.

daylight and heat begin to decline, while night and the cold, wet season gradually increase until they reach their peak at the winter solstice—both the longest night of the year and the sun's southernmost point. The *tropai*, then, can be understood as both spatial limits and something like quantitative maxima and minima: heat and light at one end, cold and darkness at the other. And at the solstices, day and night alternately dominate without, of course, fully eliminating the other—just like the maxima and minima in *Regimen*'s cycle.

The connection to the solstices has been noted before, but for the most part without sufficient emphasis.[22] *Regimen* seems to take its solstitial model very seriously—so seriously, in fact, that the author apparently used a current meteorological theory to explain how the cycle works.

The theory receives an unfavourable mention in Aristotle. He dismisses as ridiculous—though evidently influential enough to warrant a rebuttal—the claim made by some unnamed predecessors of his that the sun, like any fire, is sustained by rising moisture.[23] And this, they say, is why—over the course of the year—it moves be-

---

22 Gomperz 1898: 230–231 was the first to recognise that the model in *Regimen* is a sun-cycle, and to stress its importance: fire and water, at their maxima and minima, behave like day and night at the solstices. He even pointed to Parmenides as a source, on the grounds that in the *Doxa* part of his poem, all things in the sensory world are mixtures of Light and Night—*Parmenides* B9 DK: πᾶν πλέον ἐστὶν ὁμοῦ φάεος καὶ νυκτὸς ἀφάντου / ἴσων ἀμφοτέρων, ἐπεὶ οὐδετέρωι μέτα μηδέν. While few have explored the significance of the solstice pattern in depth, Camden 2023: 217–218 presses this connection further—without endorsing the Parmenidean link—and emphasises in particular that the same cycle of dominance and defeat structures the cosmos as a whole.

23 There has been some debate over the identity of those "predecessors". Since Aristotle cites Heraclitus in this context, it seems clear that Heraclitus must be among those who held the theory that the sun feeds. Cherniss 1935: 133 n. 541 took the extreme view that only Heraclitus is meant. Marcovich 2001: 315, by contrast, argues that Aristotle has an entire group of early *physikoi* in mind. The fact that this theory also appears in *Regimen* strengthens the case for Heraclitean influence—despite Marcovich's and Kirk's (1954: 265–267) doubts about both the text's evidentiary value for Heraclitus and its intellectual worth more generally. While the idea that the sun feeds on moisture likely goes back to Heraclitus (though it was not unique to him; cf. Bartoš 2015: 126 n. 92), the accompanying explanation of the solstices probably does not. The Heraclitean fragment Aristotle quotes—"the sun is new every day" B6 DK—implies that the sun extinguishes at sunset and rekindles at dawn. This fits better with the older poetic cosmology of a flat earth encircled by Okeanos, into which the sun plunges at night. On a spherical earth model, where the sun passes beneath the earth, the notion of a "new sun" each day becomes implausible. Likewise, the idea that the sun moves from tropic to tropic in search of nourishment presupposes a spherical earth divided into hemispheres by the ocean. On a flat earth, it's unclear why fuel depletion would occur specifically in the north and south, where the sun actually draws nearer to the Okeanos. It is possible that this explanation of the solstices—later adopted by the Stoics (Cleanthes *SVF* I 501; Cicero, *De natura deorum* III 37—is itself a somewhat later adaptation of Heraclitean meteorology, in which *anathymiasis* plays a key role, to a spherical earth. But of

tween the tropics: it can't feed in one place forever, so it travels to wherever moisture is available. Once the supply runs out, it turns back.

> So, it is absurd to believe, as some of our predecessors have, that the sun is fed by moisture. Indeed, some say that this is the cause of the solstice, as the same regions cannot always provide it with nourishment yet nourishment it must have or of necessity perish, just as the fire we can see burns as long as it has fuel to feed it, and moisture is the only fuel that will feed fire. This supposes that the moisture which is drawn up reaches as far as the sun and that it rises in the same way as flame does; for this theory of the sun is based on the analogy of fire. But in fact, there is no such analogy. Flame is the result of a constant metabolism of wet and dry: it is not a thing that can be fed, for it can hardly be said to remain one and the same for any length of time. But this cannot be true of the sun: for if it were fed in the same way as a flame, as they say, clearly there would not only be, as Heraclitus says, a new sun every day, but a new sun every second. (*Meteorologica* II 2.354b33–355a15)[24]

> διὸ καὶ γελοῖοι πάντες ὅσοι τῶν πρότερον ὑπέλαβον τὸν ἥλιον τρέφεσθαι τῷ ὑγρῷ· καὶ διὰ τοῦτ' ἔνιοί γέ φασιν καὶ ποιεῖσθαι τὰς τροπὰς αὐτόν· οὐ γὰρ αἰεὶ τοὺς αὐτοὺς δύνασθαι τόπους παρασκευάζειν αὐτῷ τὴν τροφήν· ἀναγκαῖον δ' εἶναι τοῦτο συμβαίνειν περὶ αὐτὸν ἢ φθείρεσθαι· καὶ γὰρ τὸ φανερὸν πῦρ, ἕως ἂν ἔχῃ τροφήν, μέχρι τούτου ζῆν, τὸ δ' ὑγρὸν τῷ πυρὶ τροφὴν εἶναι μόνον, – ὥσπερ ἀφικνούμενον μέχρι πρὸς τὸν ἥλιον τὸ ἀναγόμενον τοῦ ὑγροῦ, ἢ τὴν ἄνοδον τοιαύτην οὖσαν οἵανπερ τῇ γιγνομένῃ φλογί, δι' ἧς τὸ εἰκὸς λαβόντες οὕτω καὶ περὶ τοῦ ἡλίου ὑπέλαβον. τὸ δ' οὐκ ἔστιν ὅμοιον· ἡ μὲν γὰρ φλὸξ διὰ συνεχοῦς ὑγροῦ καὶ ξηροῦ μεταβαλλόντων γίγνεται καὶ οὐ τρέφεται (οὐ γὰρ ἡ αὐτὴ οὖσα διαμένει οὐδένα χρόνον ὡς εἰπεῖν), περὶ δὲ τὸν ἥλιον ἀδύνατον τοῦτο συμβαίνειν, ἐπεὶ τρεφομένου γε τὸν αὐτὸν τρόπον, ὥσπερ ἐκεῖνοί φασιν, δῆλον ὅτι καὶ ὁ ἥλιος οὐ μόνον καθάπερ Ἡράκλειτός φησιν, νέος ἐφ' ἡμέρῃ ἐστίν, ἀλλ' ἀεὶ νέος συνεχῶς.

Aristotle's objections are twofold: first, the theory's mechanism is flawed—fire does not feed on moisture. Second, the analogy does not hold: if the sun really did feed like ordinary fire, it would be in constant flux. But even the theory's own proponents don't go that far—Heraclitus, for instance, says the sun is "new every day", not every instant.

There can be little doubt that *Regimen* adopts this very theory: the author says explicitly that fire feeds on water, and that this explains its movement. But he seems to turn the idea on its head, inverting the fire–sun analogy that Aristotle found so objectionable. It is, implausibly, fire that—like the sun—travels between the *tropai*.

---

course, this remains speculative. An older view (Fredrich 1899; note 17 above) holds that the Heraclitean material in *Regimen* may have come through later Heracliteans, such as Cratylus—a possibility that is both plausible and impossible to prove. But there is no reason the author of *Regimen* couldn't have been such a figure himself: a later Heraclitean reworking and updating Heraclitus' theories.

24 Trans. Lee 1952.

Regimen's element cycle is modelled on the sun's yearly journey from solstice to solstice—it's the clearest way to account for some of the cycle's odder features, above all the paths and turnings of fire, and the maxima and minima. To explain how the cycle works, the author repurposes a meteorological theory originally used to account for the sun's motion—that the sun feeds on moisture and travels in search of nourishment.

But the result is decidedly awkward. *Regimen*'s attempt to combine the fire-feeding explanation with back-and-forth elemental change is creaky at best,[25] and the *tropai* seem to demand an entirely new Anaxagorean theory of change just to make sense. So why use this pattern at all? Why imagine an element cycle as a yearly sun-path?

2

Here, comparison and context may help. The most instructive parallel is with *Nat.Hom.*, a near-contemporary of *Regimen* that famously imagines the body as a kind of yearly 'element' cycle. The two texts are clearly related in some way, though the exact nature of their relationship is difficult to determine.[26] But because *Regimen*'s own yearly pattern has gone largely unnoticed, its similarity to *Nat.Hom.*'s is still underappreciated—even in the most sympathetic readings.[27] What I want to do here is bring that resemblance out more clearly, and in doing so, sharpen our sense of what *Regimen* is actually up to.

In what was to become an immensely influential psycho-physiological theory,[28] *Nat.Hom.* says that the body is constituted by four humours—blood, phlegm, and yellow and black bile—though Polybus—unusually for a 'Hippocratic' text, its at-

25 The notion that fire feeds on water—or more broadly, that heat draws nourishment from cold—is, of course, ancient and fairly ubiquitous in the medical texts (e.g., *Natura pueri* 1 (= VII.486 L.): θερμὸν τῷ ψυχρῷ τρέφεται; *De carnibus* 6 (= VIII.592 L.)). What's notable is that *Regimen*, though it could have simply invoked this familiar model, opts instead for its specifically meteorological version.

26 For a summary of the debate, see Craik 2015: 212. There is no consensus on the question of priority, and both texts are tentatively dated, at the earliest, to the late fifth century BCE. Either may depend on the other—or, less economically, on a common source. For reasons discussed below, I lean toward reading *Regimen* as subtly responding to *Nat.Hom.* But my argument does not depend on that assumption.

27 Especially Jouanna 2002: 52–54; Bartoš 2015: 74–77.

28 For a detailed account of its influence, see Jouanna 2012.

tested author—generally avoids the term.[29] And much like *Regimen*, *Nat.Hom.* seems unsure about their status. On the one hand, the humours seem to be the body's basic elements, each defined by a pair of properties: yellow bile, for example, is hot and dry—like *Regimen*'s fire—while phlegm is cold and moist, like water. On the other, the humours are apparently also somehow degradable into the same hot, cold, dry, and wet, since the body is said to come from them, and to return to them at death—"ashes to ashes", so to speak.[30] So, again like *Regimen*, *Nat. Hom.* wants it both ways: there are 'elements' of the body that are not actually elemental that have properties that are not quite properties but vie with them for the status of genuine primitives.

Now for the cycles themselves. In *Nat.Hom.*, just as the cosmos undergoes its yearly cycle of *seasons*, so does the body cycle through its constituents.

> Thus, all these elements always exist in the human body, but as the seasons turn, they increase and decrease in turn, each according to its nature. For just as the year partakes, throughout its course, of all the elements—the hot, the cold, the dry, and the moist (since nothing in this world could endure even for a moment without all of them present, and if even one were to fail, all would vanish, for by the same necessity all things are held together and nourished by one another)—so too, in the human being, if any one of these original elements were to fail, it could not live. (*Nat.Hom.* 7.7–8 = CMG I 1,3 p. 184–6 (= VI.48–50 L.))
>
> ἔχει μὲν οὖν ταῦτα πάντα αἴδια τὸ σῶμα τοῦ ἀνθρώπου, ὑπὸ δὲ τῆς ὥρης περιισταμένης τοτὲ μὲν πλείω γίνεται αὐτὰ ἑωυτῶν, τοτὲ δὲ ἐλάσσω, ἕκαστα κατὰ μέρος τε καὶ κατὰ φύσιν. ὡς γὰρ ὁ ἐνιαυτὸς μετέχει μὲν πᾶς πάντων καὶ τῶν θερμῶν καὶ τῶν ψυχρῶν καὶ τῶν ξηρῶν καὶ τῶν ὑγρῶν· οὐ γὰρ ἂν μείνειεν οὐδὲν οὐδένα χρόνον ἄνευ πάντων τῶν ἐνεόντων ἐν τῷδε τῷ κόσμῳ, ἀλλ' εἰ ἕν τί γε ἐκλίποι, πάντ' ἂν ἀφανισθείη· ἀπὸ γὰρ τῆς αὐτῆς ἀνάγκης πάντα συνέστηκέ τε καὶ τρέφεται ὑπ' ἀλλήλων· οὕτω δὲ καὶ εἴ τι ἐκ τοῦ ἀνθρώπου ἐκλείποι τούτων τῶν συγγεγονότων, οὐκ ἂν δύναιτο ζῆν ὥνθρωπος.

The analogy is dense and somewhat muddled, but ultimately seems to work like this: just as the year moves through its seasons—each a mixture of hot, cold, dry, and wet—so too does the body move through its humours, which are made up of the same qualities-cum-components. *Regimen*, if we strip it down to basics, does

---

29 The only mention in *Nat.Hom.* 15 = CMG I 1,3 p. 204, 13 (= VI.68 L.) ἐνεόντων χυμῶν is most likely a gloss. With Jouanna's commentary ad. loc.

30 See Lloyd 1964: 92–94, however, who juxtaposes *Nat.Hom.* and *Regimen*, and claims that in the former, hot, cold, dry, and wet are themselves elements, while in the latter they are merely associated with the elements. *Pace* Enache 2019, who maintains they are qualities in both cases. Yet, as Primavesi 2009: 37–38 notes, *Nat.Hom.* explicitly treats the hot, cold, dry, and wet as elemental: they themselves, not hot and cold *things* like the humours, revert back to the environment when the body disintegrates—otherwise one would have to assume the existence of cosmic reservoirs of blood and bile.

something similar: the body cycles through fire and water, but ultimately through hot, cold, dry, and wet—with a kind of summer, when hot and dry fire dominates, and a winter, when cold and wet water does.

The passage also sheds some light on the purpose—or at least one purpose—of this kind of analogy. It is obviously a type of macrocosm–microcosm analogy, but it emphasises not structural similarity between body and cosmos, but shared process: they are alike in that they undergo regular, cyclical change.

One thing it can do is offer some conceptual 'scaffolding' for thinking of the body as balance—specifically, as *dynamic* balance that maintains stability through continual, regular change. And at the same time, the yearly cycle also serves as a *tekmērion*, a kind of loose analogical demonstration, that this is indeed how the body works.[31]

Nat.Hom. gets at this in a somewhat roundabout way by inviting us to imagine a disruption in the cosmic balance: if hot or cold were to dominate and the cycle of change were to stop—say, if we ended up in an unending winter or summer—catastrophe would ensue,[32] and life, as we know it, would cease; on a smaller scale, one can see this in the devastating effects of droughts or winter floods on the agricultural cycle. So, too, the body's stability—its life, and its health—must depend on the regularity of its change. The implicit point here, I take it, is to suggest a model of pathology as imbalance: a cosmic disruption leads to catastrophe; a bodily one, to disease and death.[33]

Regimen seems to say much the same in a very similar context, and the phrasing is close enough to *Nat.Hom.* that coincidence seems unlikely: in *Vict.* I.3.3 (= VI.474 L.), neither fire nor water can gain complete dominance, and if they did, "nothing of what now exists would be as it is now" (οὐδὲν ἂν εἴη τῶν νῦν ἐόντων ὥσπερ ἔχει

31 Since Regenbogen's study on the use of analogy by early Greek physicians, it has been recognised as a kind of heuristic technique and a method of hypothesis formation—under the Anaxagorean motto of "glimpsing the unseen from the visible". According to Regenbogen 1930: 131, an unobserved process or phenomenon is compared to an observed one, and it is through this comparison that we gain "special insight" into the former. This "special insight" broadly means that analogies serve both as heuristic devices—tools that help formulate an account in the first place—and as loose proofs of that account once it is in place. See Lonie 1981: 79 for a review of the discussion and use of analogy.

32 For a similar point, see Kahn 1960: 189; Camden 2023: 217–218.

33 *Aer.* 10.1–2 (= II.42 L.) draws an explicit connection between health and seasonal balance. The year is said to be healthy—that is, there are the fewest diseases—if it is μέτριος, with seasons that are not ὑπερβάλλων τὸν καιρόν, neither too hot nor too cold, and rains that are timely and not excessive. At the same time, the passage hints at something like a reversal of the analogy: the year itself can be called healthy, insofar as it is regular and moderate.

νῦν). Only because they are always in motion and in tension does the world persist in its current form.[34]

Here the contrast with *Nat.Hom.* becomes clear—in how *Regimen* structures its cycle and configures the body–year analogy. First, *Regimen* treats its fire–water cycle as both cosmic and bodily, shifting between these levels without much ado: in the same breath, the author calls fire and water the elements of all living things and also says they are "sufficient for *all things*" and that fire "moves *all things* always" (πάντα διὰ παντός).[35] As a result, the author doesn't need to spell out the analogy's target (the body), as *Nat.Hom.* does. But it also feels less effective: the disruption of a *yearly* cycle is a vivid, concrete image; the disruption of some large-scale theoretical element-cycle, much less so.

Second, while *Nat.Hom.* makes the year analogy explicit (ὡς γὰρ ὁ ἐνιαυτὸς . . .), *Regimen* keeps it implicit. And finally, in *Nat.Hom.* the yearly cycle means the changing seasons, while in *Regimen* it means the sun's movement,—thus, the process behind this change.

To close this section, let me briefly take stock of the main points of comparison. It should by now be clear that *Regimen* and *Nat.Hom.* follow the same basic template. Both reduce the body to a small number of components—four humours in *Nat.Hom.*, fire and water in *Regimen*—and both treat those components sometimes as basic and sometimes as made up of even more basic entities: hot, cold, dry, and wet, which, rather implausibly, also function as qualities. Most significantly, both texts rely on a particular version of the micro–macrocosm analogy—one that amounts to: as the year, so the body. But *Regimen* handles the analogy differently, and far less directly, than *Nat.Hom.* Instead of a simple elements–seasons match-up, we get what looks like two cycles—or rather, a single fire–water cycle that plays out on both cosmic and bodily scales. That cycle, in turn, is modelled on the year; though not the year as a sequence of seasons, but as the sun's path between the solstices.

3

3.1

At this point, we can, if nothing else, restate our original question in more concrete terms: why structure the cycle this way? Why bring in, as it were, an 'extra'

34 Cf. *Nat.Hom.* 7.8 (CMG I 1,3 p. 184–186 = VI.48–50 L.) οὐ γὰρ ἂν μείνειεν οὐδὲν οὐδένα χρόνον ἄνευ πάντων τῶν ἐνεόντων ἐν τῷδε τῷ κόσμῳ, ἀλλ' εἰ ἕν τί γε ἐκλίποι, πάντ' ἂν ἀφανισθείη.

35 As Schluderer 2018: 32–33 observes, *pace* Bartoš 2015: 77; see also Enache 2019: 181–184 above.

cosmic cycle—and why model it on a yearly cycle in *this* way, when a more straightforward and much clearer 'seasons-elements' model, as *Nat.Hom.* shows, was already available?

To make sense of this—and ultimately of both *Regimen* and *Nat.Hom.*—we now need to consider what the analogy is doing: what is it meant to achieve? It's a microcosm–macrocosm analogy, so its overall purpose, obviously, is to connect the two in some way, and in this case, to connect body balance to cosmic balance. As I have argued, one way *Nat.Hom.*, and to some extent *Regimen*, does this is by using the yearly cycle as a kind of paradigm—one that is especially easy to grasp—of a regular, ongoing, dynamic balance that, through change, maintains stability and sustains life. Yet that is certainly not *all* they do.

I will begin with *Nat.Hom.* because here too, it provides not just a useful but a decisive *comparandum*. Although it doesn't quite share *Regimen*'s more theoretical interest in the mechanisms and possibility of elemental change, it is still concerned with how one humour gives way to another.

I would argue that the way *Nat.Hom.* addresses this question has major implications for its overall medical project. When it tries to explain humoural change, it shifts from analogy—"as the seasons, so the humours"—to causation. This comes through most clearly in *Nat.Hom.* 7:

> That winter fills the body with phlegm you will know from the following: it is in winter that sputum and nasal discharge in humans contain the most phlegm; it is also during this season that swellings become white and other diseases phlegmatic. In spring, phlegm still retains some strength in the body, while blood increases because the cold subsides and rains come on. Blood, therefore, increases under the effect of showers and warm days, as these are the conditions of the year that are most suited to it [blood]; for it is moist and warm.[36]

So, a humour increases with its corresponding season: in cold and moist winter, cold and moist phlegm accumulates; in warm and moist spring, warm and moist blood begins to rise, and so on. *Nat. Hom.* does not explain the exact causal mechanism, but it appears that the body draws in more of the now available cold and moist stuff from the surroundings—probably because these are, in some sense,

---

36 *Nat.Hom.* 7.3–4 = CMG I 1,3 p. 182 (= VI.46–48 L.) ὅτι δὲ ὁ χειμὼν πληροῖ τὸ σῶμα φλέγματος, γνοίης ἂν τοῖσδε· οἱ ἄνθρωποι πτύουσι καὶ ἀπομύσσονται φλεγματωδέστατον τοῦ μὲν χειμῶνος, καὶ τὰ οἰδήματα λευκὰ γίνεται μάλιστα ταύτην τὴν ὥρην, καὶ τἆλλα νοσήματα φλεγματώδεα. τοῦ δὲ ἦρος ἔτι μὲν ἰσχυρὸν τὸ φλέγμα ἐστὶν ἐν τῷ σώματι, καὶ τὸ αἷμα αὔξεται· τά τε γὰρ ψύχεα ἐξανιεῖ καὶ τὰ ὕδατα ἐπιγίνεται, τὸ δὲ αἷμα αὔξεται ὑπό τε τῶν ὄμβρων καὶ ὑπὸ τῶν θερμημεριῶν· κατὰ φύσιν γὰρ αὐτῷ ταῦτ' ἐστὶ μάλιστα τοῦ ἐνιαυτοῦ· ὑγρόν τε γάρ ἐστι καὶ θερμόν.

elemental—by means of the familiar fifth-century principle of like attracting like. The same applies, with suitable adjustments, to the other humours.[37]

This suggests that the body's dynamic balance—and thus its life and health—depends above all on the cosmic seasonal rhythm. It also implies a particular model of the body: one defined by its relation to the environment and to seasonal time. In essence, the body is synchronised with the annual cycle and thus keeps seasonal time itself. As the author notes, in winter there is more phlegmatic discharge; in autumn, vomiting will produce more bile. The body, in other words, becomes a kind of time-telling device.[38] What emerges, then, is a biological—more precisely, circannual—clock model of the body, in which the humoral cycle acts as an oscillator, responsive to yearly environmental changes.

Seeing the body as a seasonal clock has clear consequences for medical practice. Since disruption of its internal rhythm leads to disease, the physician's main clinical task is to maintain that rhythm. In a bio-clock model, this means ensuring that it stays in step with the seasonal cycle, and resetting it according to the seasons if it falls out of sync. The method is dietetics; the guiding principle, to counteract opposite with opposite.[39]

Before therapy—even in diagnosis and prognosis—it is the seasons that determine which diseases are likely to occur, since each one 'promotes' the humour that shares its qualities. In autumn, for instance, when black bile is dominant, a particular kind of fever associated with it is more likely to appear.[40]

In a circannual bio-clock model, then, seasonal time becomes the primary factor a doctor must attend to. And indeed, *Nat.Hom.* lists what looks like a standard set of influences on the body's internal state—innate constitution, age, and season.[41] But season is the one that stands out.

There's a short text—only eight chapters long—that is transmitted alongside *Nat.Hom.* and appears under the title *Regimen in Health* (*Salubr.*). Whether it is part

37 *Nat.Hom.* seemingly appeals to this principle at 6.3 (= CMG I 1,3 p. 180 = VI.46 L.), using the example of plants drawing from the earth the nourishment that is "suited to their nature" (ἕλκει ἕκαστον τὸ κατὰ φύσιν αὐτῷ ἐνεὸν ἐν τῇ γῇ).

38 Not that one needs to observe phlegm to tell that it's winter, but one could imagine some (admittedly not very likely) scenario where one could tell the advent or predict the duration of a season by some such somatic indicators.

39 *Nat.Hom.* 9.2 (= CMG I 1,3 p. 188 = VI.52 L.) καὶ τὰ συντείνοντα λύειν, καὶ τὰ λελυμένα συντείνειν.

40 *Nat.Hom.* 9.2 (= CMG I 1,3 p. 188 = VI.52 L.) the doctor must counteract the established character of diseases (ἐναντίον ἵστασθαι τοῖσι καθεστηκόσι νοσήμασι), of constitutions, of seasons, and ages—relaxing what is tense, and tightening what is slack (καὶ τὰ συντείνοντα λύειν, καὶ τὰ λελυμένα συντείνειν).

41 *Nat.Hom.* 9.4 (= CMG I 1,3 p. 190 = VI.54 L.).

of *Nat.Hom.*, an inserted addendum, or less likely, an independent work is debated.[42] But whatever its status, it seems close enough to *Nat.Hom.* in that it shares its—or at least a similar—synchronisation model.

Salubr. prescribes a (mainly prophylactic) regimen organised by season. In summer and winter—the seasonal extremes—patients are told to eat foods that offset the season's heating and drying, or cooling and moistening, effects—presumably to avoid pushing the body further into that state and disrupting its rhythm. In spring and autumn, they are meant to prepare for the extremes ahead.

> During summer, one should eat soft barley bread, drink plentiful diluted beverages, and consume exclusively boiled dishes. Indeed, such a regimen is necessary during summer so that the body remains cool and soft, as this hot and dry season makes bodies burning and parched. Therefore, one must guard against these conditions through such measures.[43]

Such season-bound dietetics—where seasonal time signals the appropriate intervention (in this case, prophylaxis), and where, to boot, the body heats and cools with the seasons—makes most sense if, as in *Nat.Hom.*, the organism is synchronised with and dependent on the seasonal cycle.[44]

---

42 In Jones' and Littré's editions of the Hippocratic writings, it's printed as a separate piece. But already in Ermerins 1864 and in Jouanna 2002—whose edition makes what is now the most widely accepted case for unity—it's included as part of *Nat.Hom.* It's not transmitted as a standalone work, but rather as a distinct section (with marginal headers). It's also much too short to stand on its own. While the shift to dietetics may seem abrupt, as Craik (2015: 208, 210) shows, it fits into a three-part thematic structure: basic bodily composition, pathology, and practical therapeutic-prophylactic advice (regimen). Joly (Joly and Byl 2003: 43) is skeptical about "l'unité si stricte", though he doesn't deny single authorship; in any case, this doesn't affect the argument here.

43 *Salubr.* I.2 = *Nat.Hom.* 16 CMG I 1,3 p. 206 (= VI.72 L.) τοῦ [δὲ] θέρεος τῇ τε μάζῃ μαλθακῇ καὶ τῷ πόματι ὑδαρεῖ καὶ πολλῷ καὶ τοῖσιν ὄψοισι ἑφθοῖσιν πᾶσιν· δεῖ γὰρ χρῆσθαι τούτοισι, ὅταν τὸ θέρος ᾖ, ὅπως τὸ σῶμα ψυχρὸν καὶ μαλθακὸν γένηται· ἡ γὰρ ὥρη θερμή τε καὶ ξηρή, καὶ παρέχεται τὰ σώματα καυματώδεα καὶ αὐχμηρά· δεῖ οὖν τοῖσιν ἐπιτηδεύμασι ἀλέξασθαι. In addition to diet proper, the regimen also includes exercise, bathing, and even more invasive measures such as emetics.

44 Seasonal dietetics may well reflect a traditional pattern of thought that predates *Salubr.* (Ducatillon 1969: 40). I'm not claiming that such a model depends entirely on a physiological theory of an internal biological clock—only that it aligns especially well with one. It's also possible that the logic ran the other way: that the practice of adapting diet to the seasons may have helped prompt or justify the development of such a physiological model.

3.2

What, then, does *Regimen* do with its year analogy? At first reading, the author appears to draw broadly the same clinical lessons from it as *Nat.Hom.* and *Salubr.* In chapter 68, he gives season-specific recommendations—ranging from food and exercise to baths and emetics. The advice is essentially the same as in *Salubr.*, only more detailed, and *Regimen* likewise insists that diet should counter the particular nature of the season, apparently to prevent any one constituent from becoming too dominant.

> In winter, therefore, to counteract the cold and congealed season, it is appropriate to adopt the following regimen [. . .] consume drying, astringent, and warming foods. [. . .] And I will explain the reason: since the season is cold and congealed, living beings also become more or less the same.
>
> ἐν μὲν οὖν τῷ χειμῶνι συμφέρει πρὸς τὴν ὥρην, ψυχρήν τε καὶ συνεστηκυῖαν, ὑπεναντιούμενον τοῖσι διαιτήμασιν ὧδε χρῆσθαι. [. . .] τοῖσι δὲ διαιτήμασι χρῆσθαι τοῖσι ξηροῖσι καὶ αὐστηροῖσι καὶ θερμαντικοῖσι [. . .] διότι δὲ οὕτως ἔχει φράσω· τῆς ὥρης ψυχρῆς ἐούσης καὶ συνεστηκυίης, παραπλήσια πέπονθε καὶ τὰ ζῶα [. . .] (*Vict.* III.68.3–6 = CMG I 2,4 p. 196 (= VI.594–598 L.))

What stands out, however, is that *Regimen* reserves its seasonal recommendations for the *polloi*—those who lack the time or resources to fully devote themselves to their health. For those who can, the author offers something more refined: a form of dietetics focused on balancing food and exercise with as much precision as possible. It demands constant observation and calculation, and above all functions as a kind of prophylaxis-cum-diagnostics—a method for detecting latent imbalances and, in doing so, predicting and preventing disease.

The author's attitude here seems openly classist—in a way that may feel familiar: maintaining proper health is treated as a matter of time and resources, and essentially a privilege of the rich. But it's a curious move: why, exactly, is the seasonal diet reserved for those who, as he puts it, "must live their lives haphazardly out of necessity"?

One suggestion—which considerably softens the classism—is that the seasonal regimen is simply a basic one: easy to follow and universally applicable, especially for the lower classes, while those who can afford it receive something more sophisticated on top.[45] This may well be true, but the author's tone is hardly

45 *Vict.* III.69 (= VI.606 L.). According to Joly (Joly and Byl 2003: 285), *Regimen* is not genuinely interested in the *hoi polloi* because the lifestyle recommendations—such as nightly walks—are too demanding for ordinary people to follow. Ducatillon (1969: 39) counters that some of the advice is in fact easy to implement, suggesting the diet may have been intended for both rich and

neutral. If that were all he meant, he could have said so. I suspect there is a deeper reason behind the supercilious tone: it reflects a physiological model — subtly but significantly different from *Nat.Hom.*'s biological clock.

The real contrast between *Regimen* and *Nat.Hom.* lies in their accounts of cyclical change. *Nat.Hom.*, as discussed, relies on top-down causation, but as a mechanism it has serious limitations: it might make sense on the microcosmic level—the body pulling in more cold during winter—but it's harder to see how this applies to macrocosmic change. For one, where would the cosmos draw in the extra hot or cold to effect its change? And if this macro-change happens through transformation rather than increase, then why wouldn't transformation also apply on the bodily level?

Regimen seems to recognise the problems posed by a scheme like *Nat.Hom.'s*. Its own model, as it were, deconstructs that scheme. On the surface, *Nat.Hom.* straightforwardly matches the humoural with the seasonal cycle. But since it treats hot, cold, dry, and wet as constitutive elements of both seasons and humours ("just as the year partakes . . ."), it ultimately implies that the same cycle operates at both the cosmic and the bodily level. That is precisely the route *Regimen* takes: rather than adding another element cycle to *Nat.Hom.'s* nominally simpler structure, it drives home the point that body and cosmos are governed by the same process of periodic heating/ drying and cooling/ moistening.

If that's the implication—and if there really is one universal process operating on both levels—then it needs a single mechanism of change to account for it. *Nat.Hom.*'s top-down causation wouldn't do; so *Regimen* finds such a mechanism in a "fire feeding on moisture" theory.

An important consequence of this universal mechanism is that the cycles are self-powered. This means they may synchronise to some extent—the atmospheric conditions obviously influence the state of the body, hence the seasonal diet—but they do not have to, because there is no primary causal dependence of the microcosm on the macrocosm.

When the body is synchronised with the seasons through a direct causal relationship, seasonal time naturally takes precedence in diagnosis, prognosis, and intervention. But if the body's cycles can run autonomously, then seasonality is re-

poor. But this doesn't explain why the seasonal diet, in particular, is singled out as the baseline. If, *pace* Joly (Joly and Byl 2003: 42), *Regimen* here depends on *Salubr.*, that might clarify the move: the aim may be to downgrade a rival's work as too simplistic, suitable only for non-elites. Joly acknowledges that *Regimen*'s recommendations are more complex and detailed, but this could just as well suggest that *Salubr.* is the source, rather than an abridgement. Moreover, in *Vict.* III.67 and III.69, *Regimen* only claims as its own discovery the προδιάγνωσις πρὸ τοῦ κάμνειν, and not the dietetic recommendations, as Joly suggests.

duced to just one influence among many. It remains the easiest to observe and can still serve as a rough guide—it's perfectly reasonable to assume that summer heat will dry the body and shift its balance, so counteracting it through diet makes sense, especially for those who cannot afford to treat health as a full-time job.

In a physiological model like this—where bodily balance isn't strictly governed by the seasons—a physician would naturally focus on the most immediate levers of regulation: food that replenishes and exercise that depletes. And indeed, the author devotes nearly all of Book II to nutrition (*Vict.* II.39–56 = VI.534–570 L.) and exercise (II.57–66 = VI.570–588 L.), while seasonal diet is treated in just one (albeit lengthy) chapter, aimed at the less fortunate.

Let me briefly restate the point. In *Nat.Hom.*, at any rate, it's clear what a seasons analogy can do for a medical writer. By establishing a top-down causal relationship between the macrocosmic and microcosmic cycles—effectively by abandoning the analogy—*Nat.Hom.* constructs a 'circannual clock' model of the body. In such a model, where the body essentially keeps seasonal time, time itself—understood qualitatively, as *kairos*, the right time for any particular intervention— becomes the primary index for therapy, prevention, and diagnosis. Accordingly, *Nat.Hom.* and *Salubr.* can build a practicable dietetic project: a set of recommendations tied to the time of year, aimed at keeping the body in step with its environment and thereby maintaining its balance.

Regimen, as I've tried to show, uses the same year analogy as *Nat.Hom.*, but arrives at a different mechanism: a curious blend of qualitative change and rearrangement of immutable primitives to explain how the cycles work. This mechanism seems, at least in one respect, more theoretically sound—it can account for both microcosmic and macrocosmic change. But it also entails that the body's cycle is not primarily dependent on the environment—and, as a consequence, not necessarily synchronised with it. The result is a far more complex and less straightforward medical project.

Regimen imagines the body as a rhythm, of course, so *kairos* should, in principle, still matter.[46] But because the large and small cycles run independently, *kairos* becomes uncoupled from 'external' time. And *Regimen* effectively ends up with a body-clock that doesn't quite work.

Put differently: unlike *Nat.Hom.*, *Regimen* posits an internal, unobservable, self-powered rhythm. This rhythm is both highly individual, shaped by inborn

46 *Regimen* (I.7.2 = CMG I 2,4 p. 130) makes the point that vital processes like digestion work as rhythms that rely on timely shifts—and that when these happen παρὰ καιρόν, the whole process breaks down.

constitution and age, and constantly influenced by external factors like nutrition and environment. Dietetics, accordingly, becomes a matter of precision: the exact 'dose' of food and exercise relative to each other, and the timing of their administration, must be tailored to the individual—an ideal that proves extremely difficult to realise in practice. *Regimen* even acknowledges that the ideal dietetic project is essentially utopian. It would mean monitoring the body constantly and adjusting its fire-water balance in real time through an individual, and continually adapted, regimen.

> For if it were possible [. . .] to determine for the *physis* of each individual an exact proportion of food and exercise—one that contains neither excess nor deficiency, neither too much nor too little—then health would have been precisely discovered for human beings. As it stands, however, even if all the previously mentioned matters have been discovered for what they are, this one thing remains impossible to discover. If someone were present and able to observe a person as he undresses and exercises in the gymnasium, he could maintain the individual's health—subtracting here, adding there. But without being present, it is impossible to determine food and exercise with precision.[47]

Practically speaking, the body's own *kairos*—the *status quo* of its cycle at any given moment—is hard to catch; to pinpoint it exactly is impossible. The physician is left to work in approximations. Factors like seasonal time offer *some* but clearly crude and insufficient shortcuts.

It is therefore understandable that *Regimen* is interested in finding a more sophisticated way of assessing the state of the body's balance. And the author indeed proudly advertises as his own medical discovery a divination-like method of gaining insight into the state of the body's balance by means of certain medically prophetic dreams; which if interpreted correctly, may indicate subtle disturbances to the balance before they manifest as full-blown diseases.[48]

47 *Vict.* I.2.3 (= CMG I 2,4 p. 124 = VI.470 L.): εἰ μὲν γὰρ ἦν εὑρετὸν ἐπὶ τούτοισι πρὸς ἑκάστου φύσιν σίτου μέτρον καὶ πόνων ἀριθμὸς σύμμετρος μὴ ἔχων ὑπερβολὴν μήτε ἐπὶ τὸ πλέον μήτε ἐπὶ τὸ ἔλασσον, εὕρητο ἂν ἡ ὑγιείη τοῖσιν ἀνθρώποισιν ἀκριβέως. νῦν δὲ τὰ μὲν προειρημένα πάντα εὕρηται, ὁποῖά ἐστι, τοῦτο δὲ ἀδύνατον εὑρεῖν. εἰ μὲν οὖν παρείη τις καὶ ὁρῴη, γινώσκοι ἂν τὸν ἄνθρωπον ἐκδύνοντά τε καὶ ἐν τοῖσι γυμνασίοισι γυμναζόμενον, ὥστε φυλάσσειν ὑγιαίνοντα, τῶν μὲν ἀφαιρέων, τοῖσι δὲ προστιθείς· μὴ παρεόντι δὲ ἀδύνατον ὑποθέσθαι ἐς ἀκριβείην σῖτα καὶ πόνους. Cf. *Vict.* III.67 (= CMG I 2,4 p. 194 = VI.592 L.).

48 *Regimen* devotes all of Book 4 to diagnosis through dreams. While the author, as he himself says, is happy to borrow ideas he agrees with from others, there's a case to be made that he sees this procedure as his own distinctive contribution; see van der Eijk 2004.

3.3

We have seen what year-analogies can do in medical texts: for one thing, they help conceptualise the body as a dynamic balance of contraries (hot, cold, dry, wet), disease as *im*balance and therapy as its correction— you restore the equilibrium by acting on a contrary with a contrary.

But depending on how one handles it, the analogy can produce quite distinct body-models. By making the relationship between cosmic and body balance causal, one can get seasonal clock-like body models.

Regimen, which does not quite take this route, is only marginally interested in seasonal time, and arguably ends up with a far more complex and demanding medical (especially diagnostic) project than *Salubr*. So, then we need to ask: why use the year analogy at all, *if time is not of the essence*? So, for the final time, why use a seasonal analogy and why make its source part, the year cycle, a sun path?

To understand what *Regimen* wants with (this version of) the year model, we need to consider how the author approaches the micro-macrocosm analogy more generally. It is the text's basic conceptual framework: the fact that the body is in some way like the cosmos—*Regimen* calls this relationship *mimesis*—determines what can and should be done with it medically. But how exactly they are alike, and what *mimesis* means, is a point of contention in *Regimen* scholarship.

On one reading, *mimesis* should be taken at face value: the cosmos is an exemplar of which the body is an imperfect copy.[49] The medical goal then, much like in Plato's *Timaeus*, is to make the body resemble its exemplar as closely as

---

49 As Schluderer 2018 argues. The interpretation hinges on an embryological passage (*Vict.* I.10 = VI.484–486 L.), where fire in a kind of demiurgic capacity arranges the embryonic body as an ἀπομίμησις τοῦ ὅλου—stomach like the sea, flesh like earth, and so on. This suggests that the body is a copy of the whole. Yet even this passage doesn't make the hierarchy clear. We know from texts like *De hebdomadibus* that body–cosmos analogies can be bi-directional, but Schluderer insists that "nothing of the kind is said in *Vict.*" (Schluderer 2018: 41 n. 58). However, *Regimen* also says that fire arranges the body μικρὰ πρὸς μεγάλα καὶ μεγάλα πρὸς μικρά (*Vict.* I.10): Ἐνὶ δὲ λόγῳ πάντα διεκοσμήσατο κατὰ τρόπον αὐτὸ ἑωυτῷ τὰ ἐν τῷ σώματι τὸ πῦρ, ἀπομίμησιν τοῦ ὅλου, μικρὰ πρὸς μεγάλα καὶ μεγάλα πρὸς μικρά. Cf. Jones 1931: 247: "the small after the manner of the great and the great after the manner of the small." The phrase is somewhat ambiguous and can be taken to mean that the body's larger parts are proportioned to its smaller ones, but this reading seems forced. In fact, the demiurgic fire that does the arranging is also described in the same passage in ambiguous terms—as a fire in the body, but also, apparently, as a cosmic fire that "governs all things always". So, there is good reason to think that the same structuring process is happening on both the micro- and macro-scale: fire arranges the cosmos on the large scale and the body on the small. Neither is strictly a copy of the other.

possible, which practically would mean to make and keep its cycle as regular as the cosmic ones, but by means of dietetics, not philosophy.[50]

On a different, more "egalitarian" interpretation, *mimesis* does not mean that the body imitates the cosmos directly, but that both are 'imitations' of the same paradigm, though it remains somewhat vague on what it is, and even if there's an overarching one.[51] In the case of the element cycle(s), this take seems to be supported by a crucially important—yet often misinterpreted—passage that comes right after the author sets up the cycles:

> All things, human and divine, move[52] up and down by turn. Day and night, to the maximum and minimum; just as the moon to its maximum and minimum; the advance of fire and of water; just as the sun has its longest and its shortest course—all things are the same and not the same. (*Vict.* I.5.1 (= VI.476 L.))
>
> Χωρεῖ δὲ πάντα καὶ θεῖα καὶ ἀνθρώπινα ἄνω καὶ κάτω ἀμειβόμενα. Ἡμέρη καὶ εὐφρόνη ἐπὶ τὸ μήκιστον καὶ ἐλάχιστον· ὡς σελήνη ἐπὶ τὸ μήκιστον καὶ ἐλάχιστον, πυρὸς ἔφοδος καὶ ὕδατος, <οὕτως> ἥλιος ἐπὶ τὸ μακρότατον καὶ βραχύτατον, πάντα ταὐτὰ καὶ οὐ ταὐτά.

---

50 Schluderer, then, argues not for passive resemblance but for a dynamic conception of mimesis. I suggest that in *Regimen*, mimesis is indeed prescriptive—but its object is not the cosmos itself, but rather the law that governs it: a subtle, but in my view necessary, distinction. The parallels with the *Timaeus* are many and well documented; for detailed discussion and a review of the extensive literature, see Bartoš 2015: 231–240.

51 The 'egalitarian' reading originates with Burkert 1972: 44–45 and has since been taken up and fully developed by Bartoš 2015: 129–132.

52 There is a long-standing problem concerning the interpretation of χωρεῖ. First, it is not the original manuscript reading, but Bernays' 1848 emendation of the nonsensical χωρίς. The correction is supported by the Latin translation found in manuscript P, which represents a tradition independent of the two main Greek families and reads *complectitur*—'to encircle, enclose'—a literal rendering of χωρεῖ in its primary sense, 'to give space to' or 'contain.' Second, the passage is often translated as "everything flows" or "everything is in flux" (Joly (in Joly and Byl 2003: 129): "toutes choses [. . .] s'écoulent"; Jones 1931: 237: "all things [. . .] are in a state of flux"). While χωρεῖν can mean 'to run' (as in streams), it doesn't straightforwardly mean 'to be in flux'. LSJ lists that sense but relies on this very passage to justify it. The flux reading likely stems from the assumption that the line quotes Heraclitus. Plato (*Phaedo* 90c5), glossing Heraclitus, equates πάντα χωρεῖ with πάντα ῥεῖ, describing an up-down flux using the image of the Euripus Strait. However, as Lebedev (1985: 143–145) argues, Plato was likely conflating different Heraclitean images—namely, a path upward and downward (cf. ἄνω κάτω περιχωρέοντα καὶ ἀμειβόμενα, cited in Lucian, *Vitarum auctio* 14 and Philo, *De aeternitate mundi* 110) and the famous river fragment (B12 DK). In short, there is no reason to take πάντα χωρεῖ ἄνω κάτω ἀμειβόμενα in *Regimen* as a statement about flux. The examples that follow in *Regimen* concern cosmic motion, not instability. It may even preserve a genuine Heraclitean fragment.

The passage requires some unpacking. It begins by stating a kind of universal cosmic law of change. Importantly it is stated in terms of *motion* and—in another clear reference to Heraclitus—*up-and-down path*: everything, on both the large and the small scale, moves in a rhythm, from maximum to minimum and then back again. When one extreme is reached, things reverse—one opposite gives way to the other.

The author proceeds with a list of observable 'cosmic' examples: the cycle of the sun, the phases of the moon, the alternation of day and night—so at first glance, the microcosm, the human half of the "human and divine", seems to be missing. However, the list also includes *pyros ephodos kai hydatos*—the advance of fire and water—which can hardly refer to anything directly visible. Instead, it points back to the fire–water cycle discussed earlier in *Regimen*, which, as we have established, plays out in both the body and the cosmos. This, then, accounts for the human side.

But the point of including *pyros ephodos kai hydatos* is not just to round out the list. It's to show that this very cycle—fire and water taking turns—is what drives the others. Differently put, the movements of the sun and moon, the rhythm of day and night are visible expressions of the same underlying process. And that process, in turn, is itself an instance of the *anō–katō* law—the patterned reversal between opposites that, for *Regimen*, governs all change.

Then, the immediate purpose of the micro–macrocosm analogy, I take it, is to show that body and cosmos are alike not through imitating one another, but in that both are subject to, or rather instantiate, the same universal law. This law is made visible through a number of illustrative cases: cosmic cycles, as we have just seen, but also—somewhat unexpectedly—human crafts. As I mentioned, *Regimen* is especially fond of one in particular: two carpenters sawing wood, their movements tracing a path up and down between maximum and minimum.[53]

So how does the year analogy fit into all this? Just like *Nat.Hom.*, *Regimen* seems to be reworking a traditional thought pattern: the parallelism between elements and elemental change and the cycle of seasons.[54] *Nat.Hom.* sets out the

---

53 See note 9.

54 Analogies between the seasons and the elements are cross-cultural. Greek examples are relatively late and typically arise in discussions of seasonal *harmonia*. Aristides Quintilianus (*De musica* III.19) attributes to Pythagoras a detailed correspondence between the seasons, cosmic elements, and musical intervals—likely derived from the *Timaeus* (31b–c), though the idea itself is older (*Euripides* fr. 943). On this, see Burkert 1972: 356. Among the Heraclitean testimonia, a fragment from the 4th-century iambic poet Scythinus—who reportedly produced a versified version of Heraclitus' book—describes a cosmic lyre played by Apollo, using the sun as a plectrum to strike three or four seasonal strings. The image also appears in Cleanthes (*SVF* I 502–503).

analogy more explicitly, but *Regimen* draws a deeper lesson from it—namely, that both body and cosmos are kept going by a regular shift of opposites: fire (hot and dry) and water (cold and wet).

Regimen then tries to understand how this process works and offers a remarkably inventive Heraclitean–Anaxagorean[55] account of fire and water transforming into each other without mutual destruction. But more importantly, *Regimen* infers that there must be a deeper principle behind this kind of change: something by virtue of which opposites, in general, are bound to shift back and forth.

For this *Regimen*—perhaps inevitably—turns to Heraclitus, who famously held that the cosmos is governed by tension and unity of opposites through reversal.[56] And it explicitly casts its universal law in Heraclitean terms: the shift of opposites is a *hodos anō katō*, a back-and-forth path between limits. This clearly alludes to DK 60 (ὁδὸς ἄνω κάτω μία καὶ ὡυτή), Heraclitus' formula for the identity of opposites—though, as ancient sources show, it was also taken to describe elemental transformation.[57]

This, then, is the broader context in which *Regimen* uses the year analogy. In *Nat.Hom.*, it helps build a kind of biological clock model of the body. Within this model, seasonal time serves as a heuristic shortcut: for instance, summer means that yellow bile should be dominant, and everything else follows from there. The model also sets the therapeutic goal—to synchronise the body with the seasons, and, in essence, to assimilate it to its environment.

Regimen uses the body–year analogy for heuristic purposes too, but in a different way: to reveal—through tangible examples like the sun's journey through the year—the universal law of the regular shift of opposites. And to show how this law governs the cycle, that is the rhythm of heating and drying, cooling and moistening, that sustains both body and cosmos.

---

55 I could find no clear parallel for such an amalgam, though—as Heidel 1911: 142 notes—exhalation theories like Heraclitus' can be seen as proto-corpuscular, and thus lend themselves to reinterpretations of the kind found in *Regimen* (the fire–water cycle, alternating between hot/ dry and cold/ wet phases, does resemble Heraclitean anathymiasis, as Lebedev 2014: 34 argues).

56 Notably, the *Symposium* (186e4–187b7) features a semi-fictional example of a 'heraclitising' doctor. Eryximachus, much like *Regimen*, quotes Heraclitus B51 DK on the harmony of opposites. Craik (2015: 275) notes the parallels and argues that Plato based the speech on *Regimen*—a plausible suggestion, as Plato was likely familiar with it (Craik 2001). It may also reflect a broader medical interest in Heraclitus. *De Alimento* refers to him extensively, though its date may be relatively late.

57 Unless *Regimen* is quoting Heraclitus directly (see note 52). In any case, ancient sources almost universally understood the ἄνω κάτω path as referring to elemental transformation: Diogenes Laertius IX.9; Philo *De aeternitate mundi* 109; Cicero De *natura deorum* II 84; Epictetus fr. 8. On this, Vlastos 1955: 310–313.

A doctor needs to understand this law because the body's fire–water rhythm varies from case to case, is shaped by many factors, and cannot be directly observed. Unlike in *Nature of the Human Being*, the season offers no reliable shortcut to the body's internal state. The shortcut, if there is one, is knowing the basic principle of how the rhythm works.

The law also, in a sense, guides medical practice—it is what the doctor must work to enact. Making and keeping the body healthy does not mean keeping it "on time", but ensuring that its internal fire–water rhythm ticks steadily (something that requires complex diagnostics). This, *Regimen* suggests, is what the doctor must aim to do: act on contraries with contraries, to ensure their regular interchange. Much like, according to *Regimen*, a builder achieves their technical aim—making bricks—by *hygra xērainein, xēra hygrainein*; or like a carpenter who, to cut wood, moves the saw up and down from maximum to minimum in rhythm. Medicine, in this sense, is itself—as the author would say—an imitation of the universal law.[58]

3.4

In a study of the microcosm–macrocosm analogy in early medical and meteorological thought, Frédéric Le Blay[59] made an observation that has not received enough attention: that one can roughly identify two tendencies in early Greek medical writing depending on how the analogy is treated. Those who use it to establish direct influence, like *Nat.Hom.*, are "meteorological"—that is, concerned with how the body interacts with and depends on its environment. Those who emphasise homology or structural parallelism, like *Regimen*, fall more on the "philosophical" side.[60]

But when applied to Greek medicine, "philosophical" is a particularly fraught label. It has been challenged on several grounds: it is too vague and amorphous; it presupposes the early existence of two well-defined, bounded fields—medicine and philosophy; and it implies a one-way path of influence from philosophy to

58 *Vict.* I.15.2 (= VI.490 L.), of course, lists medicine among its nature-imitating crafts.

59 Le Blay 2005: 252–253.

60 Le Blay doesn't spell out exactly what he means by "philosophical", but the implication seems to be that the body–cosmos analogy allows for inferences from the cosmos to the body. In this way, cosmological reasoning becomes useful—indeed necessary—for understanding the body, and thus for medical practice. As he puts it, "medicine cannot be an autonomous science but directly depends on philosophical knowledge and cosmological theories".

medicine.[61] Overall, it does little to help us understand why some early medical texts engage in speculation about the origins or fundamental structure of the cosmos.

A more recent alternative—*cosmological medicine*—aims to remedy that. What marks certain medical texts as cosmological is their appeal, in medical explanation, to the first principles of all things. On this view, *Regimen* and *Nat.Hom.*—both of which adopt more or less the same parsimonious ontology— would be seen as part of the same intellectual project, driven by a shared impulse toward universality.[62]

But this misses something essential about the difference in aim between *Regimen* and *Nat.Hom.*—a distinction that Le Blay's own rough-and-ready typology nonetheless manages to capture. Both start from the same microcosm–macrocosm analogy, but the latter develops it into a medical project whose goal is to assimilate the body to the cosmos. *Regimen*, by contrast, uses the analogy to induce a metaphysical law (with the cosmos, in fact, just one of the means), which then becomes the standard for medical practice.

Which, then, is (more of) a cosmological project? *Regimen* certainly seems more "philosophical" in a general anachronistic sense than *Nat.Hom.* But again, one might ask: what exactly do these labels capture—and how useful are they, really?

The trouble with such *a priori*, teleological classifications—like "cosmological"—is precisely that they are teleological: they ascribe intent or a shared impulse in response to some perceived common problem, which must then be read into what are sometimes highly heterogeneous texts. And even in cases where texts appear close, attributing the same impulse may not ultimately explain very much.

There are alternative approaches that suggest medical authors, for reasons that may be quite individual and varied, chose to participate in what had become by the mid-fifth to fourth century a well-established mode of inquiry: *peri physeōs*

61 For discussion of the relationship between medicine and philosophy, see van der Eijk 2018: 304–307; Camden 2023: 4–10, which also offers a comprehensive overview of the scholarship.

62 Camden 2023: 3 argues that "medical writers were attempting to base the art of healing on a limited number of principles, generalized to the highest possible degree". But this risks conflating cosmology with first philosophy—or more narrowly, with ontological minimalism. Anaxagoras, who influenced *Regimen* and likely other medical writers, posits an infinite number of principles. More broadly, the idea that cosmology is essentially about finding *archai* may reflect a later philosophical perspective more than the actual concerns of early Greek thinkers. When Anaximander speaks of the *apeiron*, or Empedocles of love and strife and the four roots, their aim is not merely to reduce everything to a few substances, but to explain change, differentiation, and structure. As Menn (forthcoming) puts it, they were primarily concerned with "the problem of how the present world-order arose, complete with all of its characteristic constituents, including the earth and the rotating heavens and also living things".

historíē.[63] This was, broadly, a generative mode of explanation—an account of the *physis* of a thing that explains what it is by showing how it came to be that thing—best exemplified by cosmogonies, since Anaximander, which describe the origins and development of the cosmos and all its parts including living beings. But we should think of such accounts as an open and flexible category, not one reserved exclusively for supposed 'cosmologists' or 'philosophers'. In other words, texts like *Regimen* or *De carnibus* or indeed *Nat.Hom.* need not be seen as responding to some shared issue; rather, they may have adopted—each for its own reasons—an approach broad and popular enough to accommodate a range of projects.

Arguably *Regimen*'s first book bears the hallmarks of a generative *peri physeōs* account: it begins with *archai*, proceeds to describe how the human being is generated from or by them, and concludes with how the human functions depending on their original constitution. *Nat.Hom.* omits the embryological portion but likewise explains the body's workings in terms of *archai*, both as origin and as principle.

Yet within the *peri physeōs* 'genre' their aims, models, even their notion of human *physis* is different. In *Nat.Hom.* *physis* is the things from which it comes and which make it up and which ultimately explain its functioning. One can argue that within the micro-macrocosm analogy *physis* is well on its way to becoming a more universal sort of concept, not just *physis* of any particular individual. And *Regimen* goes further: the concept subtly moves away from "stuff from which a thing is made and which explains how it works" and moves towards a more universal transcendent principle. *Physis* in *Regimen* is actually closer to "universal law that everything obeys": to 'imitate' nature means to realise the universal principle of unity-and-shift of opposites. So, *Regimen*, by reconfiguring a traditional thought pattern, contributes to the expansion and universalisation of the concept of *physis* itself. It is a project that deserves a philosophical label but on individual merit not as representative of a supposed tendency.

Bibliography

Primary Sources

Bernays, J. *Heraclitea* I. Doct. Diss. University of Bonn, 1848.

Ermerins, F. Z. (ed./trans./comm.) *Hippocratis et aliorum medicorum reliquiae*. Vol. 3, Utrecht: Kemink & Zn, 1864.

63 The approach was first sketched out by Kahn 1960: 200–209.

Joly, R., and S. Byl. (ed./trans./comm.) *Hippocrate.* Du Régime. (CMG I, 2, 4) Berlin: Akademie Verlag, 2003[2].
Jones, W. H. S. (trans.) *Hippocrates, Vol. IV. Heracleitus* On the Universe. Loeb Classical Library 150. Cambridge, MA: Harvard University Press, 1931.
Jouanna, J. (ed./trans.) *Hippocrate.* La nature de l'homme. (CMG I, 1, 3) Berlin: Akademie Verlag, second edition 2002.
Kirk, G. S. *Heraclitus. The Cosmic Fragments*. Cambridge: Cambridge University Press, 1954.
Laks, A., and G. W. Most (eds.) *Early Greek Philosophy.* Vol. VI: *Later Ionian and Athenian Thinkers, Part 1.* (LCL 529). Cambridge, MA: Harvard University Press, 2016.
Lee, H. D. P. (trans.) *Aristotle*. Meteorologica. (LCL 397). Cambridge, MA: Harvard University Press, 1952.
Lonie, I. M. (trans./ comm.) *The Hippocratic Treatises "On Generation", "On the Nature of the Child", "Diseases IV": A Commentary*. Berlin/Boston: De Gruyter, 1981.
Marcovich, M. (ed./ trans./ comm.) *Heraclitus: Greek Text with a Short Commentary*. Sankt Augustin: Academia Verlag, 2001[2].
Schiefsky, M. J. (trans./ comm.) *Hippocrates: On Ancient Medicine*. Leiden: Brill, 2005.

Secondary Literature

Barnes, J. *The Presocratic Philosophers*. London: Routledge, revised edition 1982.
Bartoš, H. "The analogy of auger boring in the Hippocratic *De victu*". *The Classical Quarterly* 62.1, 2012: 92–97.
Bartoš, H. *Philosophy and Dietetics in the Hippocratic* On Regimen*: A Delicate Balance of Health*. (*Studies in Ancient Medicine* 44). Boston/Leiden: Brill, 2015.
Brunn, L. von. "Hippokrates und die meteorologische Medizin". *Gesnerus* 3, 1946: 151–173; 4, 1947: 1–18 and 65–85.
Burkert, W. *Lore and Science in Ancient Pythagoreanism*. Cambridge, MA: Harvard University Press, 1972.
Burnet, J. *Early Greek Philosophy*. London: A. & C. Black, 1920[3].
Camden, D. H. *The Cosmological Doctors of Classical Greece: First Principles in Early Greek Medicine*. Cambridge: Cambridge University Press, 2023.
Cherniss, H. *Aristotle's Criticism of Presocratic Philosophy*. Baltimore: Johns Hopkins University Press, 1935.
Craik, E. M. "Plato and medical texts: *Symposium* 185c–193d". *The Classical Quarterly* 51.1, 2001: 109–114.
Craik, E. M. *The 'Hippocratic' Corpus: Content and Context*. London/New York: Routledge, 2015.
Ducatillon, J. "Collection Hippocratique. Du Régime, Livre III. Les deux publics". *Revue des études grecques* 82, 1969: 33–42.
Enache, C. "Ontology and meteorology in Hippocrates' *On Regimen*". *Mnemosyne* 72.2, 2019: 173–196.
Enache, C. "The typology of human constitutions in Hippocrates' *De Victu* 1, 32". *Wiener Studien* 124, 2011: 39–54.
Fredrich, C. *Hippokratische Untersuchungen*. Berlin: Weidmannsche Buchhandlung, 1899.
Gesner, J. M. *De animabus Heracliti et Hippocratis ex huius libro I de diaeta disputatio*. Göttingen, 1752.
Gomperz, T. *Griechische Denker. Eine Geschichte der antiken Philosophie*. 3 vols. Leipzig: Veit and Comp. 1896–1902.

Halliwell, S. *The Aesthetics of Mimesis: Ancient Texts and Modern Problems*. Princeton: Princeton University Press, 2002.

Heidel, W. A. "Antecedents of Greek corpuscular theories". *Harvard Studies in Classical Philology* 22, 1911: 111–172.

Jouanna, J., "The legacy of the Hippocratic treatise *The Nature of Man*: The theory of the four humours". In *Greek Medicine from Hippocrates to Galen: Selected Papers*, 335–359. Boston/Leiden: Brill, 2012.

Kahn, C. H. *Anaximander and the Origins of Greek Cosmology*. New York: Columbia University Press, 1960.

Le Blay, F. "Microcosm and macrocosm: The dual direction of analogy in Hippocratic thought and the meteorological tradition". In *Hippocrates in Context*, ed. P. J. van der Eijk, 251–269. Leiden: Brill, 2005.

Lebedev, A. V. *The Logos of Heraclitus: A Reconstruction of His Thought and Word* (English translation of *Логос Гераклита: реконструкция мысли и слова*, 1996). St. Petersburg: Nauka, 2014.

Lebedev, A. V. "The cosmos as a stadium: agonistic metaphors in Heraclitus' cosmology". *Phronesis* 30.2, 1985: 131–150.

Liewert, A. *Die meteorologische Medizin des Corpus Hippocraticum*. Berlin/Munich/Boston: De Gruyter, 2015.

Lloyd, G. E. R. "The hot and the cold, the dry and the wet in Greek philosophy". *The Journal of Hellenic Studies* 84, 1964: 92–106.

Menn, S. "Anaxagoras, Empedocles, Leucippus: The origins of the cosmological crisis". Forthcoming.

Peck, A. L. *Pseudo-Hippocrates Philosophus: or, The Development of Philosophical and Other Theories as Illustrated by the Hippocratic Writings, with Special Reference to the De victu and the De prisca medicina*. Doct. Diss., University of Cambridge, 1928.

Primavesi, O. "Medicine between natural philosophy and physician's practice: a debate around 400 BC". In *Quo Vadis Medical Healing: Past Concepts and New Approaches*, ed. S. Elm and S. N. Willich, 29–40. Dordrecht: Springer, 2009.

Regenbogen, O. "Eine Forschungsmethode antiker Naturwissenschaft". *Quellen und Studien zur Geschichte der Mathematik*, B.1, 1930: 131–182.

Schluderer, L. R. "Imitating the cosmos: the role of microcosm–macrocosm relationships in the Hippocratic treatise *On Regimen*". *The Classical Quarterly* 68.1, 2018: 31–52.

Sider, D. (ed./comm.) *The Fragments of Anaxagoras*. Sankt Augustin: Academia Verlag, 2005^2.

van der Eijk, P. J. "Divination, prognosis, prophylaxis: the Hippocratic work "On Dreams" (*De victu* 4) and its Near Eastern background". In *Magic and Rationality in Ancient Near Eastern and Graeco-Roman Medicine*, ed. H. F. J. Horstmanshoff and M. Stol, 187–218. Leiden: Brill, 2004.

van der Eijk, P. J. *Medicine and Philosophy in Classical Antiquity: Doctors and Philosophers on Nature, Soul, Health and Disease*. Cambridge: Cambridge University Press, 2005.

van der Eijk, P. J. "The Role of Medicine in the Formation of Early Greek Thought". In *The Oxford Handbook of Presocratic Philosophy*, ed. P. Curd and D. W. Graham, 385–412. New York: Oxford University Press, 2008.

van der Eijk, P. J. "Medicine in Early and Classical Greece". In *The Cambridge History of Science*, ed. A. Jones and L. Taub, 293–315. Cambridge: Cambridge University Press, 2018.

Vlastos, G. "On Heraclitus". *The American Journal of Philology* 76.4, 1955: 337–368.

Zeller, E. *Die Philosophie der Griechen in ihrer geschichtlichen Entwicklung*. Vol. 1.2. Leipzig: O. R. Reisland, 1892.

Annette Heinrich

Hippokrates, *De internis affectionibus*

Diagnostik von Krankheitsphasen und therapeutische Synchronisation bei akuten versus chronischen Erkrankungen

Abstract: Dieser Beitrag beschäftigt sich mit einem antiken griechischen medizinischen Text über innere Erkrankungen. Die konzeptuelle Vorgehensweise in der hippokratischen Schrift *De internis affectionibus* soll hinsichtlich der Synchronisation von Körper und antikem ärztlichen Handeln analysiert werden. Es geht um die Frage, ob oder inwieweit bereits in diesem Text eine Klassifizierung in akute und chronische Zeitphasen von Krankheit oder Verlaufsformen vorgenommen wurde, und ob und auf welche Weise die ärztliche Therapie stringent mit solchen Verlaufsformen synchronisiert wurde. Der Beitrag führt zunächst überblickend in die Schrift *De internis affectionibus* und prognostisch-diagnostische Methoden darin ein. Dann wird anhand der Gruppe der Typhuserkrankungen exemplarisch eine Übersicht über einzelne, beschriebene Verlaufsformen erarbeitet, in deren Folge sich im Text jeweils entsprechend synchronisierte Therapie-Grundsätze finden. Die Methodik aus diesen exemplarischen Passagen spiegelt sich prinzipiell auch in den anderen beschriebenen Krankheitsgruppen des Textes, in dem 54 innere Erkrankungen systematisch abgehandelt werden.

Keywords: Hippokrates, innere Erkrankungen, akute Erkrankungen, chronische Erkrankungen, Prognostik, Therapeutik

Während bereits wissenschaftliche Arbeiten zu zeitlichen Aspekten von Krankheit und Therapie in der antiken Medizin vorliegen,[1] konzentriert sich dieser Beitrag auf die therapeutischen Bemühungen antiker griechischer Ärzte, den Körper des Kranken in eine Synchronität mit den Erscheinungen des Krankheitsverlaufs zu bringen. Insbesondere geht es um die Adaptation der Therapie in der Behandlung chronischer Krankheiten. Diesen Themen soll hier am Beispiel des hippokratischen Textes über innere Erkrankungen nachgegangen werden. Die antike griechische Schrift Περὶ τῶν ἐντὸς παθῶν (*De internis affectionibus*) eignet sich in besonderer Weise für eine solche Untersuchung, da sie sich ausführlich mit einer großen Zahl von einzelnen inneren Erkrankungen beschäftigt, welche in exzellenter Systematisierung dargeboten werden. Dieser Beitrag beginnt mit einer kurzen

1 Forschungsliteratur zu chronologischen Fragen in der Medizin, z. B. Miller 2023, Singer 2022, Cooper 2011.

 | https://doi.org/10.1515/9783112235690-003

Einführung zu seiner Textgrundlage. Dann wird die Rolle der ärztlichen Prognostik für die Klassifizierung von Krankheiten in kürzere oder längere zeitliche Verlaufsformen beleuchtet. Der Zeitpunkt der Entscheidung der Krankheit, die *krisis*, führt den antiken Arzt weiter zur Erkenntnis von optional wechselnden Krankheitsverläufen. Die Ätiologie einer Krankheit spielt für die therapeutische Synchronisation im Sinne eines Gegensteuerns eine Rolle. Die Krankheitsgruppe *Typhos* der inneren Erkrankungen wird im Beitrag exemplarisch bezüglich der therapeutischen Synchronisation betrachtet. Anhand der jeweiligen Heilungsmaßnahmen des antiken Arztes bei kurzen oder langen Krankheitsphasen soll untersucht werden, welche Prinzipien der therapeutischen Synchronisation im Text *De internis affectionibus* dargelegt sind.

1 Einleitung zum Text Hippokrates, *De internis affectionibus* (*Int.*)

Die Schrift *De internis affectionibus* (*Int.*) stammt aus dem 4. Jahrhundert vor Christus und gehört zum hippokratischen Textkorpus.[2] *Corpus Hippocraticum* steht dabei für die Gruppe der in der heutigen Forschung als hippokratische Schriften zusammengefassten antiken griechischen Texte, zwischen denen jedoch keine intrinsische Kohärenz angenommen werden darf. Sie stammen von verschiedensten Autoren, aus verschiedenen Zeiten und haben verschiedenste Ursprünge und Themen. Ihre Kollektion zu einem „Corpus" ist als ein Produkt späterer Kanonisierung anzusehen. Die hippokratischen Texte stellen sich sehr unterschiedlich dar, sie überlagern und ergänzen sich teilweise, andererseits widersprechen sie sich aber auch – sie stehen vermutlich auf älteren Traditionsformen von Medizin.[3]

Die Schrift *Int.* ist ein wichtiges Zeugnis der medizinischen Behandlung von inneren Erkrankungen in der antiken griechischen Medizin. Die heutige Forschung nimmt als Autor von *Int.* einen sehr erfahrenen und fachkundigen Mediziner an.[4] Der Name des Autors ist unbekannt, doch teils wird ein Arzt namens Eu-

2 *Int.*: Περὶ τῶν ἐντὸς παθῶν, siehe Fichtner 2022: 61, Nr. 42; Littré Band VII: 165–303. Die jüngste vollständige Edition der Schrift *Int.* ist die von Paul Potter (1988) mit englischer Übersetzung. Jouanna 2009 hat eine textkritische Teil-Edition von *Int.* mit französischer Übersetzung und textkritischem Kommentar erarbeitet. Es handelt sich um die Kapitel *Int.* 1, 6, 7, 8, 21, 23, 37 in Relation zu *De Morbis* II, sowie *Int.* 35, 52, 53 in Relation zu *De Morbis* III.

3 Siehe dazu auch van der Eijk 2016; Überblick zur antiken Heilkunst, siehe Kollesch und Nickel 1994: 9–49; vgl. Krug 1985: 23–24.

4 Dazu z. B. Craik 2015: 140.

ryphon als Autor angenommen.[5] Der Text gibt Informationen zur Ätiologie für jede beschriebene Krankheit und leitet aus der Ätiologie und den Symptomen die Behandlung ab. Die meisten Krankheiten werden mit einer Prognose versehen und mit der Einschätzung ihrer Schwere bewertet. *Int.* beschreibt in 54 Kapiteln je eine innere Erkrankung. Die einzelnen Krankheitsbeschreibungen sind in zusammengehörige Gruppen gegliedert. (Zur Einteilung der Inhalte der 54 Kapitel und in die Krankheitsgruppen, siehe Übersicht im Anhang.) In jedem einzelnen Kapitel wiederum gibt es ein typisches internes Expositionsschema, d. h. die Abhandlung einer Krankheit folgt prinzipiell immer der gleichen Struktur: Name, Nummer oder ätiologischer Typ der Krankheit innerhalb der jeweiligen Krankheitsgruppe; Ätiologie; Symptome; Behandlung; verschiedene mögliche Verlaufsformen mit den jeweiligen Behandlungsempfehlungen oder auch Prognosen; abschließende Prognose in Zusammenhang mit der Einschätzung der Schwere dieser Krankheit. Dieses Expositionsschema bei der Beschreibung einzelner innerer Erkrankungen weist ein hohes Maß an chronologischer Orientierung auf.

2 Prognostik in *Int.* als Orientierung für die Therapie

In der Schrift *Int.* gründet sich die Prognostik auf die Annahme von Krankheit als eine bestimmte, festgelegte Entität, die von einer Reihe von beobachtbaren Symptomen definiert ist. Diese Symptome sind von externen oder internen Faktoren verursacht, und diese haben bei allen Patienten die gleiche Wirkung. Deshalb erscheint es dem Autor möglich, *generelle* Zeiträume für den Krankheitsverlauf vorauszusagen, d. h. Prognosen zu erstellen.[6] Anmerkungen zur Ätiologie werden in jedem Kapitel hinzugefügt, jedoch nicht weiter theoretisch unterlegt.[7] Gute Prognostik gehörte bereits in der Antike zu den Grundvoraussetzungen ärztlicher Kunst. Um ein inneres Krankheitsbild auf eine solche Art und Weise beschreiben zu können, dass es alle wesentlichen Informationen enthält, und für den Nutzer des Textes praktikable Hinweise sowohl für die Diagnostik und Prognostik als auch für die Therapie liefert – dazu wird eine umfassende Sammlung empirischer Daten benötigt. Eine solche akribische Sammlung hält die Schrift *Int.* bei der Beschreibung von Symptomen und Zeitabschnitten

5 Dazu Jouanna 2009: 13, 17, 690–699; Craik 2018: 36.

6 Vgl. Asper 2015: 26.

7 Zu antiker Ätiologie siehe Hankinson 2018; zur Ätiologie in *Int.* siehe Jouanna 2009: 175–269.

der Krankheiten schriftlich fest und erstellt daraus eine systematisierte Anleitung zur Erkennung, Prognostik und Behandlung innerer Erkrankungen. In der Schrift *Int.* schlägt sich die Ungewissheit der Prognostik in der Form nieder, dass jeweils verschiedene mögliche Verlaufsformen für die gleiche Krankheit angenommen werden. In der Antike war man sich der Verbindung des menschlichen Körpers mit der Natur und mit bestimmten, festgelegten Rhythmen bewusst. Krankheiten wurden auch als Störungen natürlicher körperlicher Rhythmen wahrgenommen. Die genaue Deutung dieser Asynchronien wurde in verschiedener Art und Weise vorgenommen, doch war in *Int.* akzeptiert, dass sich bestimmte pathologische Erscheinungen in immer den gleichen Zeiträumen zeigten.

3 Kurze, akute Krankheitsphasen in *Int.* und hippokratischen nosologischen Texten

Prinzipiell enthält jede einzelne Krankheitsbeschreibung, d. h. jedes Kapitel in *Int.*, chronologische Marker. Solche Marker für akute, frühe Krankheitsphasen sind z. B. τὸ μὲν πρῶτον (zuerst) oder κατ' ἀρχὰς (zu Beginn). Diesen zeitlichen Markern folgt dann die weitere Symptombeschreibung:

> ***Int.* 1 Lungenkrankheit**
> zuerst befällt ihn ein trockener Husten.[8]
>
> τὸ μὲν πρῶτον βὴξ ἴσχει ξηρή. (P.VI.70=L.VII.166)
>
> ***Int.* 1 Lungenkrankheit**
> und Frieren und Fieber greifen [den Kranken] an, und zwar zu Beginn der Krankheit heftig.
>
> καὶ ῥῖγος καὶ πυρετὸς ἐπιλαμβάνει, κατ' ἀρχὰς μὲν τῆς νούσου σφόδρα. (P.72=L.166)
>
> ***Int.* 2 Lungenkrankheit**
> Folgendes nun leidet er [der Kranke]: zu Beginn der Krankheit [...]
>
> τάδε πάσχει· κατ' ἀρχὰς τῆς νούσου [...] (P.78=L.172)

Im hippokratischen Textkorpus generell, sowie auch in der Schrift *Int.* selbst, findet sich für akute Zustände der Begriff “scharf” (ὀξύς), der heftige Krankheitssymptome charakterisiert und meist mit akuten Phasen von Krankheit oder Rückfall in akute Phasen in Zusammenhang steht:

8 Übersetzungen zu *Int.* sind von mir.

***Int.* 16 Nierenkrankheit III**

Danach lässt der Schmerz nach, doch kurz darauf greift er wieder akut an.

ἔπειτα ἀνῆκεν ὁ πόνος, καὶ αὖθις ἐπέλαβεν ὀξὺς δι' ὀλίγου. (P.122–124=L.204)

***Int.* 1 Lungenkrankheit I**

Wenn er sich nämlich irgendwie belastet, dann quälen die Beschwerden akuter und der Husten mehr, und das Frieren und das Fieber greifen heftiger an.

ἢν γάρ τι πονήσῃ, ὅ τε πόνος ὀξύτερος καὶ ἡ βὴξ μᾶλλον ἢ τὸ πρότερον πιέζει, καὶ τὸ ῥῖγος καὶ ὁ πυρετὸς μᾶλλον ἔχει. (P.72=L.168)

Für die Krankheitsentwicklung zu einem hochakuten Zustand findet sich im hippokratischen Korpus mehrfach der Terminus (πάροξυς) – in den *Epidemien*-Büchern oft im Zusammenhang mit Jahres- oder Tageszeiten, in den nosologischen und prorrhetischen Schriften teils im Zusammenhang mit Fieber,[9] aber auch mit anderen Zeichen, wie Schaum vor dem Mund, Koma, Spasmen, oder unspezifischen Zeichen:

Hipp., *De victu acutorum spurium*

So ist das Kaltwerden der Füße nämlich sehr häufig ein Zeichen dafür, dass das Fieber gerade im Begriff ist, hochakut zu werden.

ὡς γὰρ ἐπὶ τὸ πολὺ σημεῖόν ἐστι μέλλοντος παροξύνεσθαι τοῦ πυρετοῦ ψύξις ποδῶν· (*Acut. spur.* 13=7 L., P.276=L.II.420).

Auch ärztliche Behandlungsfehler werden bereits in hippokratischem Rahmen für das Entstehen hochakuter Krankheitszeichen in Betracht gezogen (nicht direkt in *Int.*). So können etwa Fehler in der Ernährung des Patienten die Krankheit verschlimmern und diesen Zustand dann durch weitere Ernährungsfehler zusätzlich verstärken. Im folgenden Beispiel kritisiert der Autor ärztliche Kollegen, die durch ihre unrichtigen Ernährungsverordnungen die Krankheit verschlimmert haben und die gerade an den wichtigen Zeitpunkten, wenn eine Krankheit nun hochakut (πάροξυς) geworden ist, eine Richtung bei der Ernährungsverordnung anstreben, welche er genau umgekehrt für hilfreicher hält:

Hipp., *De victu acutorum*

[...] dass die Ärzte die Kranken bezüglich der Ernährung nicht richtig anleiten. [...] gerade zu solchen Zeitpunkten stellen sie vom Fasten auf Krankensuppen um, wo es doch oft hilfreicher ist, sich von den Krankensuppen dem Fasten anzunähern, wenn sich die Krankheit nun auf diese Weise [durch die falsche Ernährung] hochakut verschlimmert hat.

9 Vgl. Singer 2022: 108; Fieber wurde in antiken Texten mehr als eigenständige Krankheit verstanden, und weniger als Symptom.

> [...] ὅτι οὐκ ὀρθῶς ἄγουσιν ἐς τὰ διαιτήματα οἱ ἰητροὶ τοὺς κάμνοντας· [...] ἐν τοῖσι τοιούτοισι καιροῖσι μεταβάλλουσιν ἐς τὰ ῥυφήματα ἐκ τῆς κενεαγγίης, ἐν οἷσι πολλάκις ἀρήγει ἐκ τῶν ῥυφημάτων πλησιάζειν τῇ κενεαγγίῃ, ἢν οὕτω τύχῃ παροξυνομένη ἡ νοῦσος. (*Acut.* 41 (L.11), Joly 53.17–26=L.II.308–312)

Der Terminus *paroxys* erscheint auch später in den galenischen Krankheitsdefinitionen. Noch heute werden fulminante, hochakute Krankheitszeichen als paroxysmal bezeichnet, z. B. *paroxysmale Tachykardie.*

4 Lange, chronische Krankheitsphasen in *Int.*

Wenn sich dann nach der ersten, akuten Zeit eine verlängerte Krankheitsphase ankündigt, dann erscheinen im Text *Int.* wiederum Marker für *chronos* (χρόνος, Zeit), die die Chronifizierung indizieren, wie z. B. χρονίζειν, χρόνιος, πολυχρόνιος. Dann zeigen sich die Symptome anders, als wenn Heilung in Aussicht ist. Einige Symptome können dann stärker auftreten, andere aber auch milder, wie es sich etwa bei dieser Lungenkrankheit nach den ersten zehn Tagen zeigt:

> ***Int.* 2 Lungenkrankheit II**
>
> Wenn die Krankheit aber langdauernder sein wird, dann spuckt er viel mehr eitrigen Auswurf und die sonstigen Beschwerden in seinem Körper sind viel stärker. Doch die Fieber greifen milder an als zu Beginn.
>
> ἢν δὲ μέλλῃ πολυχρόνιος ἡ νοῦσος ἔσεσθαι, τά τε πῦα πολλῷ πλείω ἀποπτύει, καὶ ὁ ἄλλος πόνος ἐν τῷ σώματι πολλῷ ἔνι πλείων· αἱ δὲ θέρμαι βληχρότερον ἔχουσιν ἢ τὸ πρίν. (P.80=L.172–174)

Die milderen Fieber in Kombination mit dem vermehrten Sputum im Beispiel oben werden als Zeichen für Chronifizierung gewertet. Die chronische Phase der o. g. Lungenkrankheit in *Int.* 2 kann mit guter Behandlung überwunden werden. Jedoch besteht hier die Gefahr, dass sie nach einer Genesungsphase zurückkehrt und sich mehr und mehr verlängert. Eine Verlängerung der Krankheit gibt es in vielen *Int.*-Kapiteln, z. B.:

> ***Int.* 25 Wassersucht IV von der Milz**
>
> Diesem [Kranken], wenn sich die Krankheit chronifiziert [...]
>
> τούτῳ ἢν χρονίσθῇ τὸ νόσημα [...] (P.156=L.230)

> ***Int.* 27 Leberkrankheit I**
>
> Diese Krankheit ist aber schwer und chronisch.
>
> ἡ γὰρ νοῦσος χαλεπὴ καὶ χρονίη. (P.170=L.240)

***Int.* 51 Ischias**

Diese Krankheit ist aber chronisch.

ἡ δὲ νοῦσος χρονίη. (P.250=L.298)

5 Zeitpunkt der Entscheidung der Krankheit – *Krisis*

Zu Beginn jeder Krankheitsbeschreibung in *Int.* werden also zunächst die unterschiedlichen akuten Krankheitszeichen aufgezählt. Zur Prognostik in *Int.* gehört stets neben der Aussage, *wie* sich die Krankheit entwickeln wird, auch die Vorhersage der Zeiträume für die Entwicklung der Krankheit. So prognostiziert *Int.* (wie auch verwandte nosologische Texte) oft einen bestimmten Zeitraum bis zur Entscheidung der Krankheit, *krisis* (κρίσις). Über theoretische Hintergründe zur *krisis* äußert sich *Int.* nicht.[10] Der Zeitpunkt der Krisis ist in *Int.* derjenige, an dem die Krankheit nach der akuten Phase entweder heilt, oder sich chronifiziert, oder der Patient daran verstirbt:

***Int.* 27 Lebererkrankung I**

[Die Krankheit] entscheidet sich aber meistens innerhalb von sieben Tagen, in denen zeigt sie nämlich, ob sie tödlich ist oder nicht.

κρίνεται δὲ μάλιστα ἐν ἑπτὰ ἡμέρῃσιν, ἐν ταύτῃσι γὰρ ἀποδηλοῖ εἰ θανάσιμος ἢ οὔ. (P.166–168=L.238)

Hier wird also ein genauer Zeitraum von sieben Tagen bis zur Krisis der akuten Phase angegeben. Die Krankheit kann töten oder nicht. Im Weiteren kann sie mittels Therapie geheilt werden und zurückkehren. Oder auch nicht zurückkehren. Die Krankheit insgesamt wird als schwer und chronisch eingeschätzt:

***Int.* 27 Lebererkrankung I**

Wenn er sich davor hütet, dann wird die Krankheit nicht wieder zurückkehren. Die Krankheit ist aber schwer und chronisch.

ταῦτα ἢν φυλάσσηται, οὐχ ὑποτροπιάσαι πάλιν ἡ νοῦσος. ἡ γὰρ νοῦσος χαλεπὴ καὶ χρονίη. (P.168–170=L.240)

---

10 Zum hippokratischen Konzept der Krisis siehe die hippokratische Schrift *De crisibus*; zum Begriff der Krisis in der antiken Medizin vgl. Singer 2022: 102–106; zur weiteren Tradition des antiken Verständnisses von Krankheitsverläufen siehe auch Cooper 2011.

Im nächsten Kapitel, bei der zweiten Lebererkrankung, wird gar kein genauer Zeitraum bis zur Krisis angegeben:

***Int.* 28 Leberkrankheit II**

wenn aber die Tage vorübergegangen sind, in denen sich die Krankheit entscheidet, dann lassen die Beschwerden nach.

ὅταν δὲ αἵ τε ἡμέραι παρέλθωσιν ἐν ᾗσι κρίνεται τὸ νόσημα, ὅ τε πόνος ἐλάσσων ἔχῃ. (P.170=L.240)

Die Zeitspanne bis zur Krisis wird jedoch auch bei der Beobachtung bestimmter ähnlicher Anfangssymptome nicht immer als bereits sicher vorhersagbar eingeschätzt, sodass dementsprechend für die Krankheit auch verschiedene zeitliche Optionen des Verlaufs genannt werden. Krankheitsbeschreibungen mit variablen Zeitangaben bis zur Krisis oder variablen Verlaufsmöglichkeiten stellen sich in *Int.* dann z. B. so dar:

***Int.* 1 Lungenkrankheit**

Und so wird er sehr schnell gesund. Die Krankheit erfordert aber viel Behandlung, denn sie ist schwer. Wenn er nicht betreut wird, nachdem er gesund geworden ist, und wenn er sich nicht vorsichtig verhält, ist die Krankheit zu vielen zurückgekehrt und hat sie vernichtet. Wenn sich der Patient mit dieser Behandlung erholt, dann gut. Wenn nicht, dann sollst du ihm, nachdem du ihn mit Milch gekräftigt hast, den Brustkorb und den Rücken brennen. Wenn du Erfolg mit dem Brennen hast, dann besteht Hoffnung für ihn, der Krankheit zu entkommen.

καὶ οὕτως τάχιστα ὑγιὴς ἔσται, ἡ δὲ νοῦσος θεραπείης δεῖται πολλῆς, χαλεπὴ γάρ. ἢν δὲ μὴ θεραπεύηται ὑγιὴς γενόμενος καὶ ἢν μὴ ἐν φυλακῇ ἔχῃ ἑωυτὸν, τοῖς πολλοῖς ὑποτροπάσασα, ἡ νοῦσος ἀπώλεσεν. οὗτος ἢν μὲν ὑπὸ ταύτης τῆς θεραπείης λήξῃ,[11] ἄλις· εἰ δὲ μὴ, παχύνας αὐτὸν γάλακτι καῦσαι τά στήθεα καὶ τὸ μετάφρενον· ἢν γὰρ τύχῃς καύσας, ἐλπὶς ἐκφυγεῖν τῆς νούσου. (P.78=L.172)

6 Variable zeitliche Krankheitsphasen – Verlaufsformen

Nach der Einschätzung der Zeit für die *krisis* folgen in *Int.* nun die Symptombeschreibungen für die verschiedensten weiteren möglichen Verlaufsformen der jeweiligen Krankheit, mit deren Ablauf das therapeutische Handeln in engem Zusammenhang steht. Bereits die erste Krankheitsbeschreibung einer Lungenkrankheit, *Int.* 1, zeigt die Prinzipien der Einteilung in verschiedenen Zeitphasen sehr gut, und

11 Handschriften: Θ λήξῃ; M ἰηθῇ, geheilt wurde.

die therapeutischen Maßnahmen für die einzelnen Phasen sind im Text jeweils detailliert beschrieben und angeleitet: zuerst kann die Krankheit nach einer kurzen Phase schnell heilen. Sie kann aber auch bestehen bleiben, es kann Fieber hinzukommen. In dem Fall entscheidet sich die Krankheit in etwa 14 Tagen. Sie kann danach vergehen. Oder sie kann weiter bestehen bleiben und Schmerzen im gesamten Brustkorb verursachen. Falls sich das Befinden danach nun bessert, kann der Kranke schrittweise aufgebaut und mehr belastet werden. Falls er aber noch keine Nahrung verträgt und wieder Fieber auftritt, muss er weiter behandelt werden. Nun soll wieder ein schrittweiser Aufbau versucht werden, aber nur, solange dem Kranken dies bekommt, und solange es ihm nicht noch schlechter geht. Ein Rückfall nach vorheriger Besserung kann jetzt tödlich verlaufen. Für dieses Krankheitsbild wird am Ende des Kapitels eine Rezeptur für eine Suppe angefügt, für den Fall, dass der Kranke keinen Appetit hat und schwach ist. In chronischen Verlaufsphasen kann der Patient Honigmilch, Schmerzmittel und Hustenmittel erhalten, deren Substrat und Anwendung im Kapitel genau beschrieben sind. Sollte es dem Kranken schließlich sehr schlecht gehen, bleibt als letzte Hoffnung die Methode des Brennens, die angewendet werden soll, wenn es um Leben oder Tod geht, um überhaupt eine Chance auf Überleben zu erhalten (ἐλπὶς ἐκφυγεῖν). Im Folgenden sollen noch weitere, ähnliche Beispiele für verschiedene mögliche Verlaufsformen in *Int.* gezeigt werden:

***Int.* 39 Typhus I**

Die Krankheit entscheidet sich in sieben Tagen oder in 14. Viele entfliehen aber auch bis zu 24 (Tagen). Wenn er nun diesen entflohen ist, ist er gesund, denn in diesen Tagen zeigt sich, ob (die Krankheit) tödlich ist oder nicht.

ἡ νοῦσος κρίνεται ἐν ἑπτὰ ἡμέρῃσιν ἢ τεσσερακαίδεκα· πολλοὶ δὲ διαφεύγουσι καὶ ἐς τὰς τέσσαρας καὶ εἴκοσιν· ἢν οὖν ταύτας ἐκφύγῃ, ὑγιής ἐστιν, ἐν γὰρ ταύτῃσι τῇσιν ἡμέρῃσι διαδελοῖ εἰ θανάσιμος ἢ οὔ. (P.200=L.262)

***Int.* 48 Dicke Krankheit II**

Sie entscheidet sich aber innerhalb von höchstens 40 Tagen, ob sie tödlich ist, oder nicht. Bei vielen aber, als die Krankheit schon zu Ende war, ist sie wieder zurückgekehrt. Wenn sie nun zurückkehrt, besteht die Gefahr, dass er zugrunde geht. Die Krankheit entscheidet sich aber innerhalb von sieben Tagen, wenn sie zurückkommt, ob sie tödlich ist, oder nicht. Wenn er diesen entflieht, dann stirbt er wahrscheinlich nicht, sondern bei den meisten vergeht sie, wenn sie behandelt wird.

κρίνεται δ' ἐν τεσσεράκοντα ἡμέρῃσι τὸ μακρότατον, εἰ θανάσιμος ἢ οὐ. πολλοῖσι δὲ ἤδη τοῦ νοσήματος πεπαυμένου πάλιν ἡ νοῦσος ὑπετρόπασεν· ἢν οὖν ὑποτροπάσῃ, κίνδυνος αὐτὸν διαφθαρῆναι· κρίνεται δ΄ ἡ νοῦσος ἐν ἑπτὰ ἡμέρῃσιν, ἢν ὑποτροπάσῃ εἰ θανάσιμος ἢ οὔ. ἢν δὲ ταύτας ἐκφύγῃ, οὐ μάλα θνῄσκει, ἀλλὰ τοῖσι πολλοῖσι μελεδαινομένη ἐξέρχεται. (P.236=L.288)

Diese Beispiele lassen einige prognostische Optionen offen. Der antike Arzt stand zwischen den Aussagen des Patienten zu seinem Befinden, bzw. seinen Beobachtungen an bewusstlosen Patienten und seinen klinischen Untersuchungsergebnissen. Das subjektive Erleben konnte die Anamnese des Patienten bzw. seiner Angehörigen in der Wertigkeit verändern und es war schwierig, zu objektiven Ergebnissen zu kommen. Mit solchen Prognosen, die sich teils festlegen, teils aber auch hochgradig variable Angaben zu den Zeiträumen bis hin zur Krisis zulassen, konnte sich ein Arzt die Option freihalten, ganz entsprechend dem, was er am Krankenbett vorfand, therapeutisch zu handeln – und gleichzeitig seinen eigenen Voraussagen treu zu bleiben.

7 Einfluss der Ätiologie auf die Verlaufsform

Die Prognostik in *Int.* steht in engem Zusammenhang mit Fragen nach den Ursachen, welche eine Krankheit auslösen, d. h. mit der Ätiologie der Krankheit. Als Ursachen für Krankheiten nennt *Int.* u. a. Ansammlung, Vermehrung, Stase und Veränderung von Säften, meist Galle oder Schleim, in Organen. Oder äußere Einflüsse, wie etwa eine bestimmte Lebensweise, z. B. im Spätsommer grünes Obst zu essen oder sumpfiges Wasser zu trinken. Oder zu hohe körperliche Belastung, etwa ein zu langer Marsch im Winter, mechanische Schädigungen des Körpers durch innere oder äußere Verletzungen und Wunden (z. B. auch in der Lunge), saisonale oder witterungsbedingte Einflüsse u. v.m. Doch neben externen oder körperinneren Ursachen für den unterschiedlichen Verlauf von Krankheiten gibt es ätiologisch auch den Aspekt des Verhaltens des Kranken selbst. Der Kranke kann die Dauer seiner Krankheit selbst beeinflussen, bzw. er könnte das Auftreten seiner Krankheit überhaupt erst selbst ausgelöst haben. Mit diesem Aspekt zusammenhängende mögliche Grenzen der Prognostik beschreibt z. B. der Autor der hippokratischen Schrift *Prorrhetikon* (*Vorhersagen*) II.1–4,[12] indem er ausführt, dass der Verlauf von Erkrankungen nicht immer sicher vorhersagbar ist, und dass dieser Umstand sehr häufig von Fehlern in der Lebensweise des Kranken abhängt, sodass man den Kranken lange und genau in seinem täglichen Umfeld beobachten muss – und das unabhängig davon, was der Kranke dem Arzt sagt.[13]

12 Hipp., *Prorrh.* II.1–4 (L.IX.6).
13 Hipp., *Prorrh.* II.1–4 (L.IX.14–20).

***Int.* 28 Leberkrankheit II**
Dieses erleidet er manchmal heftig, manchmal aber schwächer. Und wenn die Tage vergangen sind, in denen sich die Krankheit entscheidet, und der Schmerz weniger angreift, muss er gewissenhaft dieselbe Diät anwenden wie auch vorher. Wenn er sich nämlich über das Maß betrinkt oder Geschlechtsverkehr hat oder irgendetwas anderes unpassendes macht, wird seine Leber sofort hart und schwillt an und vibriert vor Schmerz. Und wenn er sich ein wenig anstrengt, dann schmerzen plötzlich die Leber und der ganze Körper.

Ταῦτα πάσχει τοτὲ μὲν σφόδρα, τοτὲ δὲ ἧσσον. ὅταν δὲ αἱ τε ἡμέραι παρέλθωσιν ἐν ᾗσι κρίνεται τὸ νόσημα, ὅ τε πόνος ἐλάσσων ἔχῃ, ἀναμάρτητον διαιτᾶσθαι χρὴ τῇ τοιαύτῃ διαίτῃ, ᾗ καὶ πρόσθεν· ἢν γὰρ μεθυσθῇ παρὰ καιρὸν ἢ λαγνεύσῃ ἢ ἄλλο τι ποιήσῃ μὴ ἐπιτήδειον, τὸ ἧπαρ παραχρῆμα γίνεται αὐτοῦ σκληρὸν, καὶ οἰδέει, καὶ σφύζει ὑπὸ τῆς ὀδύνης, καὶ ἤν τι σπεύσῃ, πονέει ἐξαπίνης τὸ ἧπαρ καὶ τὸ σῶμα ἅπαν. (P.170–172=L.240)

Solchen Verstößen gegen eine gesunde Lebensweise steuert die Schrift *Int.* gewissermaßen gegen, indem sie sehr genaue Anweisungen für das Verhalten des Kranken für jeweils bestimmte Zeiträume gibt, an die er sich zu halten hat, bzw. therapeutische Maßnahmen verordnet (mit genauen Maßangaben für Rezepturen oder für die Gehstrecke zur körperlichen Kräftigung) die genau auszuführen sind. Einen theoretischen Rahmen zur Diätetik im Allgemeinen legt *Int.* nicht dar, doch lehnen sich die Empfehlungen in *Int.* an die Inhalte anderer hippokratischer Schriften an, deren Kenntnis der Autor von *Int.* offensichtlich voraussetzte.[14]

8 Krankheit in *Int.* als autarkes „Wesen" – welchen Einfluss hat der Arzt?

Zur Ätiologie gehört in *Int.* auch die Krankheit selbst. Denn neben inneren oder äußeren ätiologischen Faktoren sowie dem Einfluss des Menschen selbst auf seine eigene Gesundheit durch seine Diätetik, d. h. seinen Lebensstil, zeigt sich die Darstellung der Krankheit als eine Art personifizierter Entität. Dieses „Wesen" wird mit Verben charakterisiert, wie: die Krankheit greift an, hält fest, lässt nach, geht, kehrt wieder, lässt nach oder tötet. Diese aktiv handelnde „Personifizierung" zieht sich von der ersten Krankheitsbeschreibung an durch die gesamte Schrift *Int.* Die Krankheit selbst beeinflusst also den Verlauf und die zeitliche Ausdehnung der Leiden des Kranken. Die Benennung des Zeitraumes vom Beginn der Krankheit bis zur Heilung

14 Z.B. Hipp., *De diaeta* I–IV. *De diaeta* III.67–69 (L. VI.592–606) gibt einen allgemeinen Überblick über Therapien bzw. Prävention im hippokratischen Sinne, d. h. im Zusammenhang mit Jahreszeiten, Säften, Sport, Ernährung und allgemeiner Lebensweise; Hipp., *De diaeta salubri*; Zur Diätetik in der hippokratischen Medizin siehe auch Jouanna 2012: 137–153.

oder zum Tod erfolgt in *Int.* teilweise ohne genaue Festlegung und macht sich stattdessen am Auftreten bestimmter Symptome fest, die variabel sein können. So werden für die Nierenkrankheiten I–III keine Zeiträume genannt, nur für die Nierenkrankheit IV wird ein Jahr angegeben. Neben den oben angedeuteten möglichen Verlaufsformen erscheint in *Int.* noch das Bild von einer Krankheit, die mit dem Patienten altert, die bis zum Lebensende bei ihm bleibt oder erst gemeinsam mit ihm stirbt:

***Int.* 26 Wassersucht V vom Wassertrinken**

Bei vielen (Kranken) altert die (personifizierte) Krankheit mit.

τοῖσι πολλοῖσι συγγηράσκει ἡ νοῦσος. (P.162=L.236)

***Int.*14 Nierenkrankheit I**

Die (personifizierte) Krankheit stirbt gemeinsam mit dem Patienten.

ἡ νοῦσος τῷ ἀνθρώπῳ συναποθνήσκει. (P.120=L.202)

***Int.* 19 Gefäßkrankheit linke Seite**

Wenn er nicht gebrannt wird, aber von selbst gesund wird, dann ist bei vielen in zwölf Jahren die (personifizierte) Krankheit wieder zurückgekehrt, und hat, wenn sie die Milz erfasst, vielen eine Wassersucht gemacht.

ἢν δὲ μὴ καυθῇ, ὑγιὴς δὲ γένηται ἀπὸ ταὐτομάτου, τοῖσι πολλοῖσι μετὰ δυοκαίδεκα ἔτη ἡ νοῦσος αὖθις ὑπετροπίασε, καὶ ἢν λάβηται τοῦ σπληνός, τοῖσι πολλοῖσιν ὕδερον ἐποίησεν. (P.134=L.214)

In solcher Form ist die Krankheit als „Wesen" aus sich selbst heraus handlungsfähig. Allerdings sieht sich die ärztliche Kunst in *Int.* in der Lage, die Stärke und den Einfluss angreifender Krankheit zu verringern. Und der Erfolg des ärztlichen Handelns in der Beeinflussung der Krankheit ist stets eng an die Ausführung der ärztlichen Verordnungen geknüpft. Dem Kranken in *Int.* wird im Rahmen der Prognostik aber nur dann eine Gesundung in Aussicht gestellt, wenn er die Anweisungen des Arztes sehr genau befolgt und die therapeutischen Maßnahmen genauso ausführt bzw. zulässt, wie der Arzt es vorschreibt. Dies schlägt sich in *Int.*, wie auch oben in den Texten bereits gesehen, häufig in prognostischen Formulierungen nieder, die eine strenge Compliance des Patienten inkludieren. Wenn er die Heilkunst des Arztes annimmt, dann wird er sehr schnell gesund werden, bzw. wenn der Arzt genau so therapiert, dann wird er erfolgreich heilen:

***Int.*17 Nierenkrankheit IV**

Wenn er dies tut, wird er sehr schnell gesund sein.

ταῦτα ἢν ποιέῃ, τάχιστα ὑγιὴς ἔσται. (P.126.=L.208)

***Int.* 24 Wassersucht III von der Leber**

So kannst du ihn sehr schnell gesund machen.

οὕτω γὰρ ἂν τάχιστα ὑγιέα ποιήσαις. (P.154=L.228)

Der Krankheitsverlauf hängt also eng mit der ärztlichen Behandlung zusammen. So wird im Gegensatz zum (akuten) Typhus I, der in sieben oder 14 Tagen vergehen kann, der Typhus IV mit einer Dauer von bis zu 20 Jahren prognostiziert.[15] Doch selbst nach dem Ablauf von 20 Jahren wird für eine solche schwere Krankheit für einige Patienten noch Heilung in Aussicht gestellt – vorausgesetzt, sie wurden von Beginn an behandelt:

***Int.* 43 Typhus IV**

Dieser, wenn er so behandelt wird, wird meistens innerhalb von zwei Jahren gesund. [...] Diese Krankheit befällt [Menschen], die über zwanzig Jahre alt sind. Wenn sie aber auftritt und nicht von Beginn dieser Krankheit an therapiert wird, dann vergeht sie nicht wieder, bevor weitere 20 Jahre vergangen sind, sondern hält an. Danach vergeht sie bei einigen, wenn sie behandelt wird. Die Krankheit ist aber schwer.

οὗτος οὕτω μελετώμενος μάλιστα ἐν δυσὶν ἔτεσιν ὑγιὴς γίνεται. [...] αὕτη ἡ νοῦσος λαμβάνει πρεσβύτερον εἰκοσαετέος· ὅταν δὲ λάβῃ, ἢν μὴ κατ' ἀρχὰς τοῦ νοσήματος μελετηθῇ, οὐκ ἐκλείπει, πρὶν ἂν εἴκοσιν ἔτεα ἄλλα παρέλθῃ, ἀλλὰ προσίσχει· ἔπειτα ἐνίοισι μελετωμένη ἐξέρχεται· ἡ δὲ νοῦσος χαλεπή. (P.218=L.274)

9 Exemplarisch: Verlaufsformen von *Typhos* in *Int.*

Um überblickend die Prinzipien der Herangehensweise aufzuzeigen zu können, soll hier nun beispielhaft die Krankheitsgruppe *Typhos* betrachtet werden, das sind die Kapitel *Int.* 39–43.[16] Hier finden sich verschiedenste Verlaufsformen, sowohl was die Symptome betrifft als auch hinsichtlich der zeitlichen Ausdehnung der Krankheit. Das Spektrum der aufgezählten Symptome beim „Typhus“ in diesen *Int.*-Kapiteln reicht von Fieber, Schwäche, Durchfall (Typhus I) über Tertian- und Quartanfieber,[17] Kopfschmerz, Erbrechen, Blässe, geschwollene Füße, An-

15 Dabei ist der antike Krankheitsbegriff τῖφος nicht mit dem heutigen Verständnis der Krankheit Typhus gleichzusetzen.

16 Um diese Kapitel in das Gesamtbild der Krankheitsgruppen von *Int.* einordnen zu können, siehe Anhang.

17 πυρετὸς τριταῖος ἢ τεταρταῖος (*Int.* 40 P.202 = L.264). Zu zyklischen Fiebern: Die antiken Beschreibungen könnte man mit dem vergleichen, was heute dem Krankheitsbegriff Malaria zugeordnet ist, die durch Plasmodien (Parasiten) verursacht wird, welche zyklische Fieber auslösen. Der Entwicklungszyklus der Plasmodien ist an den Wechsel Mücke-Mensch-Mücke gebunden. Es

schwellen des ganzen Körpers mit Schmerzen in Brust und Rücken, Verdauungsstörungen, Auswurf, Heiserkeit, Halsentzündung und Orthopnoe (Typhus II), Geschwulst an Gelenken, Lähmung (der Beine), intermittierende Schmerzen (Typhus III), Durchfall viele Tage lang (Typhus IV) bis hin zu Blässe, Austrocknung, Schwäche, Auszehrung, sehr dunkle Haut, starre Augen, jagt die Fliegen von der Bettdecke, hat mehr Appetit, freut sich am Geruch der verlöschenden Lampe, oder hat erotische Träume (Typhus V). Allein dieses beschriebene Symptomspektrum für die Krankheit Typhus in *Int.* ist äußerst komplex und keinesfalls auf einen bestimmten, einzelnen Patienten übertragbar oder gar als festgelegtes Krankheitsbild analog dem heutigen Verständnis von Typhus definierbar: Heute versteht man unter *Typhus abdominalis* verschiedene bakterielle, zyklische Infektionskrankheiten mit *Salmonella enterica* (*typhi*), welche weltweit auftreten und sich am gesamten Körper manifestieren können. *Typhus abdominalis* wird über Nahrungsmittel, Milch oder Wasser übertragen. Die Letalität beträgt heute unbehandelt 15%. Als Symptome werden beschrieben: Kopfschmerz, langsam ansteigendes, dann wochenlang sehr hohes Fieber mit ausgeprägten Wahrnehmungsstörungen, morgendliche Fieber-Remissionen, grau-gelbe Zunge, Hauterscheinungen wie *Roseola typhosa* (rötliche Flecken) auf der Bauchhaut, Haarausfall, Milzvergrößerung u. a. Heute bekannte Komplikationen können sein: Darmblutungen, Meningitis, Bronchopneumonie, Dekubiti (Druckgeschwüre) u. a. Doch zurück zum antiken Typhus. Zunächst der Versuch einer graphischen Darstellung der verschiedenen Verlaufsformen.

9.1 Typhus Verlaufsformen Übersicht

Int. 39 Typhus I

Typhus I[18] tritt im Hochsommer auf, mit Symptomen wie Fieber, Schwäche und Durchfall (Abb. 1).

---

entstehen, zeitlich parallel zum Entwicklungszyklus des Erregers, typische Fieber-Rhythmen (bis zu ca. 40 Grad Körpertemperatur), bei Malaria tertiana alle 48h, Mal. quartana alle 72 h, Mal. tropica unregelmäßiges Fieber. Komplikationen können sein: akutes Nierenversagen, zerebrale Schäden, Gerinnungsstörungen, Hämolyse (Zerfall roter Blutkörperchen), Multiorganschäden u. a.

18 *Int.* 39, P.200 = L.260.

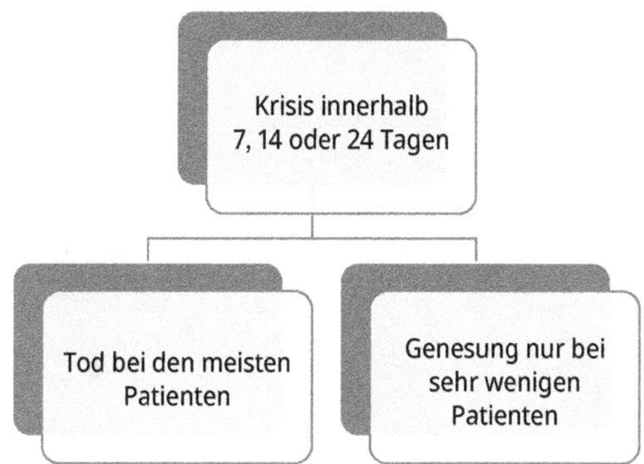

Abb. 1: Verlauf Typhos I.

Int. 40 Typhus II

Typhus II[19] tritt in allen Jahreszeiten auf, mit Symptomen wie Tertian- und Quartanfieber, Kopfschmerz, Erbrechen, Blässe, geschwollene Füße, Anschwellen des ganzen Körpers mit Schmerzen in Brust und Rücken, Verdauungsstörungen, Auswurf, Heiserkeit, Halsentzündung und Orthopnoe (Abb. 2).

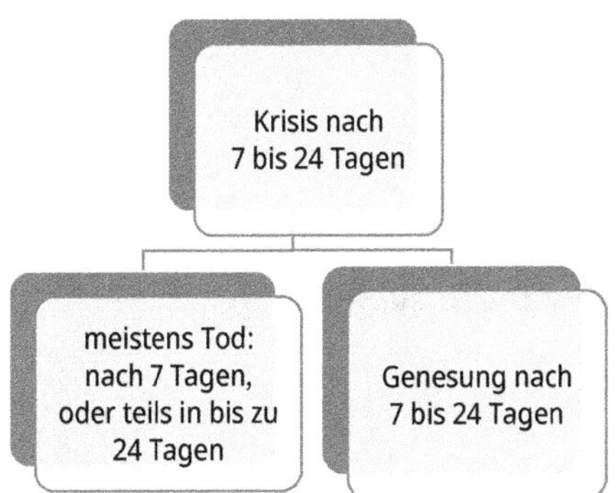

Abb. 2: Verlauf Typhos II.

19 *Int.* 40, P.202 = L.264.

Int. 41 Typhus III

Für Typhus III[20] wird keine bestimmte Jahreszeit angegeben. Er scheint jedoch zu jeder Jahreszeit auftreten zu können, da geraten wird, Milch je nach Saison zu trinken und da die Krankheit über Jahre hinweg anhalten kann, mit Symptomen wie Gelenkschwellungen, Lähmung (der Beine), intermittierende Schmerzen (Abb. 3).

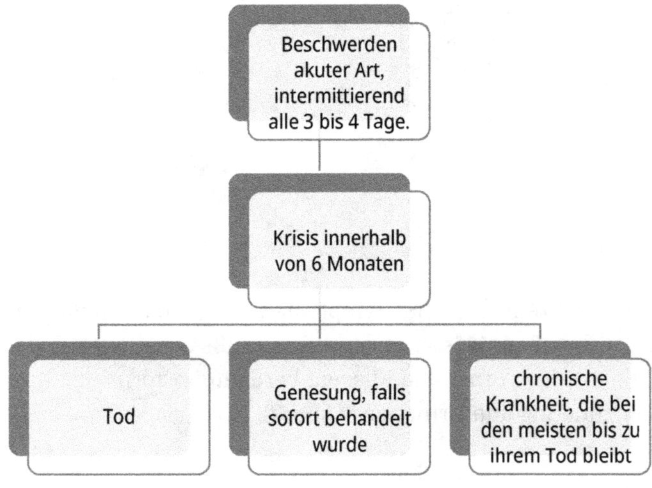

Abb. 3: Verlauf Typhos III.

Int. 42 Typhus IV

Typhus IV[21] tritt meist im Spätsommer auf, mit Durchfall, viele Tage lang (Abb. 4).

Int. 43 Typhus V

Auch für Typhus V[22] wird keine bestimmte Jahreszeit angegeben. Er scheint jedoch auch zu jeder Jahreszeit auftreten zu können, da therapeutisch wiederum geraten wird, Milch je nach Saison zu trinken und da er da er sehr lange anhalten kann, mit Symptomen wie Blässe, Austrocknung, Schwäche, Auszehrung, sehr dunkle Haut,

---

20 *Int.* 41, P.206 = L.266.
21 *Int.* 42, P.210 = L.270.
22 *Int.* 43, P.214 = L.272.

starrer Blick, Fliegen von der Bettdecke jagen, teils mehr Appetit, freut sich am Geruch der verlöschenden Lampe, hat erotische Träume (Abb. 5).

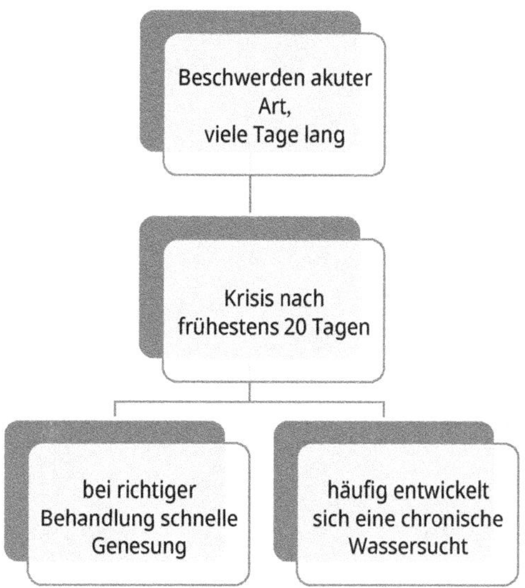

Abb. 4: Verlauf Typhos IV.

9.2 Typhusformen Therapie

Die Therapie für die einzelne Typhusformen in *Int.* erweist sich deutlich als zu den spezifischen Krankheitsphasen synchronisiert. Die sprachliche Ausdrucksform ist in *Int.* recht effektiv und knapp gehalten. Teilweise wird der ärztliche Kollege direkt angesprochen.

Int. 39 Typhus I

Akute Phase
In den ersten Tagen nicht baden, sondern auf dem Lager liegend mit warmem Öl und Wein salben. Nur leichte, kühle Krankensuppen. Trockenen, dunklen Wein trinken, falls der ihm bekommt. Falls nicht, dann stark verdünnten trockenen Weißwein. Bei Durst häufig Wasser zum Trinken geben und den Kranken dazu bringen, dies wieder zu erbrechen, und zwar zwei- bis dreimal nacheinander. Auf der Höhe starken Fiebers kalte Wickel, die aber bei Schüttelfrost wieder ent-

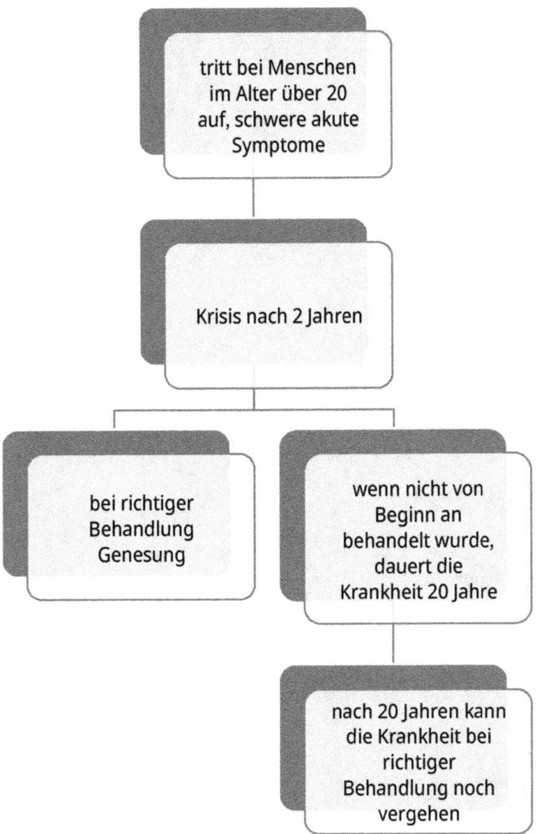

Abb. 5: Verlauf Typhos V.

fernt werden sollen.[23] Bei Todesgefahr durch starke Schmerzen die gleichen Pharmaka gegen die Schmerzen geben, wie beim Pleuritispatienten:[24] *Silphion-Saft* (σιλφίου ὀπός, adstringierende Pflanze, Dioscorides III.80) und *Aristolochia* (ἀριστολοχία, Schlingpflanze, reinigende und wärmende Wirkung, Dioscorides III.4.) sollen mit Getreide zu Kugeln geknetet werden, täglich soll eine solche Kugel in den Wein hineingerieben werden.[25]

23 Auf der Höhe des Fiebers soll dem Kranken Hitze entzogen werden. Bei Schüttelfrost hingegen versucht der Körper, Wärme zu erzeugen, deshalb sollen dann keine kalten Wickel angelegt werden.

24 Vgl. *Int.* 23 (P.150 = L.226); Pleuritis in *Int.* findet sich in Kapitel 23, Wassersucht von der Lunge.

25 Zu therapeutischen Eigenschaften von Pflanzen siehe auch Haars 2018.

Genesungsphase
Schnelle Stärkung des Patienten mit Nahrung, Getränken und Bädern.

Int. 40 Typhus II

Akute Phase
Bis nach der *krisis* nicht baden, sondern mit warmem Wein und Öl auf dem Krankenlager salben. In den ersten Tagen leichte Krankensuppen mit Honig. Dunklen Wein in kleinen Portionen und nach Wunsch das Kranken gemischt. Kein Getreide bis nach der *krisis*, aber in Wein gekochten Tintenfisch, und die Kochsoße davon zum Trinken, Rettich, gerösteten, geriebenen, gesiebten Kressesamen, der über herben dunklen Wein gestreut und mit einer kleinen Mahlzeit früh morgens serviert werden soll. Zehn Körner *Glykysidē* (γλυκυσίδη, Pfingstrosenart, mäßig wärmende, trockene, adstringierende Wirkung) in dunklem Wein kochen und zum Trinken geben. Rübsamen (γογγυλίς *Brassica rapa*. Pflanze aus der Gattung Kohl, feuchte, brennende, blähende Wirkung) gut durchkochen und den Patienten deren Kochsaft trinken lassen, der vorher mit ungesalzenem Käse, Mohn, Öl, Salz und *Silphion* bestreut und mit Essig versetzt werden soll. Falls ein abführendes Pharmakon gegeben werden soll, dann Knidische Beere[26] trinken lassen. Nach dem Abführen drei Becher sahnige Mehlsuppe zum Austrinken geben.[27] Dann weiter den gleichen Wein geben.

Genesungsphase
Die vorgeschlagenen Behandlungsmaßnahmen können beliebig ausgewählt oder kombiniert werden und können Heilung bringen. Allerdings werden trotzdem wenige Patienten überleben, die Krankheit ist schwer.

Int. 41 Typhus III

Akute Phase bis zum 24. Tag
Intermittierende Beschwerden. Bei akuten Schmerzen den Körper mit Öl salben und warme Umschläge anwenden. Nach dem Nachlassen der Schmerzen zunächst ein Ganzkörper-Dampfbad anwenden, danach das Pharmakon Hellebor

26 Κνίδιος κόκκος Knidische Körner, knidische Beere. Seidelbast-Art, Frucht der Pflanze θυμελαία. Purgative Wirkung als Getränk.

27 Dies konnte nach der pharmakologischen Purgation der Darmberuhigung und der Kräftigung des Kranken dienen.

(ἐλλέβορος, wärmende und trocknende Wirkung, Dioscorides IV.1.) zum Abführen trinken lassen.[28] Am nächsten Tag zwei große Krüge gekochte Ziegenmolke zum Trinken geben, den einen mit Honig, den anderen mit Salz, dies abwechselnd Tasse für Tasse trinken lassen, bis er alles ausgetrunken hat. Am Abend, nach dem Abführen soll er einen Becher Linsensuppe schlürfen, und einen Becher fette Rüben mit darüber gestreutem Mehl aufessen, sowie Fleisch vom jungen Hahn, von Taube, Turteltaube, Schaf oder fettem Schwein. An den Tagen zwischen der Hellebor-Gabe gut durchgebackenes Brot und Gerstenkuchen, dazu ungesalzenes, gebackenes Vogelfleisch, sonst gekochtes ohne Käse, Sesam oder Salz. Oder gekocht und mit Majoran und Öl darüber. Der Patient soll Weißwein trinken, wenn der ihm guttut, sonst dunklen. Milch und Molke soll er die ganze Zeitlang immer entsprechend der Saison trinken. Wenn es dir richtig erscheint, gib ihm auch gekochte Eselsmilch. Tagsüber soll er sich mit Rundgängen belasten, auch am Nachmittag und morgens. Hellebor sollst du alle sechs Tage verabreichen. Wenn er anschwillt, dann zieh Blut mit einem Schröpfkopf ab, falls das am Knie ist, dann stich mit einer dreieckigen Nadel ein, aber stich nicht an anderen Gelenken.

Genesungsphase
Wenn er es übersteht, dann kann die Krankheit unter dieser Behandlung innerhalb von sechs Monaten vergehen. Er soll sich von Kälte und Hitze fernhalten und sich nicht mit Nahrung überfüllen. Sonst besteht die Gefahr, dass die Krankheit zurückkehrt. Die Krankheit ist schwer und bleibt bei den meisten Patienten bis sie sterben.

Int. 42 Typhus IV

Akute Phase
An den ersten Tagen gekochte, abgekühlte Mehlsuppe mit Honig und herben, dunklen Wein geben. Nach dem Ende der Diarrhoe-Phase soll der Kranke drei halbe Krüge Linsensaft mit Salz trinken. Wenn er diese wieder ausgeschieden hat, soll er gegen Abend einen Becher kalte, ungesalzene Linsensuppe mit viel darübergestreutem *Silphion* ausschlürfen, außerdem soll er eine Schüssel ungesalzene fette Rüben mit darübergestreutem Mehl essen. Er soll in kleinen Portionen trockenen Weißwein trinken. Danach weiter die gleiche Ernährung, und

28 Nieswurz, *Hellebor*. Wirkung als Emetikum (weiße Art, Dioscorides IV.148 ἐλλέβορος λευκός), und Laxans (schwarze Art, Dioscorides IV.162. ἐλλέβορος μέλας) durch Alkaloide bzw. Saponin. Tödliche Dosis für Menschen: ca. 2 g Drogenpulver.

dazu gut durchgebackenes Brot und besonders Gerstenkuchen. Diese Ernährung weiterführen, bis die Krankheit aufhört. Sollte der Bauch sich nicht von allein entleeren, dann als Pharmakon *Hippophaes* (ἱπποφαές/ἱππόφεως, der Saft der Pflanze enthält Gifte, die Erbrechen und Durchfall auslösen, Dioscorides IV.159). Oder als Pharmakon *Knidische Beere* verwenden (Κνίδιος κόκκος, Seidelbast-Art, *Daphne cnidium*, Dioscorides I.472).[29] Dann abends das Gleiche verabreichen, wie bei den Kranken, bei denen sich der Bauch spontan entleert hat (siehe oben, akute Phase). Wenn der Kranke am nächsten Tag fiebert, dann Bettruhe halten und den gleichen Wein in möglichst kaltem Wasser geben. Wenn er nicht fiebert, dann kann er eine möglichst feuchte und kräftigende Diätetik anwenden und entsprechend seinen Speisen spazieren gehen.[30]

Falls sich nach der Krisis eine Wassersucht entwickelt

Dies geschieht in vielen Fällen. Dann eine bestimmte Klistierrezeptur aus Honigwasser und *Thapsia* (θαψίη, beißend, stark wärmend, zieht Säfte aus der Tiefe und zerteilt das Herausgezogene, Dioscorides IV.153) anwenden, dann wird es dem Kranken schnell besser gehen.[31]

Int. 43 Typhus V

Akute Phase
Bei schweren Symptomen, den Oberbauch mit dem Pharmakon *Hellebor* reinigen (hier als Emetikum). Den Unterbauch mit dem Pharmakon *Skammonia* (σκαμμονίη, *Convolvulus scammonia*, Kletterpflanze, Clematis, auch als "orientalische Purgierwinde" bezeichnet, wirkt abführend durch Toxine, Dioscorides IV.170.) abführen. Zum Abführen kann auch Eselsmilch verwendet werden. Nach der Reinigung die gleiche Ernährung wie bei den Patienten vorher. [...] Und Molke und Milch von Kuh oder Ziege nach Saison geben.

Genesungsphase
Bei dieser Behandlung kann er in meistens innerhalb von zwei Jahren genesen.

Krankheitsphase bis zu zwanzig Jahren
Er darf die Nahrung essen, die er bevorzugt, und so viel davon, wie er möchte. Er soll spazieren gehen und die Gehstrecke soll entsprechend seiner Nahrungsmenge festgelegt werden.

29 Vgl. Haars 2018: 263, zu 12,32K.
30 περιπατείτω πρὸς τὰ σιτία τεκμαιρόμενος *Int.* 42 (P.214=L.272).
31 Die Wurzel von *Thapsia* ist stärker als die Frucht und gibt einen milchigen Saft ab, der Histamin freisetzende Stoffe enthält, vgl. Haars 2018: 108, 237–238.

10 Therapeutische Synchronisation bei akuten versus chronischen Krankheitsphasen in *Int.*

Anhand dieser selektiven Veranschaulichung an der Typhusgruppe ist für die Schrift *Int.* erkennbar, dass akute und chronische Phase nicht stets gleichartig nacheinander ablaufen, sondern dass sich die beschriebenen Krankheitsverläufe hoch variabel gestalten. Nicht immer sind die Zeitphasen überhaupt klar bemessen. Sie können kurz, lang oder intermittierend sein und jede dieser Phasen kann akute oder abgemilderte Symptombilder mit sich bringen. Bestimmte Verlaufsformen können sich über sehr lange Zeiträume hinweg erstrecken, sie können über Jahre, Jahrzehnte oder bis zum Lebensende des Kranken anhalten. Bei bestimmten äußeren Einflüssen oder bei Diätetik-Fehlern des Kranken können auch die langdauernden Krankheiten erneut in akute Phasen übergehen und eine neue Krisis wiederum zu verschiedenen Verlaufsformen mit sich bringen. Um die Behandlung zu den Symptomen zu synchronisieren, beschreibt der Autor möglichst genau die Zeiträume, in denen sich die Krankheitsphasen bei einer großen Zahl von Patienten entwickeln. Die Synchronisierung des Körpers durch therapeutische Maßnahmen muss ein Versuch gewesen sein, den Krankheitsverlauf zu beeinflussen und eine zeitliche Harmonisierung zu erreichen. Am Beispiel der Typhusgruppe in *Int.* zeigt sich bereits, wie genau auf den Punkt der Arzt sein therapeutisches Handeln entsprechend dem Zustandswechsel des Kranken zu synchronisieren hatte.

Auch in der Krankheitsgruppe Typhus hängt die Wahl der Heilmethoden neben zeitlichen Aspekten genauso eng auch mit der Ätiologie zusammen. Die Heilprogramme werden außerdem stets entsprechend der aktuell wechselnden körperlichen Situation des Kranken synchronisiert. Dies alles führt zu komplexen prognostischen Möglichkeiten in *Int.* und erlaubt kaum eine dogmatische Einteilung von Krankheiten in einen Beginn mit akuter Phase, dann Heilung oder Übergang in chronische Phase. Diese Beobachtungsweise erlaubt primär keine klare Einteilung von Krankheiten in akute bzw. chronische Formen. Dabei ist zudem die Schrift *Int.* insgesamt bezüglich der Verlaufsoptionen nicht in allen Krankheitsgruppen stringent, sondern es erscheinen verschiedene Variationen in einzelnen Krankheitsgruppen. Trotz dieser Vielfalt, Komplexität und Variabilität sind die Prinzipien des therapeutischen Gegensteuerns in *Int.* alles andere als zufällig. Sie sind als stringent zu bewerten, d. h. die Zuordnung der Therapie unterliegt festen Prinzipien und korreliert exakt mit den verschiedenen von Zeitphasen der Krankheit.

Die möglichst akribische und hochflexible Dokumentation von Zeitphasen für therapeutische Intervalle wird in *Int.* konzeptuell verwendet, um die Periodizität von Gesundheit und Krankheit im Zusammenhang mit der Prognostik und Therapiewahl berücksichtigen zu können. In vielen Kapiteln von *Int.* wird dabei gar keine konkrete Zeitspanne angegeben, sondern es werden die potenziellen Verläufe anhand ihrer Symptome besprochen. Für die Ermöglichung therapeutischer Synchronisation des kranken Körpers mit der Phase der Krankheit dienen die in *Int.* äußerst umfassend gesammelten Symptombeschreibungen und Nennungen von Zeichen bzw. Zeiträumen für mögliche Verlaufs-Umschwünge. Anhand der Symptome, die der Arzt am Kranken wahrnimmt, kann er erfragen, beobachten und untersuchen, in welche Richtung sich die Krankheit voraussichtlich entwickeln wird. So finden sich in *Int.* bei jeder einzelnen Krankheitsbeschreibung die Vorschläge zur Heilmethode bei jeder einzelnen Krankheitsphase direkt im Anschluss an die Aufzählung der jeweiligen Symptome dieser Phase. Diese therapeutischen Mittel werden häufig mit einer bestimmten Wendung als Marker im Text eingeleitet, etwa: τοῦτον ὁκὸταν οὕτως (oder ὧδε) ἔχῃ – wenn es diesem Kranken so geht, dann (hier folgen die Verordnungen).[32]

Int. bietet somit für jede einzelne Verlaufs-Option eine adaptierte, synchronisierte Heilmethode an. Bei der Krankheitsbeschreibung folgen nach den akuten Symptomen zunächst die Maßnahmen für die ersten Krankheitstage. Dann folgen die Symptome der nächsten Zeitphase, danach die Maßnahmen für diese Verlaufsvariable, welche wiederum in sich selbst verschiedene symptomatischen Optionen mit entsprechender therapeutischer Gegensteuerung enthalten kann. Das Ziel des Arztes besteht darin, genau zur richtigen Zeit, genau die für diesen individuellen Kranken die genau richtige, adaptierte, synchronisierte Heilmethode wählen zu können.

11 Umfassende therapeutische Prinzipien in *Int.*

Mit welcher Herangehensweise strebt der Autor der hippokratischen Schrift *De internis affectionibus* danach, die medizinische Kunst (τὴν ἰατρικὴν τέχνην) mit den natürlichen Rhythmen zu synchronisieren? Die therapeutischen Mittel in *Int.* werden stets möglichst antagonistisch zu den Ursachen der Beschwerden gewählt, d. h. sie sollen den angenommenen Krankheitsauslösern entgegenarbeiten. Die Krankheiten in *Int.* sind zwar häufig einem bestimmten Organ zugeordnet, tatsächlich sind die beschriebenen Symptome aber so vielgestaltig, dass eine klare topographische Zuordnung der jeweiligen Krankheit zu einem bestimmten Organ aus heutiger Sicht kaum nachvollziehbar als möglich erscheint.[33] Dem-

32 Zu typischen Wendungen in *Int.* vgl. Heinrich 2022: 201–202.

33 Erst Herophilos (ca. 330–250 v. Chr.), der in einem historisch relativ kurzen Zeitraum mit legalisierten Sektionen an menschlichen Körpern lebte, entwickelte (neben Erasistratos 304–250

entsprechend erscheinen die allgemeinen therapeutischen Maßnahmen hinsichtlich unterschiedlicher Krankheitsbilder einerseits aus heutiger Sicht relativ übertragbar, sie sind als allgemeinen Behandlungsprinzipien einzuordnen. Andererseits erscheinen in *Int.* auch sehr krankheitsspezifische Behandlungsmethoden, wie etwa in *Int.* 1 ein Hustenmittel, in *Int.* 14 ein Kichererbsen-Getränk in großer Menge zur Ausspülung von Nierensteinen oder in *Int.* 24 die Punktion von Bauchwasser.[34] Allgemein-therapeutisch werden bei schleimigen viszeralen Erscheinungen adstringierende und ausleitende Mittel verordnet, bei Überlastung und in schweren, akuten Phasen soll der Kranke körperliche Ruhe halten. Die Therapie zielt oft auf die Ausleitung der Krankheit, bzw. des verursachenden Saftes, aus dem Körper des Kranken. Hierzu dienen Abführmittel, Klistiere, Brechmittel, Trink- und Badekuren.

Jedoch ist die Wahl der Applikationsform für die Ausleitung stets zur zeitlichen Phase der Krankheit synchronisiert, wie bereits am Beispiel der *Int.*-Typhusgruppe ersichtlich. Bei der Ausleitung von Krankheit wird zwar die Belastbarkeit des Körpers des Kranken in der akuten versus chronische Phase beachtet, doch entscheidend für die Stärke der gewählten Mittel scheint die aktuelle Stärke der Krankheit zu sein, die ausgeleitet werden muss. Dementsprechend wird die Ausleitung mit stärkeren versus milderen Varianten der Heilmittelanordnung umgesetzt. Die zeitliche Dringlichkeit der Behandlung spielt also eine Rolle. So werden in akuten Phasen neben Brechmitteln und Abführmitteln auch Dampfbäder oder Waschungen, Salbungen, Tränke oder leichte Suppen und körperliche Ruhe angeordnet. Letztere dienen dann der Erholung des Körpers des Kranken von der belastenden Prozedur der Ausleitung. In chronischen Phasen werden zum Abführen über eine lange Zeitdauer in regelmäßigen Abständen eher Milch- oder Molkekuren sowie bestimmte mildere pflanzliche Trankzubereitungen verwendet. Die den Körper des Kranken belastende pharmakologische Purgation des Patienten wird in *Int.* also tendenziell eher bei schweren Krankheiten angewendet (was aus heutiger Sicht für eine akute, schwere Krankheitsphase nicht unbedenklich erscheint). Die gebräuchlichen, meist pflanzlichen Mittel waren häufig „giftig“ und verursachten neben Durchfall und Erbrechen weitere belastende Nebenwirkungen – von Übelkeit und Schwindel bis hin zu schweren Kreislaufstörungen oder dem Tod.[35] In chronischen Krankheitsphasen wird erst dann, wenn

v. Chr.) eine systematische, auf Menschenkörpern basierende Anatomie, zu Herophilos siehe von Staden 2007.

34 *Int.* 1 Hustenmittel (P.78 = L.172), *Int.* 14 gegen Nierensteine (P.118 = L.202), *Int.* 24 Bauchwasserpunktion (P.154 = L.228).

35 Viele hippokratische Texte warnen bereits vor der Giftigkeit der Purgativa, so etwa Aphorismen, *Aphor.* V.1–4 (L. IV.502), Akute Erkrankungen, *Acut. spur.* 23 (9 L.), (P.286 = L.II.440–442),

die milderen Mittel ohne Wirkung bleiben, die pharmakologische Purgation alternativ zur Anwendung der Milchkur *vorgeschlagen* (nicht verordnet). Drastischere Maßnahmen wie Hitzeanwendung („Brennen"), Aderlass oder chirurgische Methoden werden prinzipiell nur in schweren, zeitlich verlängerten Verläufen, bzw. bei schlechter Prognose als *ultima ratio* empfohlen. Heilmethoden für chronische Krankheiten werden bei sehr langdauernden Krankheiten teils in rhythmischen Abständen, saisonal oder über das Jahr verteilt verordnet. Dabei spielt es auch eine Rolle, welche Art von Milch oder welche Pflanzen saisonal oder regional verfügbar sind. Die Stärke der anzuwendenden Maßnahmen bildet sich dabei stets im Verhältnis zum An- oder Absteigen des Krankheitsniveaus ab. Bei Chronifizierung nach der ersten Krisis einer Krankheit kann es erneut zu akuten Komplikationen mit einer erneuten Krisis kommen, nach der sich der Kranke wiederum auf einer prognostischen Palette zwischen Genesung, chronischer Krankheit und Zugrundegehen befindet. Nun werden entsprechend erneut invasivere therapeutische Mittel hinzugezogen.

Für stark verlängerte Krankheitsphasen legt der Arzt besondere Aufmerksamkeit auf ein ausbalanciertes Verhältnis von Nahrung und körperlicher Bewegung des Kranken. Bei schweren und sehr lange oder lebenslang andauernden chronischen Krankheiten besteht das Ziel der Therapie in *Int.* darin, dass der Mensch mit seiner Krankheit umzugehen und zu leben lernt und sich in seiner Diätetik, d. h. in seiner gesamten Lebensweise, auf sie einstellt. Dies erfordert eine Langzeit-Betreuung, in deren Rahmen der Arzt den Kranken anleitet, wie er mit entsprechenden Nahrungsanweisungen, Rezepturen und exakt angepassten Bewegungsplänen seinen Körper mit der langen Krankheitsphase synchronisieren kann. Die Herangehensweise in der chronischen Phase erscheint eng an allgemeine diätetische Prinzipien angelehnt, welche im hippokratischen Schriftenkreis auch für die Prävention empfohlen und theoretisch unterlegt sind, wie etwa in der Schrift *De diaeta*.

Aspekte der Synchronisation des kranken Körpers mit der Krankheitsphase in *Int.* hängen also nicht nur mit der aktuellen zeitliche Phase der Krankheit zusammen, sondern auch mit der Ätiologie, der Stärke der Krankheit selbst, der allgemeinen körperlichen und psychischen Verfassung des Kranken sowie mit den Lebensgewohnheiten des Kranken.

Zeitliche Verordnungen betreffen auch zirkadiane Aspekte, etwa dass der Patient eine Verordnung stets morgens (ἕωθεν) ausführen soll (etwa in *Int.* 3 jeden Morgen geschüttelte Pferdemilch trinken). Prinzipien der Therapiewahl in Zu-

Über Kopfverletzungen, *De capitis vulneribus* 16 (L. III.246). In Epidemien, *Epid.* II.2.22 (L. V.94) wird ein Todesfall beschrieben, vgl. Heinrich 2022: 178.

sammenhang mit der körperlichen Verfassung des Patienten erklärt die Schrift *Int.* aber nicht, da sie rein auf Praktikabilität orientiert ist und die Kenntnis des konzeptuellen Hintergrundwissens aus anderen hippokratischen Schriften vorauszusetzen scheint. Hier sei zu diesem Hintergrundwissen ein Beispiel aus der hippokratischen Schrift *De victu acutorum* genannt. Es geht um die Ernährung des Kranken im akuten Stadium einer Krankheit. Der Arzt muss wissen, welche Art von Nahrung (etwa Zubereitungsformen von Getreidesuppen) ein schwer erkrankter Körper zu sich nehmen kann. Und der Arzt muss für diese Nahrungsformen genau den richtigen Zeitpunkt erkennen, damit der Kranke nicht noch mehr Schaden nimmt:

Hipp., *Acut.* 38 (L.11)

Zusätzlich müssen auch die Stärke und die Art einer jeden Krankheit berücksichtigt werden, sowie der Natur des Menschen und der Lebensgewohnheiten des Kranken, nicht nur bei den Speisen, sondern auch bei den Getränken.

προστεκμαρτέα δὴ καὶ ἡ ἰσχὺς καὶ ὁ τρόπος τοῦ νοσήματος ἑκάστου καὶ τῆς φύσιος τοῦ ἀνθρώπου καὶ τοῦ ἔθεος τῆς διαίτης τοῦ κάμνοντος, οὐ μοῦνον σιτίων, ἀλλὰ καὶ ποτῶν. (Joly 52.4–7=L.II.302–304)

Auch in *Int.* 32 wird der richtige Zeitpunkt, der *kairos*, angemahnt:

***Int.* 32 Milzkrankheit III**

Und wenn es dir gelingt, zum richtigen Zeitpunkt (τοῦ καιροῦ) zu brennen, dann wirst du ihn gesund machen. Wenn er aber von dieser Heilmethode nicht gesund wird, dann wird er mit der Zeit zugrunde gehen und sterben.

καὶ ἢν τύχῃς καύσας τοῦ καιροῦ, ὑγιέα ποιήσεις· ἢν δὲ μὴ ὑπὸ ταύτης τῆς ἰήσιος ὑγιὴς γένηται, φθειρόμενος χρόνῳ θνήσκει. (P.184=L.250)

Dem Autor von *Int.* war in hohem Maße bewusst, dass der richtige Augenblick für therapeutisches Handeln kurz ist. Die Bestrebungen nach therapeutischer Synchronisation entsprechen auch in *Int.* dem antiken, allegorischen Bild des *Kairos*, der Allegorie vom richtigen Augenblick, vom günstigsten Zeitpunkt.[36] In bildhaften Darstellungen erscheint *Kairos* als ein junger Mann: er ist über eine Waage gebeugt, um die Balance einzuhalten. Er besitzt Flügel, sowohl am Rücken als auch an den Fersen, denn handelt man zu spät – so ist er bereits entflogen. Sein langer Schopf wächst nur oben auf dem Scheitel und da er nach vorn über die Waage gebeugt ist, kann man ihn nur von vorn ergreifen, das heißt genau in dem Moment, in dem man ihm direkt von vorn gegenübersteht und ihn als *Kairos* erkennen kann. Das Hinterhaupt des *Kairos* hingegen ist ohne Haar, d. h. wenn

36 Zum *kairos* in der Medizin vgl. Singer 2022: 102–106.

sich der richtige Moment bereits abgewendet hat, dann ist er nicht mehr am Schopf greifbar. Kairos ist in späteren mittelalterlichen Verbildlichungen häufig auch vor einer Uhr dargestellt, um seinen Zeitbezug abzubilden. Die metaphorische Figur des *Kairos* drückt exakt das ärztliche Bemühen um den passenden Moment für ihr therapeutisches Eingreifen aus. Die antiken Ärzte wussten von der Kürze des menschlichen Lebens im Vergleich mit der Ewigkeit, und von der Erfahrung, derer es bedarf, um medizinisch richtig zu handeln. Sie kannten die Flüchtigkeit des richtigen Moments, des genauen Zeitpunktes für therapeutische Intervention. Sie kannten die Schwierigkeit für den Arzt, die richtige Entscheidung zu treffen, während sich der Zustand des Kranken ständig veränderte.[37]

12 Konklusion zu *Int.*

Dieser Beitrag möchte unsere Kenntnis über antikes Verständnis von zeitlichen Phasen und entsprechendes medizinisches Handeln erweitern. Zusammenfassend kann zur Therapie in der Schrift *Int.* gesagt werden, dass sich eine Erläuterung eines klaren theoretischen Konzepts zur Einteilung von Krankheiten in eine akute und eine chronische Phase nicht findet. Das Fehlen einer konzeptuellen Hintergrunderläuterung mag jedoch an dem generellen Charakter der Schrift *Int.* liegen, welche vorrangig auf Praktikabilität der möglichst kurz gefassten Krankheitsbeschreibungen und therapeutischen Hinweise ausgerichtet ist und grundsätzlich auf theoretische Exkurse fast gänzlich verzichtet. Dennoch sind die Behandlungsprinzipien in *Int.* alles andere als wahllos oder stochastisch, nein, es finden sich klare Standards für die therapeutische Herangehensweise, je nachdem ob eine der variablen akuten oder chronischen Krankheitsphasen diagnostiziert wird. Diese Standards wiederum sind keineswegs starr oder dogmatisch. Selbst die kleinste Abweichung im Befinden des Kranken wird therapeutisch abgefedert. Die Verwendung von Terminologie, die die Krankheit in eine erste Phase und in eine dann folgende längere Phase einteilen, lässt wohl an ein Konzept des Autors mit relativ klarer Einteilung in akute und chronische Krankheitsphasen denken.[38] Betrachtet man die diffizilen Beschreibungen der einzelnen

37 Vgl. den ersten hippokratischen Aphorismus: ὁ βίος βραχὺς, ἡ δὲ τέχνη μακρὴ, ὁ δὲ καιρὸς ὀξὺς, ἡ δὲ πεῖρα σφαλερὴ, ἡ δὲ κρίσις χαλεπή [...] (I.1, L. IV.458) – Das Leben ist kurz, die Technik ist lang, der richtige Augenblick aber ist scharf (begrenzt) und die Erfahrung trügerisch und die Entscheidung schwierig.

38 Vgl. auch van der Eijk 2013: 309: "Sometimes, the conditions mentioned in the ancient texts are presented as acute [...]. Yet many of them are described in ways that would make us regard them as chronic conditions [...]".

Krankheitsphasen und die synchronisierten therapeutischen Anweisungen in dieser Schrift, so ist ein stringentes System der Behandlung in bestimmten Verlaufsformen durchaus und durchgängig erkennbar. Der Autor von *Int.* beschreibt kurze und lange Krankheitsverläufe. Letztere bezeichnet er bereits als chronisch und schätzt die chronisch Kranken als besonders betreuungsbedürftig ein. In der Schrift *Int.* erscheinen deutliche Bestrebungen, die ärztliche Therapie mit den zeitlichen Verläufen der Krankheiten zu synchronisieren.

13 Therapeutische Synchronisation in der nachfolgenden Wissenschaftsgeschichte

Was die hippokratische Schrift *De internis affectionibus* aus dem vierten vorchristlichen Jahrhundert betrifft, so ist die Sichtweise auf den Verlauf einer einzelnen Krankheit hochgradig flexibel. Hier bewegt sich die Prognostik stets direkt an der Realität entlang, die der Arzt am Krankenbett vorfindet. Dadurch wurde dieser hippokratische Text neben anderen nosologischen hippokratischen Texten für die nachfolgende Medizin zu einer Basis der späteren medizinischen Forschung, was an der Rezeption dieser Texte deutlich wird. Um günstige Zeitpunkte für ärztliches Eingreifen übersichtlich und praktikabel darzustellen, bedurfte es einer Art Übersichtswerk. Im Zeitrahmen hippokratischer Texte hatte sich schon früh ein solches etwa in Form der hippokratischen Aphorismen-Sammlungen gestaltet.[39]

Erst in viel späteren Phasen der Wissenschaftsgeschichte, etwa im 19./20. Jhd., wurden systematische Datensammlungen angelegt, um Krankheiten zeitlich zu bemessen und zu kategorisieren.[40] So finden sich in einer Dissertation von K. Piorkowski (1907) Angaben zur Krankheitsdauer von Typhus:

> Die für Typhus angegebenen Werte zeigen einen beträchtlichen Unterschied. Eine durchschnittliche Dauer von 27 Tagen erscheint sehr niedrig. Nach einer Berechnung an 1045 Fällen der Leipziger Klinik (Dissertation K. Piorkowsky 1907) hatten 83 Kranke eine Dauer bis 3 Wochen, 159 bis 6 Wochen, 282 bis 9 Wochen und die übrigen 521 Fälle (die Hälfte) eine längere Dauer. Danach beträgt der Mittelwert sicher mehr als 7,8 Wochen oder 55 Tage.[41]

39 Hipp., *Aphorismen*, Edition siehe Magdelaine 1994.
40 Vgl. Günther 1941: 114–122.
41 Zitiert nach Günther 1941: 120.

Solche statistischen Methoden sind für uns in der Antike noch nicht erkennbar. Doch häufig wurde in Form von frühen Listen, Sammlungen von Krankheitsbeschreibungen oder Einzelfall-Darstellungen versucht, die pathologischen Erscheinungen umfassend zu sammeln und möglichst überschaubar darzustellen – in unserer Überlieferung beginnend mit medizinischen Tabellen aus der Zeit vom 3. Jahrtausend bis etwa 1500 v. Chr.,[42] gefolgt von medizinischen Texten verschiedenster Epochen,[43] später gefolgt von griechischen medizinischen Texten[44] und o. g. hippokratischen Texten, wie etwa den *Epidemien*-Büchern, der *Aphorismen*-Sammlung und prognostischen Sammlungen. Letztere Werke wurden in späterer Zeit weiter genutzt und viel kommentiert. Hier seien kurz einige Beispiele genannt. Der römische Enzyklopädist Aulus Cornelius Celsus (1. Jhd. n. Chr.) kannte die griechische Tradition gut und schöpfte aus ihren Quellen.[45] Celsus legte in seinem lateinischen Werk *De medicina*[46] die Ansichten verschiedener Ärzteschulen dar, welche sich aufgrund ihrer unterschiedlichen Konzepte, und wohl auch aus kompetitiven Gründen herausgebildet hatten. Der Arzt Galenos von Pergamon (129–216 n. Chr.) erarbeitete auf der Grundlage der Werke seiner antiken Vorgänger sowie durch eigene Forschung und breit aufgestellte fachliche Polemik bereits eine systematische medizinische Theorie, die noch über viele Jahrhunderte medizinisches Wirken stark beeinflusste.[47] Im Rahmen seiner Arbeiten an früheren medizinischen Quellen findet sich auch die umfangreiche Kommentierung der o. g. hippokratischen Aphorismen-Sammlungen.[48] Aufgrund der stetigen Vergrößerung des Umfangs verfügbarer medizinischer Texte seit Galens Zeit durch Überarbeitungen und Kommentierungen strebte man wiederum übersichtlichere Formen der Wissensdarstellung an. Im Rahmen galenischer Texte gestaltete sich etwa im 2. Jhd. n. Chr. ein solcher Versuch in Form der pseudogalenischen Schrift *Definitiones medicae*.[49] Hier finden sich u. a. Bemühungen um klarere Definitionen für akute und chronische

---

42 Siehe Geller 2004.

43 Dazu siehe Asper 2015.

44 Dazu van der Eijk 2016.

45 Bekannt ist seine Einteilung der Medizin in drei Hauptbereiche: Diätetik, Pharmazeutik und Chirurgie (*De medicina* I.9); vgl. Pardon 2005.

46 Celsus, *De medicina*, Edition siehe Marx 1915, Übersetzungen zu Celsus, siehe Lederer 2016.

47 Siehe dazu Miller 2023, Singer 2022, Cooper 2011, Nickel 2005.

48 Neues Forschungsprojekt ab 2024 zur galenischen Kommentierung der hippokratischen Aphorismen-Sammlungen: Interdisziplinäres DFG-Langfristvorhaben Humboldt–Universität zu Berlin unter der Leitung von Philip van der Eijk.

49 Galen, *Definitiones medicae*, Edition siehe Kollesch 2023.

Krankheiten.[50] Die medizinischen Schriften des spätantiken Autors Caelius Aurelianus (5. Jhd. n. Chr.) beschäftigen sich schwerpunktmäßig damit, wie die Ärzte ihre Therapie an Zeiten, Rhythmen, Wachstum und Verfall anpassten. Caelius kannte ebenfalls die griechische und hippokratische Tradition gut und arbeitet auf ihrer Basis.[51] Von Caelius sind uns drei Bücher über akute Krankheiten, *Celerum passionum libri III* sowie fünf Bücher über chronische Krankheiten, *Tardarum passionum libri V* überliefert.[52] In der Spätantike hatte sich die systematische Vorstellung von akuten und chronischen Krankheiten oder Krankheitsverläufen bereits fest etabliert und gehörte zur Grundlage jeder Prognostik und Therapie. Die Bedeutung der Schrift *Int.* für nachfolgende Epochen könnte darin gesehen werden, dass hierin die sehr diffizile Beobachtung und Dokumentation aller, auch der scheinbar unwichtigsten Krankheitszeichen akribisch gesammelt und systematisiert wurde und so – vielleicht zum ersten Mal in der Geschichte – ein umfassendes Bild von inneren Erkrankungen gezeigt wurde. In diesem neu entstandenen Bild zeichnete sich die stetige Präsenz zeitlicher Krankheitsphasen und natürlicher Rhythmen nun deutlich ab und wurde vielleicht erstmals in dieser detailreichen Klarheit sichtbar. Mit dem Wissen und der Diagnostik von zeitlichen Formen der Krankheit strebte der antike Arzt nun nach der Synchronisation seiner Therapie.

14 Kurzzusammenfassung

Die starke Fokussierung auf die Synchronisation der Therapien in *Int.* mit den einzelnen zeitlichen Verlaufsformen zeigt bereits in dieser frühen Schrift der antiken griechischen Medizin ein hohes Maß an Wissenschaftlichkeit – neben der zu dieser Zeit neuartigen völligen Vernachlässigung übernatürlicher Einflüsse. Die umfassende Sammlung und Aufzeichnung von Krankheitszeichen an Patienten (nicht immer in dem Wissen, ob sie nun zu der betreffenden Krankheit gehörten, oder nicht) zeigt eine empirisch orientierte Herangehensweise an die Erkennung von Krankheiten. Damit gibt die Schrift *Int.* dem Arzt ein Instrument an die Hand, aufmerksam die zeitlichen Phasen der Krankheit zu diagnostizieren sowie für jede Phase geeignete Heilmittel zur Verfügung zu haben. Die schematischen, systematisierten therapeutischen Verordnungen hingegen zeigen eine ausgereifte

50 Die Definitionen 134–166 stellen eine Klassifikation verschiedener Aspekte von Krankheit dar und schließen die zeitlichen Rahmen von Krankheitsphasen ein (Kollesch 56.10–66.17 = §§ 133–153 Kühn XIX.386.6–392.4). Doch auch hier gibt es keine einfachen Lösungen.

51 Zu Caelius Aurelianus siehe van der Eijk 1999; Formisano 2013.

52 Caelius-Edition siehe Bendz 1990/1993 und 2002.

Methodik, die automatisch bei bestimmten Beobachtungen am Kranken und bei bestimmten ätiologischen Deutungen der Krankheit griff. Obwohl in der hippokratischen Schrift *Int.* kein klares System akuter versus chronische Krankheiten erläutert wird, so ist doch die Abhandlung der vielen einzelnen Krankheitsbilder stark zeitlich gegliedert und sind akute und chronische Phasen aus den Beschreibungen prinzipiell deutlich ableitbar. Ja sogar innerhalb der Krankheitsgruppen wird nach chronologischen Aspekten sortiert: Zuerst werden kürzere, leichter heilende Varianten beschrieben, dann Verläufe, die länger dauern können, dann schwere, chronische Verläufe. Die Entität der Krankheit erscheint in der Schrift *Int.* als eine Art Personifizierung, die aktiv kommt, geht, altert oder Symptome bewirkt. Doch trotzdem zeigt sich in *Int.* die feste Haltung, diese Entität Krankheit durch therapeutisches Können beeinflussen oder besiegen zu können – sofern der Arzt den *kairos*, d. h. den richtigen therapeutischen Zeitpunkt zu erkennen vermag. In der Schrift *Int.* zeigen sich deutliche Bestrebungen, Therapien für Krankheiten entsprechend deren chronologischen Erscheinungen möglichst angepasst, d. h. möglichst synchronisiert durchzuführen, um mit dem natürlichen Rhythmus des menschlichen Körpers bzw. seiner Krankheit mitzugehen, und zum richtigen Zeitpunkt mit dem richtigen Mittel der Krankheit entgegenwirken zu können. Die jeweilige Phase der Krankheit – ob akut oder chronisch – bildet sich in *Int.* stets verlässlich in der zeitlich synchronisierten Form der Therapie ab.

Anhang

Krankheitsgruppen in der Schrift *Int.*

Int. 1–9	Lungenkrankheiten
Int. 10–12	Lungenkrankheiten mit Phthisis
Int. 13	Krankheit des Rückenmarks
Int. 14–17	Nierenkrankheiten
Int. 18–19	Gefäßkrankheiten
Int. 20–21	Schleimkrankheiten
Int. 22–26	Wassersucht
Int. 27–29	Leberkrankheiten
Int. 30–34	Milzkrankheiten
Int. 35–38	Ikterus
Int. 39–43	Typhus
Int. 44–46	Ileus
Int. 47–50	Dicke Krankheiten
Int. 51	Ischias
Int. 52–54	Tetanus

Die 54 einzelnen Kapitel der Schrift *Int.*

Int. 1	Lungenkrankheit I
Int. 2	Lungenkrankheit II
Int. 3	Lungenkrankheit III
Int. 4–5	Lungenkrankheit IV
Int. 6	Lungenkrankheit V
Int. 7	Lungenkrankheit VI
Int. 8	Lungenkrankheit VII
Int. 9	Lungenkrankheit VIII
Int. 10	Lungenkrankheit mit Phthisis I
Int. 11	Lungenkrankheit mit Phthisis II
Int. 12	Lungenkrankheit mit Phthisis III
Int. 13	Krankheit des Rückenmarks
Int. 14	Nierenkrankheit I
Int. 15	Nierenkrankheit II
Int. 16	Nierenkrankheit III
Int. 17	Nierenkrankheit IV
Int. 18	Gefäßkrankheit rechte Seite
Int. 19	Gefäßkrankheit linke Seite
Int. 20	Schleimkrankheit I
Int. 21	Schleimkrankheit II
Int. 22	Wassersucht I Allgemeine Prinzipien
Int. 23	Wassersucht II von der Lunge
Int. 24	Wassersucht III von der Leber
Int. 25	Wassersucht IV von der Milz
Int. 26	Wassersucht V vom Wassertrinken
Int. 27	Leberkrankheit I
Int. 28	Leberkrankheit II
Int. 29	Leberkrankheit III
Int. 30	Milzkrankheit I
Int. 31	Milzkrankheit II
Int. 32	Milzkrankheit III
Int. 33	Milzkrankheit IV
Int. 34	Milzkrankheit V
Int. 35	Ikterus I
Int. 36	Ikterus II
Int. 37	Ikterus III
Int. 38	Ikterus IV
Int. 39	Typhus I
Int. 40	Typhus II
Int. 41	Typhus III
Int. 42	Typhus IV
Int. 43	Typhus V
Int. 44	Ileus I
Int. 45	Ileus II

(fortgesetzt)

Int. 46	Ileus III
Int. 47	Dicke Krankheit I
Int. 48	Dicke Krankheit II
Int. 49	Dicke Krankheit III
Int. 50	Dicke Krankheit IV
Int. 51	Ischias
Int. 52	Tetanus I
Int. 53	Tetanus II, Opisthotonus
Int. 54	Tetanus III

Abkürzungen

L. Littré, E. 1839–1861
K. Kühn, K. G. 1821–1833
P. Potter, P. 1988

Bibliographie

Primärliteratur

Bendz, G. (hrsg.) *Caelii Aureliani* Celerum passionum libri III, Tardarum passionum libri V, *edidit G. Bendz, in linguam Germanicam transtulit I. Pape; Indices composuerunt J. Kollesch et D. Nickel.* (CML VI 1) Berlin: Akademie Verlag 1990/1993 (Pars I); 2002 (Pars II).

Cooper, G. M. *Galen*, De diebus decretoriis, *from Greek into Arabic. A Critical Edition, with Translation and Commentary, of Hunayn ibn Isḥāq, Kitāb ayyām al-buḥrān*. New York: Routledge, 2011.

Haars, M. *Die allgemeinen Wirkungspotentiale der einfachen Arzneimittel bei Galen. Oreibasios, Collectiones medicae XV*. Einleitung Übersetzung, pharmazeutischer Kommentar. Stuttgart: Wissenschaftliche Verlagsgesellschaft, 2018.

Joly, R. (hrsg./ übers.) *Hippocrate*: Tome VI, 2e partie*: Du régime des maladies aiguēs. Appendice. De l'aliment. De l'usage des liquids. Texte établi et traduit.* Paris: Les Belles Lettres, 1972.

Jouanna, J. (hrsg./übers./komm.) *Hippocrate: Pour une archéologie de l'école de Cnide. 2e édition augmentée d'un article (2004) et d'une Postface (2009)*. Collection d'éudes anciennes 141. Paris: Les Belles Lettres, 2009.

Kollesch, J. (hrsg.) *[Galeni]* Definitiones medicae. (CMG V 13, 2) Berlin: De Gruyter, 2023.

Kollesch, J. und D. Nickel (hrsg.). *Antike Heilkunst. Ausgewählte Texte aus den medizinischen Schriften der Griechen und Römer*. Stuttgart: Reclam, 1994.

Kühn, K. G. (hrsg.) *Claudii Galeni Opera omnia*. 20 Bände. Leipzig: Car. Cnobloch, 1821–1833; repr. Cambridge: Cambridge University Press, 2011.

Lederer, T. (übers./komm.) *A. Cornelius Celsus*: De medicina, *Die medizinische Wissenschaft.* 3 Bände. Darmstadt: Wissenschaftliche Buchgesellschaft, 2016.
Littré, E. (hrsg.) *Oeuvres complètes d'Hippocrate.* X tomes. Paris: J. B. Baillière, 1839–1861.
Magdelaine, C. *Histoire du texte et édition critique, traduite et commentée, des* Aphorismes *d'Hippocrate.* Tomes 3. Paris. Thèse pour le Doctorat, Université de Paris-Sorbonne (Paris IV): Paris, 1994.
Marx, F. (hrsg.) *A. Cornelii Celsi quae supersunt.* (CML I) Leipzig/Berlin: Teubner, 1915.
Potter, P. (hrsg.) *Hippocrates.* Diseases 3, Internal Affections, Regimen in Acute Diseases. (LCL 473). Cambridge, MA: Harvard University Press, 1988.

Sekundärliteratur

Asper, M. „Medical Acculturation?: Early Greek Texts and the Question of Near Eastern Influence". In *The Frontiers of Ancient Science. Essays in Honor of Heinrich von Staden* (Beiträge zur Altertumskunde 338), hrsg. B. Holmes und K. D. Fischer. Berlin/Boston: De Gruyter, 2015: 19–46.
Craik, E. M. *The 'Hippocratic' Corpus. Content and Context.* London/New York: Routledge, 2015.
Craik, E. M. „The 'Hippocratic question' and the nature of the Hippocratic Corpus". In *The Cambridge Companion to Hippocrates*, hrsg. P. E. Pormann. Cambridge: Cambridge University Press, 2018: 25–37.
Fichtner, G. *Corpus Hippocraticum. Bibliographie der hippokratischen und pseudohippokratischen Werke.* Weitergeführt durch die Berlin-Brandenburgische Akademie der Wissenschaften. Erweiterte und verbesserte Ausgabe 2022/12. Berlin: Berlin-Brandenburgische Akademie der Wissenschaften, 2022. https://cmg.bbaw.de/fileadmin/Webdateien/Dateien/Hippokrates-Bibliographie.pdf (zuletzt abgerufen am 18.12.2025).
Formisano, M. „Late Latin encyclopaedism: towards a new paradigm of practical knowledge." In *Encyclopaedism from Antiquity to the Renaissance*, hrsg. J. König und G. Woolf, Cambridge: Cambridge University Press, 2013: 197–215
Geller, M. J. "West meets East. Early Greek and Babylonian Diagnosis". In *Magic and Rationality in Ancient Near Eastern and Greco-Roman medicine*, hrsg. H. F. J. Horstmanshoff und M. Stol. Leiden: Brill, 2004: 11–61.
Günther, H. „Geschichtliche Erläuterung der Ausdrücke ‚akute' und ‚chronische' Krankheit". *Sudhoffs Archiv für Geschichte der Medizin und der Naturwissenschaften* 34.1/4, 1941: 105–124.
Hankinson, R. J. „Aetiology". In *The Cambridge Companion to Hippocrates*, hrsg. P. E. Pormann. Cambridge: Cambridge University Press, 2018: 89–118.
Heinrich, A. *Studien zu Hippokrates, De internis affectionibus.* Diss., Humboldt-Universität zu Berlin, 2022. https://doi.org/10.18452/25093 .
Jouanna, J. *Greek Medicine from Hippocrates to Galen: Selected Papers.* Leiden/Boston: Brill, 2012.
Krug, A. *Heilkunst und Heilkult.* München: C. H. Beck, 1985.
Miller, K. J. *Time and Ancient Medicine, How Sundials and Water Clocks Changed Medical Science.* Oxford: Oxford University Press, 2023.
Nickel, D. „Galenos von Pergamon". In *Enzyklopädie Medizingeschichte*, hrsg. W. E. Gerabek et al. Berlin/New York: De Gruyter, 2005: 448–452.
Pardon, M. „Celsus and the *Hippocratic Corpus*: the originality of a 'plagiarist'". In *Hippocrates in context: papers read at the XIth international Hippocrates colloquium, University of Newcastle upon Tyne, 27–31 August 2002*, hrsg. P. J. van der Eijk. Leiden: Brill, 2005: 403–411.

Singer, P. N. *Time for the Ancients: Measurement, Theory, Experience.* Chronoi 3. Berlin/Boston: De Gruyter, 2022. https://doi.org/10.1515/9783110752397.
van der Eijk, P. J. „Antiquarianism and criticism: Forms and functions of medical doxography in Methodism (Soranus, Caelius Aurelianus)“. In *Ancient Histories of Medicine*, hrsg. P. J. van der Eijk. Leiden: Brill, 1999: 397–452.
van der Eijk, P. J. „Cure and (in)curability of mental disorders in ancient medical and philosophical thought“. In *Mental Disorders in the Classical World*, hrsg. W. V. Harris. Leiden/Boston: Brill, 2013: 307–338.
van der Eijk, P. J. „On 'Hippocratic' and 'non-Hippocratic' medical writings“. In *Ancient Concepts of the Hippocratic. Papers Presented at the XIIIth International Hippocrates Colloquium, Austin, Texas, August* 2008, hrsg. L. Dean-Jones und R. M. Rosen. Leiden: Brill, 2016: 17–47.
von Staden, H. *Herophilus. The Art of Medicine in Early Alexandria.* Cambridge: Cambridge University Press, 1989.

Giouli Korobili

Turbulence and Asynchrony at the Time of Orion: Ps. Aristotle's *Problemata* 26.13 in Philosophical and Medical Contexts

Abstract: This chapter explores the interplay between medicine and natural philosophy in the Peripatetic tradition, focusing on ps.-Aristotelian *Problemata Physica* 26.13 in relation to Aristotle's *Meteorologica* II 5 and Theophrastus' *De Ventis* 55. It examines how seasonal winds, especially in summer and autumn, were explained through a synthesis of astronomical, meteorological, and medical knowledge, while also accounting for popular beliefs surrounding Orion. By situating these explanations within Hippocratic environmental medicine, the chapter highlights the principle of synchrony between bodily and environmental stability. It argues that recurring attempts to rationalise turbulent seasons reveal a shared intellectual framework in which natural philosophy and medicine converged to explain the effects of environmental change on health and human life.

Keywords: ancient meteorology, astrometeorology, Orion, wind, seasons, weather and human health

1 Introduction

Medicine and meteorology were closely interrelated in ancient Greek—and subsequently in later—thought. Both disciplines belonged to a shared natural-philosophical framework, in which health and disease were conceived as linked to the movements of the heavens, the winds, and meteorological processes. The macrocosm-microcosm analogy, already present in Pre-Socratic philosophy, underpins this worldview: just as imbalances in the atmosphere were believed to produce disturbances in the natural order, so too were bodily diseases thought to result from analogous disequilibria. This analogy informs

Note: I am grateful to Philip van der Eijk, Kassandra J. Miller, and Susanne M. Hoffmann for their valuable comments and suggestions on an earlier version of this paper. The research underlying this study was conducted within the framework of the project 'Synchronizing the Body in Ancient Medicine and Philosophy', generously supported by the Berlin Einstein Center Chronoi.

Hippocratic and Galenic medicine as well as Aristotelian and Stoic natural philosophy.[1] Astrology completed the triad by mediating between meteorology and medicine, since the stars and planets were thought to exert influence both upon weather patterns (astrometeorology) and upon human health (iatromechanics).[2]

This intellectual framework emerged in part from the efforts of natural philosophers and medical writers to free humanity from fear and awe in the face of natural phenomena. Events such as thunder, lightning, storms and earthquakes, as well as eclipses, meteor showers, and unusual planetary conjunctions, were often regarded with wonder and apprehension, and were commonly interpreted by non-specialists as divine manifestations or portents of future events. In response, philosophers and physicians sought to demystify such phenomena by offering rational explanations that presented them as the products of natural laws. The concurrence of rare or extraordinary astral and meteorological phenomena, however, was regarded as particularly alarming, since it was believed to affect human life and mental health in both immediate and enduring ways.

This chapter investigates one such instance through a close reading of ps.-Aristotelian *Problemata Physica* 26.13, considered in the light of two related contexts: Aristotle's *Meteorologica* II 5 and Theophrastus' *De Ventis* 55.[3] It analyses how Aristotle and the Peripatetic school sought to explain the summer and autumn winds by drawing on astronomical, meteorological, and medical knowledge, ultimately to account for traditional beliefs concerning Orion's influence during a season perceived as turbulent and precarious for both life and health. I argue that although these explanations combine observational evidence and scientific reasoning with popular beliefs, they are grounded in and presuppose a central principle of environmental medicine: that health stability is maintained in synchrony with environmental stability, while any disruption of this synchrony negatively affects living bodies. By highlighting correspondences between these natural philosophical sources and major texts from the Hippocratic corpus, this chapter demonstrates the tacit dialogue between medicine and natural philoso-

1 See in detail the classical studies by Allers 1944 and Kranz 1967, as well as those collected in Salles 2021, particularly the chapters by Cooper, Lennox, Boys-Stones, and Hankinson; for the parallelism of external-internal imbalance, see Wee 2017; for a recent discussion of seasonal patterns and their impact on human health, see Zatta 2023.

2 See Hippocrates *De aere, aquis, locis* 2 [Diller 26.18–21 = II.14 Littré] and chapter 6 by D. Greenbaum in this volume. On ancient practices of astrometeorology and their connection to everyday life, see Lehoux 2007; cf. Hannah 2021 on the parapegma of Euktemon.

3 For *Meteorologica* (*Mete.*) I follow the text of Louis 1982 and the translation by E. W. Webster in Barnes 1984; for *De Ventis* I use Mayhew 2018; for the *Problemata Physica* (*Probl.*) I rely on Mayhew and Mirhady 2011.

phy in their shared attempt to explain the structure and functioning of the natural world, of which the living body was regarded as an indispensable part.

The texts considered here focus on winds, particularly those occurring in summer and autumn, and on the question of why this seasonal interval was commonly regarded as turbulent and indeterminate.[4] The origin of this idea is an *endoxon* preserved in all three texts, which incorporates a popular belief concerning the constellation of Orion. Although the living body and its potential symptomatology do not appear to be the central focus of these texts, it is difficult to deny that such observations were fundamentally aimed at preserving health and well-being of those affected by these phenomena.[5] As will be discussed in section 4, several Hippocratic texts argue that seasonal changes and variations in winds directly influence patterns of disease and physical constitution. Were environmental factors irrelevant to health, the systematic observations and detailed correlations found in these foundational medical works would be inexplicable. Moreover, any conceptions of weather or astral changes necessarily presuppose a perceptive, embodied observer: one cannot register a shift in the wind without feeling it on the skin, nor recognise turbulence without marking its temporal boundaries. In this sense, references to a period of turbulence in an *endoxon* are implicitly references to living bodies attempting to endure and respond to these environmental conditions.

The recurrence of the same *endoxon* across these texts, accompanied by partly distinct explanations, indicates that repeated efforts were made to account for the phenomenon—an indication that the belief retained its force among lay audiences from at least the 4th to the late 3rd ce. BCE, the approximate dates of the texts under consideration. This recurrence may further point to an earlier stage of data collection, traceable at least as far back as Aristotle. Although the extant collection of the *Probl.* is generally viewed as the product of reworking within a Peripatetic framework,[6] it is not implausible that some sections, particularly

4 Wind was a subject of considerable interest to the ancients, a fact reflected in a wide range of ancient meteorological accounts. In his appendix, Kidd 1992 provides a list of topics treated in the principal extant meteorological works (by Aristotle, Theophrastus, Epicurus, Lucretius, Seneca, the author of *De mundo*, Aëtius, and the Stoics), all of which devote substantial attention to the phenomenon of wind. See also Mayhew and Mirhady 2011: 156, and Mayhew 2026.

5 According to Flashar 1962: 316, the medical perspective is particularly prominent in the ps.-Aristotelian *Probl.* He identifies it as a unifying thread running through nearly all sections of the work—including those that appear, at first glance, to have little connection with medicine (e.g. book 18 on Philology)—thereby lending the text a certain degree of coherence.

6 A body of problemata-literature arose within the Peripatetic school and Aristotle himself wrote a work posing and solving scientific problems. Flashar 1962 dates the collection of ps.-Aristotelian *Probl.* to a period after Theophrastus (see pp. 304, 332, 356, 358), while nonetheless acknowledging that certain questions in book 26 derive from an earlier stratum and ultimately

those transmitting *endoxa*, were written down earlier in the form of a notebook.[7] Such a notebook could have served as a repository of opinions consulted by Aristotle and Theophrastus in the course of composing their explanatory works.[8]

While recent scholarship has explored aspects of Aristotelian meteorology,[9] Hippocratic environmental theory,[10] and the role of *endoxa* in Peripatetic reasoning,[11] the interconnection of these elements has received less attention. This chapter addresses this gap by showing how medical and natural philosophical perspectives converged in attempts to account for seasonal changes, with particular emphasis on the principle of synchrony between the living body and its environment. By foregrounding this notion of functional stability—and the dangers posed by turbulence or asynchrony—the discussion highlights the shared intellectual resources that informed multiple genres of writing in the 4th and 3rd ce. BCE.

The chapter is structured in four sections. The first provides a detailed overview of *Probl.* 26.13, highlighting its most complex philological and philosophical

go back to Aristotle's genuine *Problemata* (p. 336). Although he does not include *Probl.* 26.13 among the problems traceable to Aristotle's original collection (see p. 623, point 3), he argues that the passage incorporates material from another source, distinct from both Aristotle and Theophrastus but still belonging to the 4th ce. BCE (p. 681).

7 A similar view has already been advanced by A. Gotthelf with regard to Aristotle's lost *Anatomai* and, following D. Balme's suggestion, to *De mirabilibus auscultationibus*, which may "derive from a notebook that was authentic" (Gotthelf 2012: 385). This line of interpretation is developed by the research of R. Mayhew, who suspects that "the collection of data or notebook stage of inquiry was not limited to [Aristotle's] study of animals" (Mayhew 2026: 155). In Mayhew 2020: 137, Mayhew proposes that Aristotle's lost "*Zoika* was another work from the notebook stage, in which raw data about colouration, anatomy, and behaviour was recorded". And he continues, "such a work was "fluid" in that it was constantly being added to and subtracted from—this latter when the information was incorporated into the organization and explanation works" (Mayhew 2020: 138).

8 Mayhew (2026: 152–153): "[I]t seems pretty clear from [*Mete.* II 6.363a21–25] that *problemata* concerning wind were being compiled *before* the *Meteorologica* was completed." (emphasis in the original); Flashar 1962: 323: „Indem in den Probl. das Wissen der Zeit auf dem Gebiete der Natur im weitesten Sinne handbuchartig zusammengefaßt ist, bildet diese Schrift das erste Beispiel einer umfassenden Enzyklopaedie des Wissens. Bereits durch die Form der Schrift, die wir noch ausführlich betrachten wollen, ist nahegelegt, daß hier nicht neue Erkenntnisse gewonnen werden, sondern daß in der Schule bereits erarbeitete Ergebnisse in der Form des Handbuches, zunächst wohl für den Gebrauch der Schule selbst, zusammengestellt werden. Dabei hat keine andere Problem-Sammlung, die uns erhalten ist, oder von deren Aufbau wir uns eine Vorstellung machen können, jenen enzyklopaedischen Charakter, der den Aufbau des uns vorliegenden Werkes bestimmt."

9 Lettinck 1999; Taub 2003; Johnson 2009; Wilson 2013; Graham, Herzog, and Williams 2022.

10 Liewert 2015; van Tilburg 2015; Camden 2023.

11 Frede 2012; Karbowski 2015; Baltussen 2022; Mouzala 2023.

issues. Section 3 examines the seasonal winds of summer and autumn in Greece, situating them within broader meteorological and astronomical contexts. Section 4 turns to relevant Hippocratic texts, demonstrating how seasonal changes, stellar positions, and winds patterns were believed to affect living bodies and determine health outcomes—underscoring the principle of synchrony between environmental and bodily stability. The final section concludes with an analysis of *Probl.* 26.32, revisiting unresolved questions from the previous sections and offering a more integrated interpretation of *Probl.* 26.13, thereby revealing the interplay between natural philosophy and medicine in accounting for environmental and bodily dynamics.

2 Ps.-Aristotle's *Probl.* 26.13

> Why, at the time of Orion, do the days and the indefiniteness of the winds become most of all changeable? Is it because during a time of change everything is always especially indeterminate? Now Orion rises at the beginning of late summer and sets in winter, so that because one season has not yet settled—but one is coming to be while the other is ending—for this reason the winds too must be unsettled, because they share the properties of those from each season. And indeed, Orion is called difficult, both rising and setting, because of the indeterminateness of the season, since it is necessarily turbulent and inconsistent. (*Probl.* 26.13, trans. slightly revised)

> Διὰ τί ἐπὶ Ὠρίωνι γίνονται αἰόλοι μάλιστα αἱ ἡμέραι καὶ ἀκαιρίαι τῶν πνευμάτων; ἢ ὅτι ἐν μεταβολῇ ἀεὶ πάντα ἀοριστεῖ μάλιστα; ὁ δ' Ὠρίων ἀνατέλλει μὲν ἐν ἀρχῇ ὀπώρας, δύνει δὲ χειμῶνος, ὥστε διὰ τὸ μήπω καθεστάναι μίαν ὥραν, ἀλλὰ τὴν μὲν γίνεσθαι τὴν δὲ παύεσθαι, διὰ ταῦτα ἀνάγκη καὶ τὰ πνεύματα ἀκατάστατα εἶναι διὰ τὸ ἐπαμφοτερίζειν τὰ ἐξ ἑκατέρας. καὶ χαλεπὸς δὴ λέγεται καὶ δύνων καὶ ἀνατέλλων ὁ Ὠρίων διὰ τὴν ἀοριστίαν τῆς ὥρας· ἀνάγκη γὰρ ταραχώδη εἶναι καὶ ἀνώμαλον.

According to this passage, particular atmospheric conditions are said to prevail when Orion shines brightly in the sky. The days are described as especially changeable, and the winds seem unseasonable. These brief remarks raise several questions: in what sense are the days considered changeable? What kind of winds are implied? Is Orion himself regarded as responsible for this period of turbulence on Earth? Before addressing these issues, it is necessary first to clarify the time frame during which the author believes such conditions occur.

Although the text refers to changeable "days" (ἡμέραι), it should be recalled that ancient observers habitually interpreted celestial phenomena by watching the night sky.[12] In fact, during a certain part of the year Orion is visible throughout the entire night. Beginning with its heliacal rising—that is, its first appearance before dawn—on June 29,[13] Orion subsequently rises every night a few minutes earlier, so that by the winter months it remains visible all night long. Thus, when the author speaks of Orion "setting in winter", he is referring to its acronycal or cosmic setting, which takes place on the morning of 22 or 23 November, when the constellation stands in opposition to the rising sun. After this date, Orion's visibility gradually decreases, until its heliacal setting on 2 or 3 May.[14]

While determining the seasonal period of Orion's setting appears relatively straightforward in this passage, the same cannot be said for the period of its rising. The author states that Orion rises at the beginning of ὀπώρα (ἐν ἀρχῇ ὀπώρας). The Loeb translation renders this as "the beginning of autumn", which would imply a temporal gap of more than two months from the date identified earlier, namely June 29.[15] By contrast, in Theophrastus' *De Ventis* 55—where an almost verbatim reference to *Probl.* 26.13 appears—Robert Mayhew translates ὀπώρα more precisely as "late summer" (2018: 329), which shifts the date at least one month earlier, placing the rising in late July or early August. Given that celestial risings and settings could sometimes be obscured by adverse meteorological conditions, the end of July seems a closer approximation to the period indicated in *Probl.* 26.13. Towards the end of this paper, we will explain how this one-month discrepancy can be further reduced. For the present, it suffices to accept that the author observes Orion rising about an hour before dawn or earlier. The period of reference thus appears to extend from mid-July to the end of November.

---

12 Bickerman 1980^2: 53. The ancients distinguished four observable risings and settings of the stars: the heliacal setting, the cosmic setting, the heliacal rising, and the acronycal rising. The author of *De Signis* describes these phenomena as follows: "Settings are of two sorts, since their disappearances are settings, and this occurs both when the star sets at the same time as the sun and when the star sets as the sun rises. Similarly, risings are also of two sorts, those in the morning when the star rises before the sun and those at nightfall (acronychal) when it rises while the sun is setting."(*De Signis* 2, trans. Sider and Brunschön 2007)

13 This date is precise for the 3rd to the 1st ce. BCE; see Bickerman 1980^2: 113. All other dates cited below follow Bickerman's tabulation (pp. 112–113) for the same period.

14 I am especially grateful to S. M. Hoffmann for clarifying certain details of the phenomenon.

15 For the division of the year into four seasons, with autumn beginning in mid-September, I follow Singer 2022: 53 and his interpretation of *De diaeta*. In this schema, summer extends from mid-May to mid-September, with its midpoint falling from the third week of July onward. Bickerman offers a detailed account of the principal divisions of the natural year, basing them not only on the observed positions of fixed stars in the night sky but also on variations in local conditions in Greece and Rome (Bickerman 1980^2: 52–54).

This interval encompasses three seasons—summer, autumn and winter—but, as the text suggests, the principal cause of turbulence lies in the transitions from one season to the next.[16] Both the rising and setting of Orion coincide with and are perceived as synchronised with these seasonal transitions: its rising coincides with the transition from summer to autumn, while its setting marks the transition from autumn to winter. The entire period of Orion's visibility, however, is perceived as turbulent because its appearance and disappearance in the canonical positions of the sky do not align neatly with the natural boundaries marking the beginning and end of each season. Is this the full explanation, or are there additional reasons why this period was believed to be turbulent? I contend that further factors are involved, which will be explored as this chapter develops. Even at this stage, however, we may note that this 'perceived' asynchrony appears to have been firmly established in popular understanding and helps explain Orion's characterisation as "difficult" (χαλεπός): (i) its appearance could provoke anxiety, fear, or uncertainty and (ii) the extended duration of its visibility implied a prolonged negative influence on human affairs and the environment.[17]

This stellar-seasonal asynchrony manifests in remarkable 'signs' on Earth. For the authors of the three texts under consideration, this asynchrony *is not* regarded as the direct cause of any terrestrial instability. Rather, the indeterminateness of the seasons—which are influenced by the motion of the sun—is seen as responsible for irregularities such as the *akairiai* of winds mentioned in the passage cited above. Nevertheless, it is possible that common opinion perceived this asynchrony itself as *the* cause of instability. Before addressing this issue, it is helpful to clarify the types of irregularity indicated by these texts, namely (i) meteorological irregularity and (ii) 'embodied' irregularity. Meteorological irregularity, explicitly stated in all three texts and primarily associated with winds (and perhaps, by implication, with other natural phenomena), exhibits a surprisingly complex character. By contrast, irregularity as it pertains to living bodies is not explicitly discussed in any of the three texts, although, as I propose, it forms an implicit

16 This is a widely accepted view, as will be seen below. The author of *De Signis* identifies natural divisions not only during the day and night but also within the month (according to the positions of the sun and moon), and suggests that these divisions influence the weather: "for if the weather is going to change, it almost always does so at these midpoints" (*De Signis* 9, trans. Sider and Brunschön 2007).

17 Cf. *Ars rhetorica* I 6.1363a24, where *halepos* is defined in terms of these two interpretive aspects. In *Mete.* II 5.361b33, Aristotle refers to the long duration of Orion's appearance in the sky (discussed in the final section of this paper).

component of the conceptual framework that motivated the composition of *Probl.* 26.13.

3 Meteorological Irregularity: Winds (and Other Phenomena) at the Time of Orion

The central Mediterranean and the Aegean region have a temperate climate at least since the 5th ce. BCE, and the prevailing wind patterns identified today largely coincide with those of antiquity.[18] Boreas, the north wind, is regarded by the ancients as the most powerful wind in Greece and is understood to dominate the greater part of the year.[19] In visual culture it is especially prominent, conventionally depicted as a mature, bearded man—an iconographic sign of strength and authority.[20] Boreas is also believed to possess a dual nature. In the winter months, when called *bora*, it introduces the cold and uncertain season; in the summer, it becomes breezy and cooling, manifesting as the etesian winds (the modern *meltemi*), eagerly awaited by sailors as a guarantee of safe navigation. This duality is articulated not only on a yearly basis but also on a daily one.[21] Hesiod already attests in the *Opera et dies* (547–553) that the dawn is marked by chill air and gentle morning breezes, which by evening intensify into the stronger blasts of the north wind.

The heliacal rising of Sirius on July 28 (at the latitude of Athens) announces the arrival of the etesians, the transient winds that recur annually from July until mid-September, when they cease with the heliacal rising of Arcturus.[22] Dry and forceful, especially in the afternoon, the etesians typically subside overnight, in accordance with the general rhythm of most winds.[23] Although they are often as-

18 Zerefos et al. 2020: 2; Williams 2000: 3–4. This section of the paper has benefited greatly from Williams' dissertation.

19 See e.g. *Mete.* II 4.361a6–7; *De Ventis* 2 and 10; *Probl.* 26.10 and 26.15.

20 Williams 2000: 99.

21 In *De Ventis* 53, in the course of making a general point, Theophrastus notes that the two modes of alteration of wind—namely, (i) moving in a circle blowing sequentially, and (ii) reversing to blow back against the opposite wind—can be observed in many locations on a daily basis.

22 In addition, Aristotle and Theophrastus mention the counterpart of the *etesiai*: the *leuconotoi* winds, which blow in spring, are clear and cloudless, and typically go unnoticed (*De Ventis* 11). These are followed by the *ornithiai*, or 'bird' winds, which are comparatively weak (*Mete.* II 5.362a11–31). Cf. *Probl.* 26.2.

23 *Probl.* 26.51; "a fairly forceful wind (10–20 knots)" Williams 2000: 46; "[T]hey blow in the Aegean with significant intensity in some cases, reaching even that of a gale." Zerefos et al. 2020: 5.

sociated with bad weather, Apollonius Rhodius (*Argonautica* II 521–528) preserves the myth that the etesians first appeared following a sacrifice to Sirius, to whom the islanders of the Aegean prayed for relief from drought and oppressive heat.[24] Their advent was thought to be heralded by the *prodromoi*, "forerunners", light winds from the north whose sporadic attestation in the sources appears to cause confusion among ancient authors about the precise duration of their blowing.[25]

Notably, the Athenian civic calendar also aligned with these celestial and meteorological cycles: the Athenian New Year began with the heliacal rising of Sirius on July 28, just days after the start of the Panathenaea, the city's most important festival. Lasting eight days, the celebration culminated precisely on the day of Sirius' heliacal rising—and the onset of the etesians—with the great ritual procession from the Dipylon Gate to the Acropolis.[26] Boreas himself was mythologically tied to this festival: according to tradition, he abducted Oreithuia on her way to the Panathenaea at the very moment of its culmination.

At roughly the same season, another peculiar meteorological phenomenon occurs, again connected with the winds: the so-called *palimboreas* phenomenon. Theophrastus (*De Ventis* 28) describes it in connection to Chalcis in central Euboea. According to Mayhew, it is "a *bending* of the Etesians *around* the passage near Chalcis",[27] a particular instance of the broader phenomenon of *periclasis*, in which "the reverse wind blows back in an arc and reaches or makes contact with the incoming wind".[28] Theophrastus stresses the force of these contrary winds,

Theophrastus attributes the irregularity of the *etesiai* to the uneven rhythm of snowmelt (*De Ventis* 12). The naval battle of Salamis in 480 BCE was determined by the etesian winds; see Zerefos et al. 2020. One conclusion of that study is that "[t]he ancient Greeks and particularly Themistocles must have been aware of the local wind climatology since their strategic plan was carefully designed and implemented to take advantage of the diurnal wind variation" (p. 1), suggesting that even non-experts were familiar with the main characteristics of winds.

24 Cf. *De Ventis* 4: "Hence, Boreas, and even more the Etesians, are rainy for those dwelling to the south and the east; whereas Notos, and generally speaking those (winds) blowing from that location, (are rainy) for those (dwelling) to the north."

25 *Mete.* II 5.361b24; *De Ventis* 11; *Probl.* 25.16, 26.12, 26.51. According to Hünemörder (quoted in Mayhew 2018: 164), the forerunners "are supposedly cooler" than the *etesiai*. Williams 2000: 45, notes that the prodroms begin to blow about a month before the onset of the *etesiai* (see also p. 257). By contrast, Mayhew 2018: 164 n. 155 observes "The Geminus parapegma, in the entry under the 27th day of Cancer (which month falls in June–July), states: "According to Eudoxus Sirius rises in the morning, and for the next fifty-five days the Etesian winds blow. The first five (days, the winds) are called the *Prodromoi*"."

26 Burkert 1985: 228, 232 and Williams 2000: 43.

27 Mayhew 2018: 225, emphasis in the original.

28 This explanation relies on Steinmetz's (1964: 45) definition of *periclasis*, which Mayhew employs with some caution (see 2018: 224).

which can even compel ships to turn back against their intended course: "at that time [the winds] are most able to extend the farthest, when the counter-striking (wind) is massive. And in some places it happens that the wind splits by striking against (something), so as to flow one (part) here the other there [. . .]".[29] Similarly, the southerly winds that blow in opposition to Boreas during the period of the etesians are mentioned by the author of *Probl.* 26. Characterised as hot and moist, these winds create a largely suffocating atmosphere and can appear wave-like and twisting.[30] Like Theophrastus, the author of the *Probl.* affirms the orderliness of the phenomenon.[31] According to Williams (2000: 76), this brief episode of southerly winds would have been well known to inhabitants of the eastern Greek seaboard.

In addition to these types of winds, Zephyrus, the west wind, also blows in spring and autumn, particularly late in the afternoon.[32] It is described as light,[33] steady and cold—though not colder than Boreas—since it originates from the sea and open plains.[34] For the same reason, Zephyrus is called ὁμαλός, "regular", because it arises neither from mountainous terrain nor from violent discharges such as melting of snow. This steadiness contributes to its reputation as gentle and pleasant, situated, as the sources emphasise, "on the border (μεθορίῳ) between the cold and the hot winds: being near both it shares in their capacities".[35]

This description may be summarised in the table at the end of the section. The table will be revisited in the concluding part of the chapter, in light of the

29 Apart from the *palimboreas*, Theophrastus mentions another violent phenomenon, which, however, appears to be local to the north: "This is why in some places the clouds travel in an opposite direction to the winds, as indeed (occurs) around Aegeae in Macedonia when a Boreas blows against Boreas. And the explanation is that, as the mountains are high around Olympus and Ossa, the winds striking, but not rising above them, bend back in the opposite direction, so that the clouds too, being lower, travel in the opposite direction." (*De Ventis* 27; cf. *De Ventis* 30).

30 *De Ventis* 57; *Probl.* 26.16. For the characteristics of the south wind according to the author of *Probl.* 26, see 26.2, 26.16, 26.17, 26.20, 26.39, 26.46, 26.50.

31 See the opening question of *Probl.* 26.12 ("Why does the Notos blow at the time of the Dog Star, and (why does) this occur just like any other orderly winds (γίνεται τεταγμένως)?" and cf. *De Ventis* 48. See also Mayhew 2018: 304–305.

32 *Mete.* II 6.364b2–3; *De Ventis* 38 and 40; *Probl.* 26.33 and 26.52. In *Probl.* 26.21, the author notes that west air currents blow throughout summer.

33 Theophrastus, however, explains that the autumnal Zephyrus could "develop into a storm due to its power" (*De Ventis* 42). This may result from its union with another air current, on which see *De Ventis* 48: "And if (Zephyrus) picks up another (local) wind blowing as (the sun) rises, it becomes greater, because (something) has been added (to it)."

34 *De Ventis* 40; *Probl.* 26.22 and 26.52.

35 *De Ventis* 41; *Probl.* 26.31, 26.52. In *Probl.* 26.55, Zephyrus is further described as *eukratos*, "well-mixed".

immediately preceding discussion of ancient views on bodily pathologies as shaped by seasonal and astral influences. Before turning to that, it is worth noting briefly that Aristotle, in the *Meteorologica*, refers to several natural phenomena other than winds that occur in late summer and/or autumn and that may be violent or potentially dangerous. These phenomena are, in one way or another, causally connected to winds. For instance, Aristotle observes that hurricanes are most frequent in autumn and spring, "because hurricanes are generally formed when some winds are blowing and others fall on them".[36] He also includes earthquakes among the phenomena especially common in these seasons (though he notes they may also occur in times of wetness and drought), on the grounds that these are the periods during which wind is the dominant force.[37] A further example is tidal waves. Although such events are localised phenomena and Aristotle does not assign them to any particular season, he nonetheless maintains that "the combination of a tidal wave with an earthquake is due to the presence of contrary winds".[38] This confluence seems more likely to occur in the period under discussion than at times when contrary winds are rare.

These examples of violent and irregular phenomena provide additional reasons to believe that the stretch of time between late summer and the end of autumn was remembered with particular fear and anxiety, and it was imprinted in cultural memory as a season of turbulence and instability.[39] Nevertheless, *Probl.* 26.13 confines its focus specifically to winds, and for this reason winds alone will be represented in the following table:

---

36 *Mete.* II 6.365a1–5.

37 *Mete.* II 8.366b2–4. Aristotle held that earthquakes and winds share a common nature: "We say that the same stuff is wind on the earth, and earthquake under it, and in the clouds thunder. The substance of all these phenomena is the same: namely, the dry exhalation."; Wilson 2013: 217: "Earthquakes are affections of the winds, which move inside the earth and shake it. [. . .] But if we expect earthquakes to be produced by the kinds of winds we have just learned about, we will be disappointed, for in fact the winds that cause earthquakes are of a quite different sort. As we compare the properties of winds, earthquakes, and stormy phenomena, it becomes clear that they are not just modifications of one another differing merely in the places they are found. The dry exhalation itself displays a different nature in each case."

38 *Mete.* II 8.368a34–35. He further explains this occurrence in the following terms: "It occurs when the wind which is shaking the earth does not entirely succeed in driving off the sea which another wind is bringing on, but pushes it back and heaps it up in a great mass in one place. Given this situation it follows that when this wind gives way the whole body of the sea, driven on by the opposite wind, will burst out and cause a flood." (368a35–b6)

39 Cf. Mayhew 2018: 327: "[*De Ventis* 55] is devoted to an issue apparently of some interest to the Peripatetics, namely, the idea that the *weather* (including wind) is indeterminate and disorderly during the rising and setting of the constellation Orion." (emphasis added)

June		July	September	November	
June 21 Summer Solstice	June 29	July 28	September 20 Autumnal equinox	November 5 or 6	November 22 or 23
	Hel. Rising of Orion	Hel. Rising of Sirius	Hel. Rising of Arcturus	Cosm. Setting of Pleiades	Cosm. Setting of Orion
Prodroms		End of the Prodroms Start of the Etesians The *Palimboreas* phenomenon	End of the Etesians	Start of *bora*	
		Zephyrus			

4 'Embodied' Irregularity

The author of *Probl.* 26.13, like Aristotle and Theophrastus in the relevant contexts, concentrates on winds as the immediate 'recipients' of the negative effects associated with the seasonal transition marked by Orion's rising and setting. Yet there are compelling reasons to infer—despite the author's silence on the matter—that this negative influence extended to the health and well-being of living bodies. The presence of *Probl.* 1, which opens the collection by examining *hosa iatrika,* namely questions concerning the art of medicine, already testifies to the author's sustained interest in pathologies arising from climatic conditions.[40] Within the context of book 26 itself, at least two further passages explicitly examine pathological effects

40 As Flashar makes clear the ps.-Aristotelian *Probl.* cannot be dismissed as a haphazard compilation. Despite its layers, disparate themes, and varied sources, the collection exhibits a medically oriented perspective and an overarching structure that reflects a deliberate conceptual design: „So endet das Werk, wie es begonnen hat, mit vorwiegend medizinisch orientierten Fragen über Einzelheiten des menschlichen Körpers. Doch während zu Beginn der Schrift krankhafte Erscheinungen im Vordergrund der Betrachtung standen, ist es jetzt der gesunde menschliche Körper, der Thema der Untersuchung ist. So dürfen wir wohl zusammenfassend sagen: wenn auch bei diesem Aufriß der Thematik im einzelnen Verschiebungen möglich und denkbar sind, so zeigt doch der grobe Aufbau im ganzen einen Plan. Er ist nicht durch eine allmähliche Entstehung einzelner Teile und den Verlust anderer Teile oder durch ähnliche Überlieferungsschicksale zustande gekommen, sondern muß—allenfalls von einigen Einzelheiten abgesehen—im ganzen das Ergebnis einer bestimmten Konzeption sein." (Flashar 1962: 318)

of the south wind.[41] In *Probl.* 26.42 the author asks why individuals feel heavier (βαρύτερον) and weaker (ἀδυνατώτερον) when the south winds blow. His explanation is that the warmth of *Notos* liquefies bodily moisture, producing an excess that weighs down the body and diminishes its strength.[42] Similarly, in *Probl.* 26.50 he enquires why dry, non-rain-bearing south winds provoke fever. The answer, as Mayhew (2018: 334) clarifies in connection with a related passage in *De Ventis* 57, is that the south wind, still fundamentally moist though not invariably accompanied by rainfall, "implants in human bodies an excessive amount of hot moisture", thereby producing fever.

The central thesis of *Probl.* 26.13—that during Orion's season both days and winds are exceptionally changeable—is initially grounded in a general principle: "during a time of change everything is always especially indeterminate". This indeterminacy is then explained in terms of the transition between seasons, which necessitates both that the air currents be unsettled and, as will be discussed in the final section of this chapter, that Orion be perceived as difficult, since its appearance coincides with a period of turbulence and indeterminacy. I suggest, however, that this sense of indeterminacy is also informed by a broader ancient conviction—frequently articulated in Greek medical literature—that seasonal transitions correlate with bodily instability and increased susceptibility to disease.[43] A few illustrative examples of this belief are provided below:

The author of the Hippocratic *De natura hominis* maintains that diseases are caused by seasonal changes and therefore require close attention to the four bodily humours. Phlegm, blood, yellow bile, and black bile prevail respectively in winter, spring, summer, and autumn, and in turn generate seasonal diseases.[44] The mani-

---

41 In addition to the two problems discussed here, 26.17 and 26.43 focus on the effects of wind on living bodies. The former addresses putrefaction but notes that plants can benefit from south winds coming from the sea. The latter considers why people tend to consume more when the north wind blows.

42 This problem is identical to the first part of *Probl.* 1.14 and closely parallels *De Ventis* 56, a chapter which, together with the two subsequent chapters, discusses "the effects of various winds on human life" (Mayhew 2018: 330).

43 An extreme opposite of this view is offered by Herodotus (II 77), who claims that the Egyptians are the healthiest of all men because their climate remains constant throughout the year. If Herodotus here implies that the absence of (seasonal) changes ensures stability and health, he appears to receive a striking counterpoint from the author of *De aere, aquis, locis*. In chapter 19 [Diller 66.17–70.3 = II.70–73 Littré], the latter provides abundant details of the physiological corruptions of the Scythian race, who inhabit regions where (only) the north wind blows, the sun rarely appears, and the seasonal conditions resemble an everlasting winter.

44 See e.g. "Phlegm increases in a man in winter; for phlegm, being the coldest constituent of the body, is closest akin to winter". (*De natura hominis* 7.5 [Jouanna 184.4–6 = VI.48 Littré], trans. Jones 1931)

festation of humours within the body coincides with their prevalence in the natural environment, creating the impression that living bodies and their surroundings are in synchrony, undergoing the same cyclical transformations. The author of *De humoribus* reiterates that seasonal transitions are especially responsible for disease, though he adds an important qualification: seasons that shift gradually are the least harmful, since bodies can withstand and adapt to incremental day-by-day changes.[45] Similarly, the *Aphorismi* affirms the causal connection between seasonal change and disease. Autumn is singled out as the period during which illnesses are most acute and most deadly.[46]

These examples demonstrate that the belief in a correlation, and even synchronisation, between seasonal change and bodily instability—which I suggest is implicit in *Probl.* 26.13—was already deeply embedded in earlier medical thought. A confirmation of this perspective appears in *Probl.* 1.27, which explicitly describes spring and autumn as disease-producing (νοσώδη), with autumn considered far more dangerous than spring, since changes (μεταβολαί) themselves engender illness, especially when heat gives way to cold, as in autumn.[47] In *Probl.* 1.3, the author goes further, extending responsibility to winds as well: winds may intensify or alleviate disease, hasten a crisis, or even induce illness in otherwise healthy individuals.

At the same time, medical writers often caution their readers about particular days or transitional periods that might decisively affect a patient's condition. A case in point is the well-known passage from *De aere, aquis, locis,* to which we shall now turn:

> By investigating and observing such matters, a person will be able to foresee most of the consequences of the changes. One must be especially on one's guard against the most important *changes of the seasons*, and avoid giving a purgative medication or applying any cautery at all for the cavity, or incising, *before ten days are past, or even more*. Most important (sc. of the changes) are the following, and most dangerous: both solstices, *especially the summer one*, and both equinoxes (as they are reckoned), *especially the autumnal*. One must also pay attention to the risings of the stars, *especially of Sirius*, then of Arcturus, and also to the setting of the Pleiades: for diseases generally have their crises on these days, some proving fatal, others coming to an end, and all the rest changing to a different form and to a different constitution. (11 [Diller 52.15–54.3 = II.51–53 Littré]; trans. Potter 2022, emphasis added)

---

45 *De humoribus* 15 [Overwien 174.3–7 = V.496 Littré].

46 "It is chiefly the changes of the seasons which produce diseases, and in the seasons the great changes from cold or heat, and so on according to the same rule." (*Aphorismi* III.1 [= IV.486 Littré], trans. Jones 1931; cf. III.9 [= IV.488 Littré])

47 Another aspect of interpretation of νοσώδης μεταβολή appears in *Probl.* 1.15. There, the author asks why changes are disease-producing and answers that, in a process of change, the extremities—that is, the beginning (ἀρχή) and the end (τελευτή)—are volatile (εὐκίνητα) and therefore prone to decay (φθορά).

The view I suggest as implied in *Probl.* 26.13 here becomes more explicit: seasonal transitions are not merely correlated with the course of diseases but synchronised with them. Critical days of illness—those decisive moments when a condition turns toward recovery or decline—are presented as occurring in step with the critical turning points of the year.[48] In other words, the instability of the living body is thought to resonate with the instability of the surrounding environment. The medical author identifies the solstices, especially the summer solstice on June 21, and the equinoxes, above all the autumnal equinox on September 20, as the most decisive of these transitional moments. He further notes the rising and setting of particular stars between July and November—already included in the table of the previous section—as markers of medical importance. What is strikingly new in this passage, however, is the insistence that the influence of such transitions is not confined to the exact day on which the external change occurs. Rather, the period of danger extends for ten days or more, as though the body remains entrained to the turbulence of the seasonal shift. We are now in a position to examine the ps.-Aristotelian *Probl.* once more—specifically 26.32—to see how synchrony of cosmic and bodily rhythms is further elaborated.

5 Uncertain Winds: Orion, *Akrisia*, and the Vulnerable Body

At this stage, the various strands of evidence may be drawn together to clarify the content of *Probl.* 26.13. Yet, before this synthesis, attention must be given to one crucial observation the author makes in *Probl.* 26.32.[49] This problem explores the phenomenon of the south wind blowing at the time of the heliacal rising of Sirius and situates it within a broader framework of cosmological and meteorological explanations. It argues that, as with the risings and settings of all stars, a change in weather is to be expected—this change is signalled by an alteration of

48 Cf. *Epidemiarum* I.17 (= II.650 Littré), where the author states that "[t]owards (sc. the rising of) Arcturus many had a crisis on the eleventh day, and these did not suffer even the normal relapses". (trans. Potter 2022)

49 The initial *dia ti* question of *Probl.* 26.32 is identical with that of *Probl.* 26.12. On this basis, most scholars have transferred the detailed explanation (i.e. the answer to the initial question, 941b1–23) from 26.32 back to 26.12, a practice also followed in the edition of Mayhew and Mirhady 2011. As Flashar has shown, however, this move lacks manuscript support and the rearrangement is entirely unwarranted (Flashar 1962: 680–681; cf. 324–325). While I accept Flashar's position, it is nevertheless worth noting that *Probl.* 26.12 (when supplemented by the added passage) and 26.13 form a coherent thematic sequence. I thank Philip van der Eijk for this point.

winds. Because Sirius is associated with intense heat, the hottest winds are naturally set in motion, with *Notos* being the warmest among them. Following the principle that natural processes tend to shift into their opposites, the *Notos* succeeds the northern forerunner winds that precede the rising of Sirius.

The discussion further integrates astronomical temporality; this aspect deserves emphasis, as it clearly recalls the view articulated earlier in Hippocratic *De aere, aquis, locis* 11. On the fifteenth day after the winter solstice, when the sun reaches its southernmost position, the adjacent air masses are stirred, giving rise to *Notos*.[50] This does not occur immediately after the solstice—when solar movement is minimal and the solstice itself is regarded as a "certain beginning"—but only on the fifteenth day, because "this time coincides with the first impression corresponding to the change" (συμμέτρως ἔχειν τῇ κατὰ τὴν μετάστασιν πρώτῃ φαντασίᾳ).

This remark makes clear that the crucial factor is not simply the solstitial turning itself but the moment when its effects first become perceptible. The solstice is a certain beginning, but its initial changes are too slight to produce immediately noticeable effects. Only on the fifteenth day does the process coincide "in due proportion" with the first perceptible impression of the shift. This does not imply that nature delays its operations until human perception occurs; rather it emphasises that our access to natural order is mediated by perception: cosmic and meteorological change may already be underway, but it enters the horizon of human experience only when it produces a sensible impression. In this way, the passage acknowledges both the synchronism of celestial and atmospheric processes and the inevitable asynchrony between these processes and the moment of their perceptibility. The perceptive capacities of the human body register the change in co-temporality with the external wind, yet this perception is in fact asynchronous with the actual moment of generation, which may have occurred days or weeks earlier elsewhere. The rational part of the human mind, however, can reconstruct this apparent asynchrony (as the author himself shows through his interpretation), leading to the conclusion that stellar movements and wind

---

50 Aristotle's theory of wind production is notably complex. In his account, both the dry and the wet exhalations function as material causes of winds, while their efficient cause is the annual movement of the sun along the ecliptic (see Wilson 2013: 196–200 and 203). For detailed analysis of the difficulties raised by Aristotle's treatment, see Wilson 2013: 196–216. By contrast, Theophrastus attributes to the sun an important role as a συνεργῶν, "working together" with the exhalations in the generation of winds, while the moon is accorded a comparatively weaker influence (see *De Ventis* 15–17, 19, 41, and Mayhew 2018 *ad loc*, esp. pp. 177–184). In *Probl.* 26, however, the sun is identified as the primary generator of winds, although the moon is again recognised as exerting a significant role (*Probl.* 26.26, 26.18, 26.33, 26.34—In the latter two passages, air or vapour appears to function as the material cause of winds.).

changes—in particular the Sun's shift toward the southern regions—were indeed synchronised, and that what we perceive in the present reflects the consequences of this past synchrony.

The analysis of 26.32 can help us interpret and 'substantiate' the table provided at the end of section 3, and also resolve one of the puzzles raised there: namely, how to account for the one-month gap between the beginning of late summer (end of July), when the author of *Probl.* 26.13 places the rising of Orion, and the end of June, when the actual heliacal rising of the constellation occurred between the 3rd and 1st ce. BCE. Orion rises at the end of June, but winds signalling its rising could be perceived even two weeks later. Given the admittedly challenging circumstances under which ancient observers attempted to map the sky—without telescopes, under poor meteorological conditions, and without clocks to indicate the precise minutes before dawn, which would have aided identification of the 'real' heliacal risings of stars—some temporal gap between actual and assumed risings or settings is understandable. Furthermore, because the constellation is so large, it is possible that not all Greeks relied on the same star(s) within Orion to mark its risings and settings.[51] Orion's belt, its most characteristic feature for identification by non-experts, rises later than Betelgeuse, which is one of its brightest stars, and, depending on meteorological conditions, it might first become visible up to 2,5 weeks after Betelgeuse's heliacal rising, that is, in the second week of July.

On the other hand, since Orion rises not synchronously with the beginning of a season but at a transitional point, its influence—or the consequences of its rising—will be perceived by living bodies a-synchronously with the seasonal effects or the consequences of the season's prevalence. To these perceived, a-synchronous effects originating from two sources we must add a third, namely those related to winds. Winds are especially changeable due to the seasonal transition, and their mixed qualities and characteristics produce corresponding heterogeneous effects on living bodies. Such conditions seem to prevail over an extended period, largely because the size of Orion causes its rising and setting to extend over many days (*Mete.* II 5.361b30–33).

Another problematic point emerges from the table, which has not yet been addressed. All three authors examined in this chapter agree that Orion's rising initiates a period of turbulence, but only the author of *Probl.* 26.13 emphasises from the outset that this turbulence relates specifically to various winds, which are particularly changeable. At the beginning of the passage, he refers to αἰόλοι ἡμέραι, "changeable days"—and here the connection with Aiolos, the mythological lord of the winds, cannot be missed—and to ἀκαιρίαι τῶν πνευμάτων, "vari-

51 I thank Kassandra Miller for pressing me on this point.

ability of winds", according to the Loeb translation. In other words, if one reads only *Probl.* 26.13, without consulting the relevant contexts in Aristotle and Theophrastus, one might wonder why the table shows 'no signs' of turbulence for June 29 or later (similarly for November 22 when Orion sets), at least before the rising of Sirius about a month later. The table, however, appears accurate when read alongside Aristotle's relevant passage—through which Theophrastus' text also becomes intelligible at the corresponding point.

Aristotle's passage begins: "Hence calm (νηνεμία) is very apt to prevail (γίγνεται μάλιστα) about the rising of Orion (περὶ Ὠρίωνος ἀνατολὴν) and lasts until (καὶ μέχρι) the coming of the etesian winds and their forerunners." (361b23–24) By using a more restricted—and thus clearer—temporal phrase, Aristotle indicates that calm prevails about the time of Orion's rising, although, as noted above, this may last several days due to the size of the constellation.[52] Calm, he explains, continues until the arrival of the forerunners.[53] Similarly, Theophrastus uses ἐπ' Ὠριῶνος ἀνατολῇ καὶ δύσει. By contrast, the author of *Probl.* 26.13 employs ἐπὶ Ὠρίωνι, which may be translated as "at the time of Orion" or more freely "when Orion is observable", implying a longer period of influence than Aristotle's and Theophrastus' lexical constructions.

But how do Aristotle and Theophrastus communicate—similarly to the author of *Probl.* 26.13—that this period, broadly conceived, is turbulent even if it begins with no real winds blowing? Both use the concept of ἀκρισία for winds ("undecided character", "confusion"), which strongly echoes Hippocratic ideas of critical days or factors affecting the development of a disease (discussed briefly in section 4). Theophrastus' text is more straightforward: he opens the discussion by referring to πνευμάτων ἀκρισίαι, which lead to indeterminacy (ἀοριστεῖν). To be sure, ἀκρισία πνεύματος does not mean "no wind" and is therefore not identical to Aristotle's νηνεμία. However, recalling that for several Hippocratic authors—and for the author of *Probl.* 1.3—winds are among the decisive factors that 'determine' a condition, 'mark a critical point', or 'check' it, we may assume that ἀκρισία πνεύματος implies either an undetermined air current (i.e. a weak or ineffec-

52 Cf. Wilson 2013: 206: "The heat of the sun depends on the season of the year and the time of the day, and these allow Aristotle to account for the winds' periodicities. Because the sun is particularly hot at the summer tropic around the time of the heliacal rising of Orion, the wind is calm. Inter-seasonal periods of calm may also occur, because in the spring the exhalations have not yet been generated (because it is still too cold) and in the fall they have been exhausted and have not yet been replenished in the earth (2.5.361b27–30). Oddly, during these times, too, weather is unsettled, because there is a change of the season and the sun is reversing direction."

53 Here the table is inevitably unclear not only due to the scanty references to the forerunners (see n. 25 above), but also due to Aristotle's ambiguous statement a bit further down in the text: "The etesian winds blow after the summer solstice and the rising of the dog-star." (II 5.361b35–36)

tive wind) or an air current with insufficient force to determine an external condition. Aristotle, by contrast, seems not obliged to use ἀκρισία, given his literal use of νηνεμία. Nevertheless, he employs the concept when transmitting the *endoxon* that initially formed the basis of *Probl.* 26.13: Ἄκριτος δὲ καὶ χαλεπὸς ὁ Ὠρίων εἶναι δοκεῖ, καὶ δύνων καὶ ἐπιτέλλων (361b30–31). Orion seems "uncertain" or "undecided" and difficult with respect to both its setting and rising. In common opinion, Orion is undecided in the sense that its rising or setting does not initiate any significant air current—and, by implication, I propose, no noticeable change in bodily conditions, whether healthy or unhealthy. In this respect, it is also difficult, because at these temporal points external conditions remain indefinite, undetermined, stationary, and thus unpredictable in their outcomes. By extension, Orion may have been associated in popular thought with indeterminacy and ambiguity in matters of health and disease, or with precarious bodily developments leading to unpredictability and insecurity.

This idea of Orion as uncertain or undecided in its influence—whether on winds, on living bodies, or both—triggered negative feelings in humans at its appearance. It lies behind the *endoxon* transmitted through the stronger λέγεται in *Probl.* 26.13 and *De Ventis* 55, and through the weaker, though still indicative, δοκεῖ in *Mete.* II 5.361b30–31. The three authors exploit this basic idea of the *endoxon* to emphasise different aspects of the nature of winds, depending on the temporal point they wish to mark as noteworthy. For the author of *Probl.* 26.13, the whole period between Orion's rising and setting is generally regarded as turbulent, with winds especially indefinite—this is how I understand ἀκαιρία here[54]—in the sense that whether weaker or stronger, northern or mixed, they still blow at seasonal transitions, under the shadow of a star notorious for its 'difficulty' and indecisiveness in checking or determining matters of the sublunary world. For Aristotle, by contrast, Orion's characteristic ἀκρισία is harmonised with the winds' νηνεμία or calm, especially noticeable in the days around Orion's rising. Although the star appears a-synchronously with respect to the beginning of a season, its chief feature corresponds to that of the winds at this point in time, thus introducing a period of synchronised indeterminacy between weather and human conditions. Theophrastus' combined choice of ἀκρισία πνεύματος, with emphasis on both Orion's rising and setting dates, seems to confirm this interpretation.

Taken together, these readings show that Orion functioned not merely as a temporal marker but as a conceptual hinge between natural philosophy, medical theory, and lived human experience. By tracing the shifting uses of ἀκρισία and ἀκαιρία, we can see how ancient thinkers integrated cosmological observation

54 Cf. Flashar 1962: 351: „Unangemessenheit", „Unbestimmtheit".

with the language of bodily change, reflecting a principle of synchronisation that aligned celestial, environmental, and human rhythms. In this way, the *Problemata*, Aristotle, and Theophrastus participate in a broader effort to stabilise knowledge amid environmental uncertainty. The analysis demonstrates that these texts do not merely report meteorological phenomena but actively negotiate perception, interpretation, and prediction, illustrating how synchronicity structured both observation and expectation in ancient philosophy and medicine.

Bibliography

Primary Sources

Barnes, J. *The Complete Works of Aristotle. The Revised Oxford Translation*. 2 vols. Princeton, NJ: Princeton University Press, 1984.

Diller, H. (ed.) *Hippocratis.* De aere aquis locis, *edidit et in linguam Germanicam vertit.* (CMG I 1,2) Berlin: Akademie Verlag, 1999.

Flashar, H. (trans./comm.) *Aristoteles.* Problemata Physica. Aristoteles Werke in deutscher Übersetzung, Band 19. Berlin: Akademie Verlag, 1962.

Jones, W. H. S. (trans.) Hippocrates, Heracleitus. *Nature of Man. Regimen in Health. Humours. Aphorisms. Regimen 1–3. Dreams. Heracleitus. On the Universe*. Cambridge, MA: Harvard University Press, 1931.

Jouanna, J. (ed./comm.) *Hippocratis.* De natura hominis, *edidit, in linguam Francogallicam vertit, commentatus est.* (CMG I 1,3) Berlin: Akademie Verlag, 2002[2].

Louis, P. (ed./trans.) *Aristote.* Météorologiques. *Tome 1. Livres I et II.* Paris: Les Belles Lettres, 1982.

Mayhew, R. and D. C. Mirhady (eds./trans.) *Aristotle*. Problems, *Volume II*: Books 20–38. Rhetoric to Alexander. Cambridge, MA: Harvard University Press, 2011.

Mayhew, R. (ed./trans./comm.) *Theophrastus of Eresus*: On Winds. Leiden/Boston: Brill, 2018.

Overwien, O. (ed./trans./comm.) *Hippocratis.* De humoribus, *edidit, in linguam Germanicam vertit, commentatus est.* (CMG I 3,1) Berlin: De Gruyter, 2014.

Potter, P. (ed./trans.) *Hippocrates.* Ancient Medicine. Airs, Waters, Places. Epidemics 1 *and* 3. The Oath. Precepts. Nutriment. Cambridge, MA: Harvard University Press, 2022.

Sider, D. and C. W. Brunschön (eds./trans.) *Theophrastus of Eresus.* On Weather Signs. Leiden/Boston: Brill, 2007.

Secondary Literature

Bickerman, E. J. *Chronology of the Ancient World.* Ithaka, NY: Cornell University Press, 1980[2].

Allers, R. “Microcosmus. From Anaximandros to Paracelsus”. *Traditio* 2, 1944: 319–407.

Baltussen, H. “Reputable Opinions (*endoxa*) in Aristotle, Theophrastus, and Simplicius: Doxography or Endoxography?” In *Received Opinions: Doxography in Antiquity and the Islamic World*, Philosophia Antiqua 160, ed. A. Lammer and M. Jas. Leiden/Boston: Brill, 2022: 151–174.

Burkert, W. *Greek Religion: Archaic and Classical*. Translated by J. Raffan. Oxford: Blackwell Publishing, 1985.

Camden, D. H. *The Cosmological Doctors of Classical Greece: First Principles in Early Greek Medicine*. Cambridge/New York: Cambridge University Press, 2023.

Frede, D. "The *Endoxon Mystique*: What *Endoxa* Are and What They Are Not". *Oxford Studies in Ancient Philosophy* 43, 2012: 184–215.

Gotthelf, A. *Teleology, First Principles, and Scientific Method in Aristotle's Biology*. Oxford: Oxford University Press, 2012.

Graham, D. W., Z. Herzog and M. Williams. "Earth, Wind, and Fire: Aristotle on Violent Storm Events, with Reconsideration of the Terms ἐκνεφίας, τυφών, κεραυνός, and πρηστήρ". *Apeiron* 55.3, 2022: 417–442.

Hannah, R. "The Stars in Ancient Greece". In *Advancing Cultural Astronomy. Studies in Honour of Clive Ruggles*, ed. E. Boutsikas, S. C. McCluskey and J. Steele. Cham: Springer International Publishing, 2021: 211–222.

Johnson, M. R. "The Aristotelian Explanation of the Halo". *Apeiron* 42.4, 2009: 325–358.

Karbowski, J. "*Endoxa*, facts, and the starting points of the *Nicomachean Ethics*". In *Bridging the Gap Between Aristotle's Science and Ethics*, ed. D. Henry and K. M. Nielsen. Cambridge: Cambridge University Press, 2015: 113–129.

Kidd, I. G. "Theophrastus' Meteorology, Aristotle and Posidonius". In *Theophrastus. His Psychological, Doxographical, and Scientific Writings*, Rutgers University Studies in Classical Humanities V, ed. W. W. Fortenbaugh and D. Gutas. New York: Routledge, 1992: 294–306.

Kranz, W. „Kosmos und Mensch in der frühgriechischen Philosophie". In *Walther Kranz. Studien zur antiken Literatur und ihrem Fortwirken*, ed. E. Vogt. Heidelberg: Carl Winter Universitätsverlag, 1967: 165–196.

Lehoux, D. *Astronomy, Weather, and Calendars in the Ancient World. Parapegmata and Related Texts in Classical and Near-Eastern Societies*. Cambridge: Cambridge University Press, 2007.

Lettinck, P. *Aristotle's Meteorology and its Reception in the Arab World*. Leiden/Boston/Cologne: Brill, 1999.

Liewert, A. *Die meteorologische Medizin des Corpus Hippocraticum*. Untersuchungen zur antiken Literatur und Geschichte 119. Berlin/Munich/Boston: De Gruyter, 2015.

Mayhew, R. "Athenaeus' *Deipnosophistae* 7 and Aristotle's lost *Zoïka or On Fish*". In *Revisiting Aristotle's Fragments: New Essays on the Fragments of Aristotle's Lost Works*, ed. A. P. Mesquita, S. Noriega-Olmos and C. J. I. Shields. Berlin: De Gruyter, 2020: 109–139.

Mayhew, R. "*De Signis* §§ 13 and 37 and *Problemata Physica* 26.23 in the Context of Peripatetic Meteorology: Shooting Stars as Weather Signs". In *Meteorology Beyond Borders. Ancient and Modern Reflections*, Euhormos: Greco-Roman Studies in Anchoring Innovation 10, ed. G. Korobili and T. Tieleman. Leiden/Boston: Brill, 2026: 151–165.

Mouzala, M. (ed.) *Ancient Greek Dialectic and Its Reception*. Topics in Ancient Philosophy/Themen der antiken Philosophie 10. Berlin/Boston: De Gruyter, 2023.

Salles, R. (ed.) *Cosmology and Biology in Ancient Philosophy. From Thales to Avicenna*. Cambridge: Cambridge University Press, 2021.

Singer, P. N. *Time for the Ancients. Measurement, Theory, Experience*. Chronoi. Zeit, Zeitempfinden, Zeitordnungen. Time, Time Awareness, Time Management, Band 3. Berlin/Boston: De Gruyter, 2022.

Steinmetz, P. *Die Physik des Theophrastos von Eresos*. Bad Homburg: Max Gehlen, 1964.

Taub, L. *Ancient Meteorology*. London: Routledge, 2003.

Tilburg, C. van. "A Good Place to Be: Meteorological and Medical Conditions in Ancient Cities". *Mnemosyne* 68.5, 2015: 794–813.

Wee, J. Z. "Earthquake and Epilepsy: The Body Geologic in the Hippocratic Treatise *On the Sacred Disease*". In *The Comparable Body. Analogy and Metaphor in Ancient Mesopotamian, Egyptian, and Greco-Roman Medicine*, ed. J. Z. Wee. Leiden: Brill, 2017: 142–167.

Williams, S. L. *Taming the Winds in Antiquity (1400 B.C.–500 A.D.). Iconography, Cult and Literature*. Doct. Diss., University of Edinburgh, 2000. https://era.ed.ac.uk/handle/1842/23524?show=full.

Wilson, M. *Structure and Method in Aristotle's* Meteorologica. *A More Disorderly Nature.* Cambridge: Cambridge University Press, 2013.

Zatta, C. "Seasons and Human Health in the Hippocratic *Airs, Waters, and Places* and Hesiod's *Works and Days*". *Florentia Iliberritana* 33, 2023: 149–163.

Zerefos, C., S. Solomos, D. Melas, J. Kapsomenakis and C. Repapis. "The Role of Weather during the Greek-Persian 'Naval Battle of Salamis' in 480 B.C.". *Atmosphere* 11 (838), 2020: 1–16.

James Ker

Synchronizing Diachronies in Seneca's *Consolatio ad Marciam*

Abstract: In Seneca's *Consolatio ad Marciam*, the diachrony of the mother's protracted and unending grief is figured in bodily terms, both in the form of tears and through the metaphor of a wound. Responding to this problematic temporality of grief, the philosophical consoler seeks to impose a clear temporal schedule for the subject's recovery from grief. The consoler's time frame for recovery involves synchronization in two senses: (1) Marcia's grieving body is expected to synchronize with this schedule, while (2) the schedule itself includes a range of time-considerations, embedded within the discursive time of the consolation, that facilitate a more rapid recovery. Seneca thus seeks to use synchronization to transform the addressee's time experience, especially as this is encoded in her literal and metaphorical body.

Keywords: consolation, Marcia, Seneca, synchronization, tears, time, wound

1 Introduction

In this chapter I explore synchronization and the body in the context of Seneca the Younger's consolation written for the aristocratic woman Marcia following the death of her adult son Metilius. Like all other surviving Greek and Roman consolations, *Ad Marciam de consolatione* (*Marc.*) is primarily concerned with the grieving person's state of mind. What makes the work a useful case study here, however, is that Seneca's portrait of Marcia's experience of grief attends to the bodily signifiers of tears and a grief-stricken face and also to a metaphorical wound. As Seneca employs his written therapy to define a time schedule for Marcia's recovery from grief, this schedule has powerful implications both for her whole person and for her body.

Ad Marciam is Seneca's earliest surviving literary work, having been written likely in the late 30s during the reign of Caligula, and it may represent something of a debut in his philosophical writing. In focusing on this work I am building on the renewed attention it has been receiving thanks especially to the commentary by Fabio Tutrone (2023).[1] There is much in my analysis, however, that is relevant

1 Both Tutrone 2023 and Manning's (1981) earlier commentary are indispensable.

https://doi.org/10.1515/9783112235690-005

to ancient consolatory writing more generally,[2] including Seneca's second surviving consolation addressed to his mother Helvia, which I touch upon in my conclusion.

1.1 Synchronicity

As is evident from the variety of chapters in this volume, there are quite a few ways in which the body may be understood as synchronized with other rhythms or circumstances, even within the specific fields of ancient medicine and philosophy. Before I home in on the form that body-synchronization takes within Seneca's text, it will be useful to recognize the fundamental place occupied by "synchronization" and "synchronicity" in accounts of time in general as well as in studies of ancient Greek and Roman temporalities.

As simply one illustration of modern analysis, consider the opening of Thomas Luckmann's essay, "The Constitution of Human Life in Time" (1991), which encapsulates some of the main insights developed about time within the field of sociology:

> The emergence and subsequent interpenetration of several dimensions in the experience of time were a necessary condition for both the evolution and the ontogenesis of personal identity as the peculiarly human form of life. As I will try to show, these dimensions are the *non*-identical diachronies of the body, of the ongoing synchronizations of self and other in face-to-face interaction and of "history". Personal identity arises at the intersection of these dimensions in individual consciousness.[3]

Here synchronicity is manifested both in the "interpenetration" and "intersection" by which various "*non*-identical diachronies" are brought together to form the person and already in the "synchronizations" of self and other that Luckmann treats as an essential condition of social interaction.

All of Luckmann's items, however, are subject to further explanation and subcategorization, and indeed debate, not only within his own important essay (which I do not explore further here) but also across the fabric of time studies. Thus, for example, in their volume *Shaping the Day: A History of Timekeeping in England and Wales 1300–1800* (2009), Glennie and Thrift use the term 'time-discipline' as an umbrella term for a range of different notions—"regularity", "standardization", and "coordination"—each of which could be used to characterize

2 On ancient consolation in general, see Baltussen 2013, especially the opening chapter by Scourfield 2013.

3 Luckmann 1991: 151; emphasis in original.

how a given diachrony (they are thinking in particular of a person's schedule) might relate to another, and each of which, I suggest, may be described as a form of synchronicity.[4] Johannes Fabian, in *Time and the Other: How Anthropology Makes Its Object* (2014), takes the term "synchronous" to refer to "events occurring at the same physical time; *contemporary* asserts co-occurrence in what I call typological time. *Coeval*, according to my pocket Oxford dictionary, covers both ('of same age, duration, or epoch'). Beyond that, it [i.e. *coeval*] is to connote a common, active 'occupation,' or sharing of time.".[5] The denial of coevalness, or "allochronism", is the problematic phenomenon that Fabian sees recurring in the ethnographies of modern cultural anthropology. Synchronization, then, encompasses the various ways in which temporalities are matched with one another, or not, and with significant social and historical implications.

Synchronizing relations have been prominent, too, at various levels of analysis within the study of ancient Greek and Roman time. In Clarke's analysis of the meshing of linear and cyclical temporalities in a specific ancient Greek festival calendar, the term "synchronic history" captures the way in which an experience of deep diachronic time is accessed through the shallow and recurrent diachrony of the calendrical year.[6] We may compare Beard's classic characterization of the Roman *fasti*, which "offered a pageant of what it was to be Roman, which existed in 'ritual time,' in time whose sequence had collapsed into an overlapping series of stories",[7] and, with greater complexity, the syncing of different historical, solar, and biographic time schemes that Wallace-Hadrill (1987) located in the emperor Augustus's monumental complex on the Campus Martius.

Such effects are also often the product of literary endeavors. In Ovid's month-by-month didactic framework for teaching readers about the Roman *fasti*, Volk observes, "poetic and mimetic simultaneity basically fall together as the poem about the Roman year, the poet/persona's producing the poem about the Roman year, and the Roman year itself are presented as happening at the same time, 'now'".[8] In the separate dawn-labor topos in Greek and Roman poetry, where we are given a montage of all the different types of activity that different people are engaged in at one and the same time, the lens of synchronicity shines a light precisely on social heterogeneity: when Dawn arrives, the poet complains, "the traveler gets up no matter how tired, . . . you cheat boys of sleep and hand them over to schoolteachers . . . you recall [a woman's] woolworking hand to its

4 Glennie and Thrift 2009: 45.
5 Fabian 2014: 31.
6 Clarke 2008: 34.
7 Beard 1987: 12.
8 Volk 1997: 294.

tasks", and many others besides (Ovid, *Amores* I 13.13–24).[9] The topos is an example of how textual representations of simultaneous times, even as they manipulate the reader's experience of the real time of poetic aesthetics, can serve as a pageant of broader time schemes ranging from one person's form of life to the broader scales of Roman imperial history and the history of human culture.

What this range of examples shows is that synchronicity serves as a metatemporal concept or function—as a name for the various ways in which distinct temporalities can be correlated with one another (or not) in service of a specific social or rhetorical goal. In this chapter I focus on the ways in which synchronization serves Seneca's consolatory goals in *Ad Marciam*, with a focus on two specific synchronizing operations in which the body of the grieving mother Marcia is implicated. In doing so, I seek to demonstrate what can be gained from taking certain known features of this consolation in which time is a prominent theme and reviewing them through the lens of synchronization. First, I argue, an ambitious schedule for recovery from grief is charted by the consolatory text, and the conspicuous diachronies of grief are expected to either synchronize with it or be absorbed or even eclipsed by it. Second, this schedule of grief-recovery itself includes a complex embedding of times, temporalities, and narratives that are synchronized within the discursive time of the text. These are "good to think with" and can accelerate Marcia's recovery progress.

2 The Times of Consolation, and the Grief-Recovery Schedule

An essential starting point for this analysis is to observe that the grief situation portrayed in *Ad Marciam* encompasses a wide array of times, temporalities, and what I have elsewhere referred to as "mediating narratives".[10] In the opening sentence alone (*Marc.* 1.1), Seneca first characterizes Marcia's potential to overcome her grief, and to overcome her feminine weakness, in terms of a backward movement in time to an *antiquum exemplar* (with implications of aristocratic tradition);[11] then he frames the present consolation in terms of a forensic process by which Marcia, despite this being an "unfavorable time" (*tempore iniquo*), may be

9 On this topos, see Ker 2023: 124–127.

10 Ker 2009: 91.

11 Tutrone 2023: 50–51. On the gendered formulation of moral fortitude here in terms of *virtus*, see Langlands 2004: 119–121.

persuaded to "acquit" (*absolvere*) her misfortune on the model of a forensic process.[12]

During the first few pages, we encounter a succession of time perspectives that frame the consolatory scenario. There is biographic time and recent history, within which Marcia is reminded of her own brave response to the death of her father, the historian Cremutius Cordus, after his persecution by Sejanus in the year 25 CE, followed by her re-publication of his banished historical writings after the *mutatio temporum* ("changing political climate") ushered in by the new emperor Gaius/Caligula in 37 (*Marc.* 1.2–1.4). Then there is Marcia's present grief situation, an intractable crisis. The extent of Marcia's grieving is highlighted—"Three years have now passed" (*tertius iam praeterit annus*)—while her present grief is a time of acute intensification, in which, as Seneca tells her, "your mourning renews and strengthens itself each day" (*renovat se et corroborat cotidie luctus*, 1.7).

During these opening chapters there is also a focus on the prospects for a consolation process. Seneca sketches the time from Metilius' death until his consolation as one in which family members have sought to console Marcia but "[e]verything has been tried to no avail" (*omnia in superuacuum temptata sunt*, 1.6). He also points out to Marcia that "nature's own remedy, time, which heals even the greatest distress, in your case alone has proved powerless" (*illud ipsum naturale remedium temporis, quod maximas quoque aerumnas componit, in te una uim suam perdidit*, 1.6; cf. 8.2). This situation is set against an alternative timeframe, the initial opportunity for consolation that Seneca says he has missed: "I wish I could have begun this treatment in the early stages" (*cupissem itaque primis temporibus ad istam curationem accedere*, 1.8). Instead, all that Seneca can hope for is that the present consolation can challenge Marcia, with his challenging question: "Where will it end?" (*quis enim erit finis*, 1.6). The consoler aspires for her to take grief-termination into her own hands, urging: "You should renounce it yourself" (*ipsa illi renuntia*, 8.3).

In the course of the consolation, Seneca introduces a range of additional therapies and self-therapeutic options that—like his reminder to Marcia about her earlier recovery after her father's death—summon up a range of biographic, historical, and cosmic perspectives. He famously begins with a pair of recent examples from the Augustan household and Marcia's own lifetime, describing the contrasting responses of Octavia and Livia after the deaths of their respective sons Marcellus (23 BCE) and Drusus (9 BCE): "Throughout her entire life [Octavia] never brought her weeping and lamenting to an end" (*nullum finem per omne*

12 English translations of *Ad Marciam* here and below are from Hine 2014.

uitae suae tempus flendi gemendique fecit, 2.4), whereas Livia "laid both him [viz. Drusus] and her grief to rest" (*simul et illum et dolorem suum posuit,* 3.2).[13] Later examples come from the age of the Roman republic, such as that of Cornelia, who is portrayed saying: "I shall never stop saying that I am fortunate, I who gave birth to the Gracchi" (*'numquam . . . non felicem me dicam, quae Gracchos peperi'*, 16.3). Seneca summons up the temporality of the birth and death cycle across all of nature, reminding Marcia, in her identity as a mother: "You were born a mortal and you have given birth to mortals" (*mortalis nata es mortalesque peperisti,* 11.1). This notion of a natural law or contract is given a more specific analogy from historic time in which a hypothetical visitor to the scenic but politically volatile city of Syracuse is warned: "You will see the spring of Arethusa, famed in poetry" (*videbis celebratissimum carminibus fontem Arethusam,* 17.3), yet also "there you will find the tyrant Dionysius" (*erit Dionysius illic tyrannus,* 17.5).

Toward the end of the consolation, Marcia is presented with additional time perspectives on her son's life and death. One argument appeals to *opportuna mors,* the notion that a timely death can make a life happier than it would have been were it protracted (the prime example being the life of Cicero, who lived too long; 20.5). A related argument evaluates life by its quality rather than its quantity: "If you start to value him in terms of his virtues, not his years, then he lived sufficiently long" (*incipe uirtutibus illum, non annis aestimare; satis diu uixit,* 24.1).

While ancient consolation typically leaves open the possibility of a happy afterlife for the deceased, *Ad Marciam* offers an unambiguously optimistic view: Seneca assures Marcia that Metilius "was then raised up high and hurried to join the souls of the blessed. He has been welcomed by a sacred entourage, by Scipios and Catos" (*ad excelsa sublatus inter felices currit animas. excepit illum coetus sacer, Scipiones Catonesque* [. . .], 25.1). The work concludes with a description of the deceased Cremutius Cordus, who is also up there, welcoming his grandson's disembodied soul and reassuring Marcia in an imagined speech: "We also, the blessed souls . . . we too shall be a small appendage to the wholesale destruction, and we shall be returned to our original elements" (*nos quoque felices animae . . . ipsae parua ruinae ingentis accessio in antiqua elementa uertemur,* 26.7). Although this cosmic conflagration ultimately leaves no survivors—not even the "blessed souls" whom some Stoic eschatologies had allowed to persist for a long time after death—the closing image alludes to a renewing metamorphosis in the next round of the cosmic cycle.[14]

13 On the Octavia and Livia examples, see the classic analysis by Shelton 1995; also Wilcox 2006: 81–87.

14 On these closing chapters, see Ker 2022, and on Seneca's eschatologies, Williams 2021.

Any collection of heterogeneous times in a literary text always has some sort of narratological impact, and in the case of *Ad Marciam* the intended impact is explicit. These various diachronies are all in the service of expediting Marcia's full recovery. This is envisaged in terms of Marcia one day renouncing her grief and imposing an end (cf. 8.3, 1.6 above), or her ushering in a time when she can joyfully remember Metilius as he was during his lifetime (as in Livia's joyful recollection of Drusus in both public and private contexts, 3.2), rather than continuing to fixate on his death.

It does not seem controversial to say that Seneca's consolation itself establishes a "schedule" for the termination of grief. Although the time of Marcia's recovery is perhaps not expected to arrive *during* her reading of Seneca's text, the text is clearly intended to adumbrate it and to accelerate it. In Seneca's example of the philosopher Areus advising Livia, he encourages her to take up her regular duties "without being terrified, once the initial disturbance is past" (*primo dumtaxat strepitu conterrita*), and he tries to catalyze this by reminding her about her surviving son (Tiberius) as well as the grandchildren that she has from the deceased son (5.6).

3 Synchronizing Times in Consolation

Seneca's textualized consolatory therapy for Marcia, which as we have seen is distinguished by its continual reference to different time schemes and perspectives on time, activates these temporalities for therapeutic ends, I argue, through the power of synchronization. This synchronizing takes two distinct forms.

The first form of synchronization is what I would describe as imposing the schedule of recovery. The consolation sets forth an idealized, normative process for Marcia's termination of her grief, and the processes of protracted grief are expected to speed up and coincide with it. Let us look more closely at how Seneca articulates the schedule of recovery for Marcia:

> It suits the excellence of your character much better to impose an end on your mourning rather than wait for its end (*finem luctus potius facere quam expectare*), and to refuse to hold out until the day when, against your wishes, grief will fade away (*nec illum opperiri diem quo te invita dolor desinat*). You should renounce it yourself! (*Marc.* 8.3)

Here and elsewhere in his consolatory writings Seneca takes a relatively hard and fast line, among the various possible approaches listed by Cicero in his discussion of consolation and individual philosophical doctrines in the *Tusculan Disputations* (*Tusc.*):

> These, then, are the comforter's responsibilities: to remove distress altogether (*tollere aegritudinem funditus*), or to cause it to subside, or to diminish it as much as possible, or to restrain it so that it cannot spread any further, or to divert it elsewhere. (*Tusc.* III 75, trans. Graver 2002)

My first claim about synchronization is that this schedule of recovery becomes *the* schedule that other narratives of grief need to synchronize with. The most obvious alternative schedule is that of Time the Healer, which Cicero already treats as a foil in one of his consolatory letters:

> After all, there was never a woman bereaved of children so frail of spirit (*liberis amissis tam imbecillo mulier animo*) that she did not in the end set a term to her mourning (*lugendi modum fecerit*). Surely then we should apply in advance by using our reason (*consilio ante ferre*) what the passing of the days will bring (*quod est dies adlatura*); we ought not to wait for time to produce the medicine (*exspectare temporis medicinam*) which our intelligence can supply to hand (*repraesentare ratione*). (*Epistulae ad familiares* 5.16.6, trans. Shackleton Bailey 2001)

As Cicero points out in the *Tusculan Disputations*, in fact, the notion of Time the Healer is itself a misconception. If people get over grief in time, this is itself the product of a kind of accidental self-consolation:

> The disappearance of grief over time (a point on which all sides agree) is not solely a matter of duration (*hanc vim non esse in die positam*); rather, it comes of thinking for a long time about what has happened (*in cogitatione diuturna*). [. . .] What heals grief must be the length of time one spends thinking that no evil is in fact present (*cogitatio igitur diuturna nihil esse in re mali dolori medetur*). It can hardly be the passage of time in and of itself (*non ipsa diuturnitas*). (*Tusc.* III 74; cf. III 54)

The philosophical schedule for grief-recovery is simply a more proactive, more systematic, and more rapid version of the same mental process.

In Marcia's case, however, as noted above, the natural process of Time the Healer has been thwarted by a kind of psychological impasse. Seneca presents his schedule of grief-recovery as competing with schedules that on their own seem unlikely to produce healing at all. When he draws attention to the fact that her mourning has continued into the third year, as Tutrone notes, this would have sounded to the reader "like a transgression of customary norms set up by the community for the sake of social order"—one year being the legally permitted limit for mourning a child over six years of age.[15]

And when Seneca characterizes her grief as "renewing" (*renovat*) and "strengthening" (*corroborat*) itself "every day" (*cotidie*), this appears to be not

15 Tutrone 2023: 61, citing Paulus, *Sententiae* I 21.2–5 and 21.8–14.

only a form of continuation but of a growing attachment. Her grief "has established squatter's rights, and has reached the point where it thinks that it would be shameful to stop" (*iam sibi ius mora fecit eoque adductus est ut putet turpe desinere*) and "the unhappy mind finds a perverse pleasure in grief" (*fit infelicis animi prava voluptas dolor*) (1.7).

Seneca presents his consolatory therapy as a way for Marcia to impose a new, shorter schedule on the termination of her grief. As we have seen, the alternative trajectories of her grief are not only slower—various factors are leading Marcia into a process whose ending *ever* is seriously in question. It may be more accurate to refer to the grief-recovery schedule as needing to altogether eclipse or elide the more problematic diachronies of her grief, but the overall contrast between the natural recovery through Time the Healer and the philosophically catalyzed recovery schedule, along with the salience of temporal considerations in Marcia's grieving, defines an overall modality of an imposed acceleration. Marcia's recovery needs to match the pace determined by the idealized recovery schedule defined by the consolatory text—to end when it ends, and to synchronize with it.

The second form of synchronization is what I refer to as an embedding of times. The consolatory text includes a complex set of time-considerations—the series of time perspectives and mediating narratives that Seneca leads Marcia through, as mentioned above—that are "good to think with" (as a focus of reasoning, or *cogitatio*, about death and grief) and can accelerate recovery from grief. These time-considerations facilitate the timely completion of the grief-recovery schedule, and being presented within the textual plotting of this schedule, they are in that sense synchronized with it.

We may note, for example, the time-consideration mentioned above that plays an important role in Seneca's approach to Marcia: his reminding her about the time within her own life when she overcame the death of her father. More than once in the text Seneca activates that experience in Marcia's memory, reminding her of the public praise for "how you behaved in regard to your father" (*qualem te in persona patris tui gesseris*, 1.2) and even prompting her to actively revisit it: "Picture to yourself that period that caused you such pain" (*propone illud acerbissimum tibi tempus*), which is followed by a retelling of Cremutius' death by self-starvation and her final interactions with him (22.4). Seneca's apparatus for leveraging Marcia's response to her father's death includes drawing attention to the posthumous survival she ensured for his writings: "You enabled the public to have access once more to your father's literary talent, which had been the target of the punishment; you rescued him from real death . . ." (*ingenium patris tui, de quo sumptum erat supplicium, in usum hominum reduxisti et a uera illum uindicasti morte*, 1.3). The fact that she was able to bring Cremutius back to life even after the burning of his writings will also fuel Seneca's assertion at the end of the consolation that Metilius can join Cremutius in the afterlife and even that some part of us will endure beyond cosmic conflagration (cf. 26.2–7).

Or consider the extensive and rhetorically powerful Syracuse analogy. Marcia is invited to conduct a thought-experiment within a hypothetical scenario that is informed by historical time (the past existence of specific Syracusan tyrants) and is also likely informed by the literary-philosophical ambiance of Plato. Seneca echoes the last days of Socrates, particularly the *Crito*, with its reminder about the implicit terms under which we accept the risks of life along with the good things (*Crito* 50a–54d; cf. *Marc.* 17–18), and the *Phaedo*, with its focus on death as the soul's liberation from embodied life (*Phaedo* 63e–67e; cf. *Marc.* 23.1).[16]

These complex time-considerations are the sort of *cogitatio* that allows Seneca to be openly ambitious about Marcia's recovery schedule. And because they are essential to the more rapid healing process that Seneca promotes in and through his text, they are also simultaneous with it. The references to other times past and future, and to ways of thinking about time and memory and about life, death, and afterlife, are summoned up by Seneca within the discursive time of the evolving text. Their synchronization with this discursive time is expected to improve Marcia's chances of ending her grief quickly. Through this choreographing of times the text thereby serves as a kind of time technology.

4 Synchronizing the Grieving Body

Having sketched this framework for thinking about how Seneca's grief-recovery schedule relates to other times, in which alternative diachronies must synchronize with the grief-recovery process and the grief-recovery discourse synchronizes a range of time-perspectives, I turn now to discuss the times of the body that are foregrounded in *Ad Marciam*. These are, first, the mother's tears, including the effect these tears have had on Marcia's appearance, and second, the metaphorical wound that Seneca refers to in connection with Marcia's experience of loss.

16 On the relationship to *Crito*, see e.g. Inwood 2005: 241–242, 244; on *Phaedo*, Tutrone 2023: 241.

4.1 Tears and Face

Seneca mentions Marcia's feminine body and its characteristic expression of grief through crying. To the extent that Marcia has succumbed to grief and shows no sign of recovery, her bodily response continues unabated. The key mention comes in the consolation's first chapter, where Seneca makes her conscious of her gender (cf. *sexum tuum*, 1.5) and the specific physical features of her "face, which is still marred by so many years' continual sadness, just as it was disfigured by it at the start" (*vultum, quem tot annorum continua tristitia, ut semel obduxit, tenet*), as well as her "weary, exhausted eyes, which, if you want to know the truth, flow more from habit than from longing" (*defessos exhaustosque oculos, si verum vis magis iam ex consuetudine quam ex desiderio fluentis*, 1.5). The portrait of Marcia's grief is closely tied to the protracted temporality of this bodily experience.

Yet these mentions of the face and eyes are themselves embedded in Seneca's articulation of his consolatory program, which appeals to Marcia's inner resources that allow her to transcend her femininity:

> This noble-mindedness of yours (*haec magnitudo animi*) has prevented me from taking any notice of your sex (*vetuit me ad sexum tuum respicere*), or of your face, which is still marred by so many years' continual sadness, just as it was disfigured by it at the start. . . . I shall bring your weary, exhausted eyes under control (*continebo*), eyes which, if you want to know the truth, flow more from habit than from longing. (*Marc.* 1.5)

Here we see the authorial persona of Seneca averting his gaze from Marcia's body in a way that builds upon things he has already said about her capacity to overcome weakness. In the very first words of the consolation Seneca had told Marcia that he was confident precisely because, he says, "you have drawn back from the frailties of the female temperament just as much as you have from all other kinds of fault (*te . . . tam longe ab infirmitate muliebris animi quam a ceteris vitiis recessisse*)" and "people look up to your character as though it were some ancient paragon" (*mores tuos velut aliquod antiquum exemplar aspici*, 1.1)—where people's eyes look beyond Marcia's body to her interior character. He had also reminded her of what people admired about her response to her father's death, where she had exerted at least some control over her bodily comportment: "you signaled acceptance of defeat; you openly shed tears, and you swallowed your sighs, yet did not conceal them beneath a cheerful expression" (*dedisti manus victa, fudistique lacrimas palam et gemitus devorasti quidem, non tamen hilari fronte texisti*, 1.2).[17]

Seneca's appeal to the masculine moral fortitude of Marcia's *virtus* and *animus* will be complemented at the end of the work by his focus on disembodied *animae* (cf. 25.1 and 26.7) demonstrating that death is not even the end—in other words, another reason not to cry. Seneca does not at all deny Marcia's identity as a woman and a mother throughout the work, but he seeks to replace the idealization of maternal fertility often termed *felicitas* with reminders of the inclusion of birth *and* mortality within the purview of maternal Nature and also of the status of Cremutius and his grandson as *felices animae*, "blessed souls".[18]

It is useful to think of Seneca here as seeking to synchronize Marcia's body, in both the senses distinguished above. First, the bodily process of shedding tears and of signifying sadness in various other ways must be accelerated and brought to an end soon, following the schedule of recovery from grief that the consolation imposes. Body time must accommodate itself to the time of the *animus*.

Second, this synchronization of bodily time with the grief-recovery schedule is to be facilitated by the array of time perspectives that Seneca corrals for expediting it. These time perspectives are many: Marcia's inner resources are located in the temporally marked locus of an *antiquum exemplar*; the *felices animae* are figured as an enduring procession of republican heroes; and so on. Seneca's most extensive thought experiment for Marcia involves inviting her to remember the grief response of Octavia, who "throughout her life . . . behaved just as she had at the funeral" (*talis per omnem vitam fuit qualis in funere*, 2.4), and that of Livia, who quickly put aside tears and "soon recovered her usual frame of mind" (*cito animum in sedem suam reposuit*, 2.2) and was always "gladly speaking about him and hearing about him" (*libentissime de illo loqui, de illo audire*, 3.2). Seneca explicitly embeds the moment of Livia's conversion, through the advice of the philosopher Areus, within the temporality of the present discourse: "Your own circumstances were addressed on that occasion, Marcia, it was you that Areus sat beside" (*tuum illic, Marcia, negotium actum, tibi Areus adsedit*, 6.1).

Marcia's body is expected, then, both to synchronize with the expedited grief-recovery schedule of the mind's ideal response to grief and to reach this pace through the benefit of the rapid succession of time-perspectives and thought experiments that are corraled so as to facilitate this schedule's timely completion.

17 As Hine notes, "the sequence of ideas is puzzling" (2014: 37 n. 3); for full discussion, including questions about the text, see Tutrone 2023: 55. Seneca clearly claims not that Marcia entirely suppressed all physical signs of grief, but that she complied with Cremutius' decision and eventually overcame the loss.

18 On *felicitas* redefined, see Gunderson 2015: 79–87; on maternal Nature, Gloyn 2017: 19.

4.2 The Metaphorical Wound

Much as he had pointed to Marcia's tears and face as bodily symptoms of her continuing grief, Seneca also characterizes her loss and grief through the image of a "wound" (*vulnus*, 1.5). But as with tears and face, he also projects confidence in Marcia's capacity to heal herself:

> I have reminded you of sufferings that are long past (*antiqua mala in memoriam reduxi*); and so that you may realize that the present wound also needs healing (*ut scires hanc quoque plagam esse sanandam*), I have shown you the scar of an equally severe injury (*ostendi tibi aeque magni vulneris cicatricem*). (*Marc.* 1.5)

The scar referred to here—the trace of a wound that is a wound no more—is Marcia's recovery after the death of her father, including her re-publication of his histories, which Seneca mentioned just before this moment in the preface. To this extent, Seneca activates a medical analogy both in terms of what can go wrong (the wound) and in terms of healing (the scar).

But this analogy raises the question of how the diachrony from wound to healing might relate to the various time schemes of the present consolation, including Seneca's idealized schedule for Marcia's recovery from her grief over Metilius. And while the scarification of Marcia's wound after the death of her father is implied to have happened satisfactorily, or at least to have concluded some time ago, the remainder of Seneca's preface presents a more complicated prognosis for Marcia's latest wound.

As he sketches Marcia's entrenched and ever-renewing grief in chapter 2 of the consolation, Seneca expresses regret that he wasn't able to attend to her malady sooner, saying:

> I wish I could have begun this treatment in the early stages (*cupissem primis temporibus ad istam curationem accedere*): a milder medicine could have been used to check the attack while it was still building up (*leniore medicina fuisset oriens adhuc restringenda uis*); but chronic diseases need to be fought more vigorously (*vehementius contra inveterata pugnandum est*). (*Marc.* 1.8)

He proceeds from this broad illness analogy to the more specific example of a wound:

> For with wounds as well, healing is easy while they are fresh and still bleeding; but when they have festered and turned foully ulcerous, they must be cauterized and cut open again and must allow fingers to probe into them.

> *Nam vulnerum quoque sanitas facilis est, dum a sanguine recentia sunt: tunc et uruntur et in altum revocantur et digitos scrutantium recipiunt, ubi corrupta in malum ulcus verterunt.* (*Marc.* 1.8)

He uses this to explain why the present consolation needs to be more robust and violent than it would have been had Seneca been on the scene sooner: "As things stand, I cannot attack such a hardened grief by polite or gentle means: it has to be shattered" (*non possum nunc per obsequium nec molliter adgredi tam durum dolorem: frangendus est*, 1.8).

Here, of course, Seneca is deploying the already well-established analogy between philosophical consolation and medical therapy. Within this analogy, the comparison of mental distress to physical pain is relatively seamless given that the terms *lupê* in Greek and *dolor* in Latin can refer to mental as well as physical pain. Cicero makes this parallel his point of departure in *Tusculan Disputations* III, where he seeks to give philosophy the recognition it deserves as a "medicine for the mind" (*animi medicina*) alongside the art that tends to the health of the body (*Tusc.* III 1). And his discussion of consolation in that book makes reference to loss and grief in terms of wounds (*vulnera*), recovery in terms of scars (*cicatrices*), and consolation in terms of therapy or treatment (*mederi*; e.g. *Tusc.* III 54).[19]

With regard to wound care, Seneca's contrast between the treatment of a fresh wound and a neglected wound corresponds closely to the advice on wound care to be found in ancient medical texts, such as *On Medicine* (*Med.*) by his contemporary Celsus. A fresh wound, Celsus explains, is ideally treated with pressure, dressed, washed, and re-dressed, and is carefully monitored for signs of infection (*Med.* V 26.20–27). Ultimately a scar is actively formed by the doctor:

> Whatever the kind of wound, when the time has come for inducing the scar (*ubi . . . ventum ad inducendam cicatricem est*), which must be after the wound has [been] cleaned and filled with new flesh, first lint is applied, wetted by cold water while the flesh is being nourished; afterwards, when it has to be checked, dry lint must be applied until the scar is induced. (*Med.* V 26.36, trans. Spencer 1938)

In cases where the normative treatment has not been applied, however, the progression from a fresh wound to scarification is not as straightforward:

> Sometimes the wound becomes the seat of chronic ulceration (*interdum enim vetustas ulcus occupat*). It becomes hardened, and the thickened margins are a livid colour; after which whatever medicament is applied is of little service; and this commonly occurs when the

19 On the medical analogy for philosophy, see Graver 2002: 73–74 and 210–211.

wound has been carelessly treated (*quod fere neglegenter curato ulceri supervenit*). (*Med.* V 26.31)

Seneca draws metaphorically—and through explicit analogy—on these experiences of the body with and without medical treatment. They inform the expedited time frame of the consoler's recovery schedule, the protracted and even static time frames of a neglected or mistreated grief, and the violent rupture involved in a critical intervention.

These detailed correspondences are evocative for our understanding of Seneca's consolatory discourse in *Ad Marciam*. The "milder medicine" that Seneca says he might have used had he been able to intervene in Marcia's grief much earlier would have entailed a consolation that was perhaps not even written down, or at any rate more gentle or conventional. But by explicitly describing the present consolation as involving the violent intervention of "shattering" (*frangendus*) or perhaps "tearing open", suggests that many of the features of the present text are emphatically disruptive. This notion of violent intervention may include something as basic as his choice to send Marcia a written consolation in the form of a public letter witnessed by others, putting her grief in the "public eye".[20] It certainly includes the work's innovative rhetorical and argumentative tactics.

Seneca's comparison of his therapy to the medical procedure of wound rending and resetting is also suggestive for the temporal features of the consolation, and this can inform our understanding of the two forms of synchronization we have been observing in the text. First, the wound-rending analogy supplies a precise framework for understanding the schedule of grief-recovery. Seneca subjects the metaphorical wound of Marcia's grief to a treatment that involves violent rending, and even a temporary reversal, but also offers a new and more promising path to scarification. To this extent, the relatively transparent and reliable timeline of medical scarification gives new clarity to the grief-recovery schedule. And in conjunction with this, the alternative diachronies of protracted grief are expected either to yield or to accelerate, much like the alternative diachronies of the neglected wound.

Second, the surgery and manipulation involved in the resetting of a wound, which Seneca himself evokes with his mention of cauterizing, cutting open, probing, and rending, are suggestive for the specific rhetorical tactics that allow his consolatory discourse to facilitate Marcia's timely completion of the grief-recovery schedule. As we know, these tactics include the aggregation of time-perspectives that are embedded within this schedule so as to accelerate it. At this

20 Cf. Wilcox 2006: 73.

point in the work he has already disrupted time by taking Marcia back to the time of her father's death. And in the very next sentences after announcing that he must "break" Marcia's wound, Seneca describes how he must reorder the conventional components of a consolation and innovate in his treatment of Marcia:

> I know that everyone who wants to give advice begins with instructions and ends with examples. Sometimes it is useful to change this pattern.
>
> *Scio a praeceptis incipere omnis qui monere aliquem volunt, in exemplis desinere. Mutari hunc interim morem expedit.* (*Marc.* 2.1)

This sequence centering on the Livia and Octavia examples (2–5) requires Marcia to revisit events that belong within her own personal memory as well as the Roman collective memory, and to reflect upon the dichotomy between Octavia's protracted grief and Livia's rapid, public recovery—the latter to serve as a model for her own.

5 Synchronizing the Body and the Limits of the Consolatory Project

The grief-recovery schedule Seneca promotes in *Ad Marciam* is a superordinate diachrony to which other diachronies of grief and grief-recovery are expected to adapt. This adaptation is synchronization in the first sense I have defined. With regard to the body, the specific diachronies of tears and the grief-worn face are superseded by the consoler's mind-oriented interventions that will bring grief to an end more quickly. The diachrony of Marcia's grief as metaphorical ulcerated wound is subjected to the rhetorical and argumentative equivalent of aggressive surgery that rends the wound but sets it on a more secure path to healing.

To facilitate and accelerate this schedule, however, the consolatory therapy includes time-considerations, narratives, and *cogitatio* that are good to think with. The embedding of such times within the time of the consolatory discourse is synchronization in the second sense. The body is caught up in this also, since Seneca embeds time-perspectives that privilege the various diachronies of the *animus* and *animae* over those of the body such as protracted crying and other physical signs of grieving. The metaphor of the wound for Marcia's grief, along with the medical model of rending and resetting a wound for scarification, supplies her with a way to understand how the various forms of time-manipulation involved in the consolation's *cogitatio* are themselves conducive to a timely completion of the grief-recovery schedule.

Seneca's overall synchronizing strategy in *Ad Marciam* may be usefully conceived of as a kind of temporal "displacement". The term "displacement" was introduced by Fantham to characterize a number of Seneca's innovative moves within the consolations, including various kinds of generic innovation and analogies.[21] At various points in *Ad Marciam*, she observes, the discourse is commandeered with "displaced speech" in the voices of Areus, Nature, and Cremutius. Seneca's efforts to synchronize Marcia's grieving body, I suggest, equally involve displacement—displacement of the regular diachronies of grief both by the alternative accelerated schedule and by the range of time-perspectives and analogies that are to accelerate her time to recovery.

My analysis here, however, must only serve as a prequel to tracking the more complex and ambiguous dimensions of body-synchronization that ensued in Seneca's next consolation, *Ad Helviam*, written to console his mother following his banishment to Corsica. In a general sense the second consolation shares the main two synchronizing dimensions I have highlighted here, and the grieving body of Helvia is once again implicated in these. The comparison of grief to wound is multiplied and expanded there to articulate the many losses Helvia has experienced in her eventful lifetime as well as the exceptionality of her most recent loss, while Seneca's quasi-surgical inventions are themselves more elaborate. But with this expansion comes a different configuration of both time and the body—the most immediate illustration of this being that Seneca begins *Ad Helviam* in stark contrast with *Ad Marciam*:

> I realized that your grief should not be confronted while it was fresh and violently felt (*dolori tuo, dum recens saeviret, sciebam occurrendum non esse*) . . . for in diseases as well, nothing is more harmful than overhasty treatment (*nam in morbis quoque nihil est perniciosius quam inmatura medicina*). (*Ad Helviam* 1.2, trans. Williams 2021)

In fact, the prominence of the wound and Seneca's temporary concession to its time-schedule make for a consolatory scenario in which protracted time and the prominence of the wound draw attention to vulnerability and to the limits of consolation as a precarious and a potentially violent and counterproductive social discourse. In light of this, Victoria Rimell, in a superb essay on *Ad Helviam*, calls into question the presumed hegemony of the grief-recovery schedule:

> Through the figure of the wound, a tear through which the *ad Heluiam* converses with medicine from the Hippocratics to Celsus, with Greco-Roman epic, tragedy and erotic elegy, and also with a broader imaginary of the heroic or demeaning display of wounds and scars in Roman thought, the self-regulating, disembodied subject of Foucaultian consolation be-

---

21 Fantham 2007: esp. 188.

comes porous to the temporality of maternal grief and to the vulnerability encoded in the penetrable adult female body.[22]

Rimell does all that one could hope for in an exploration of consolation's limits in the light of this vulnerability. Her findings suggest that we cannot assume that Seneca succeeded in synchronizing Marcia's grieving body with his imposed recovery schedule and time-perspectives, especially when he so openly depicts the temporalities that may in the end hold a greater sway no matter what a consoler says.

Bibliography

Primary Sources

Graver, M. (trans./comm.) *Cicero on the Emotions*: Tusculan Disputations 3 *and* 4. Chicago, IL: University of Chicago Press, 2002.

Hine, H. M. (ed./trans.) "Consolation to Marcia". In *Lucius Annaeus Seneca: Hardship and Happiness*. Chicago, IL: University of Chicago Press, 2014: 3–44.

Manning, C. E. *On Seneca's* Ad Marciam. Leiden: Brill, 1981.

Shackleton Bailey, D. R. (ed./transl.) *Cicero: Letters to Friends*, Volume I: Letters 1–113. Cambridge, MA: Harvard University Press, 2001.

Spencer, W. G. *Celsus. On Medicine, Volume II: Books 5–6*. Cambridge, MA: Harvard University Press, 1938.

Tutrone, F. *Healing Grief: A Commentary on Seneca's* Consolatio ad Marciam. Berlin, Boston, MA: De Gruyter, 2023.

Secondary Literature

Baltussen, H. (ed.) *Greek and Roman Consolations: Eight Studies of a Tradition and its Afterlife*. Swansea: The Classical Press of Wales, 2013.

Beard, M. "A Complex of Times: No More Sheep on Romulus' Birthday". *Proceedings of the Cambridge Philological Society* 33, 1987: 1–15.

Clarke, K. *Making Time for the Past: Local History and the Polis*. Oxford/New York, NY: Oxford University Press, 2008.

Fabian, J. *Time and the Other: How Anthropology Makes Its Object*. New York, NY: Columbia University Press, 2014.

22 Rimell 2020: 541.

Fantham, E. "Dialogues of Displacement. Seneca's Concolations to Helvia and Polybius". In *Writing Exile. The Discourse of Displacement in Greco-Roman Antiquity and Beyond*, ed. J. F. Gärtner. Leiden: Brill, 2007: 173–192.

Glennie, P. and N. Thrift. *Shaping the Day: A History of Timekeeping in England and Wales, 1300–1800*. Oxford: Oxford University Press, 2009.

Gloyn, L. *The Ethics of the Family in Seneca*. Cambridge: Cambridge University Press, 2017.

Gunderson, E. *The Sublime Seneca. Ethics, Literature, Metaphysics*. Cambridge: Cambridge University Press, 2015.

Inwood, B. *Reading Seneca: Stoic Philosophy at Rome*. Oxford: Oxford University Press, 2005.

Ker, J. *The Deaths of Seneca*. New York, NY: Oxford University Press, 2009.

Ker, J. "It's the *Animae*, Stupid: Seneca's Ovidian Afterlives". In *The Lives of Latin Texts: Papers Presented to Richard J. Tarrant*, ed. L. Curtis and I. Peirano Garrison. Cambridge, MA: Department of the Classics, Harvard University, 2021: 149–172.

Ker, J. *The Ordered Day: Quotidian Time and Forms of Life in Ancient Rome*. Baltimore: Johns Hopkins University Press, 2023.

Langlands, R. "A Woman's Influence on a Roman Text: Marcia and Seneca". In *Women's Influence on Classical Civilization*, ed. F. McHardy and E. Marshall. New York, NY/London: Routledge, 2004: 115–126.

Luckmann, T. "The Constitution of Human Life in Time". In *Chronotypes: The Construction of Time*, ed. J. Bender and D. Wellbery. Stanford: Stanford University Press, 1991: 151–166.

Rimell, V. "The Intimacy of Wounds: Care of the Other in Seneca's *Consolatio Ad Helviam*". *American Journal of Philology* 141.4, 2020: 537–574.

Scourfield, J. H. D. "Towards a Genre of Consolation". In *Greek and Roman Consolations: Eight Studies of a Tradition and its Afterlife*, ed. H. Baltussen. Swansea: The Classical Press of Wales, 2013: 1–36.

Shelton, J.-A. "Persuasion and Paradigm in Seneca's *Consolatio ad Marciam* 1–6". *Classica et Mediaevalia* 46, 1995: 157–188.

Volk, K. "*Cum carmine crescit et annus*: Ovid's *Fasti* and the Poetics of Simultaneity". *Transactions of the American Philological Association* 127, 1997: 287–313.

Wallace-Hadrill, A. "Time for Augustus: Ovid, Augustus, and the *Fasti*". In *Homo Viator: Classical Essays for John Bramble*, ed. L. M. Whitby, P. R. Hardie, and M. Whitby. Bristol: Bristol Classical Press, 1987: 221–230.

Wilcox, A. "Exemplary Grief: Gender and Virtue in Seneca's Consolations to Women". *Helios* 33, 2006: 73–100.

Williams, G. "Eschatology in Seneca: The Senses of an Ending". In *Eschatology in Antiquity: Forms and Functions*, ed. H. Marlow, K. Pollman and H. Van Noorden. Abindgon, Oxon/New York, NY/ London: Routledge, 2021: 320–332.

Kassandra J. Miller

Untimely Women: "Clock Time" and "Women's Time" in Imperial Rome

Abstract: In the modern West, mechanical clocks and hourly timekeeping were often presented as attributes of dominant groups (such as men, the educated elite, or colonizers), while subalterns were portrayed, in contrast, as out of sync with such time. This chapter examines the extent to which similar stereotypes circulated under the Roman Empire, when hourly time told by other kinds of clocks—namely, sundials and water clocks—had also become widespread and structured time in many environments, such as the lawcourts, bath houses, and military. This chapter focuses specifically on gender dynamics, asking: how did elite male authors of this period portray female clock users in their writings? How might we problematize these portrayals? And how might Roman-period women have created pointed synchronies or asynchronies with normative "clock time"? As case studies, this chapter analyzes passages from three texts: Athenaeus' *The Philosophers at Supper*, Juvenal's *Sixth Satire*, and Galen's *On Health*. While these texts belong to different genres and have different goals and conventions, they all portray certain women, or certain kinds of women, as incompetent daily timekeepers. But, this chapter argues, behind some of these authors' complaints and caricatures we can catch glimpses of how real Roman-era women might have used or resisted "clock time" to exercise personal autonomy over their lives and bodies. Papyrological evidence from Roman Egypt provides further examples of women using hourly timekeeping in ways that, *contra* our elite male authors, are both normative and unremarkable.

Keywords: clock, women, gender, Rome, Imperial

1 Introduction

"With regard to time," James Ker has observed, "the [Roman] emperor's daily routine, occasionally glimpsed in moment-to-moment detail, might serve as a central 'clock' for the social activities of the elite, the city, and to some extent the whole empire."[1] This metaphor, of *princeps* as master clock, was cultivated by many emperors for many reasons: it could convey virtues like self-discipline and regular-

1 Ker 2023: 151.

ity, articulate the emperor's priorities (e.g., that he considered study or civic duty to be more important than sleep), and give the impression that the emperor and his reign were synchronized with the very motions of the heavens. Imperial biographers often supported these ideas by depicting emperors not only as being *like* clocks, but also as being frequent *users* of clocks, which, in this period, would have been sundials and water clocks capable of telling time down to the hour or, in rare cases, even the quarter hour.[2] Suetonius, for example, in his *Life of Augustus* (*Vit. Aug.*), gives an account of how Augustus reformed the military and established a postal system "so that what was going on in each of the provinces could be reported and known more swiftly and readily".[3] Suetonius proceeds to describe how "to all of his letters" the *princeps* "would append the exact hour not only of the day but also of the night, in order to specify when they were written", a detail which strengthens the bond between Augustus and clock time and underscores the emperor's commitment to efficiency and precision.[4] Many elite men of this era strove to imitate the emperor's association with clock time by boasting of their own daily schedules, by frequently noting the hour in their writings, and even by dedicating sundials in public spaces.[5] In this period, hourly timekeeping was also integral to areas—such as the law courts, the military, and civic administration—that were dominated by elite male interests and activity, and clocks had accrued a range of symbolic associations closely linked to elite male power and accomplishment.[6]

The trope of powerful men using clock time to articulate and reinforce their dominant positions within society is not unique to the Roman period. It also flourished in the 19th- and early 20th-centuries, when mechanical clocks, train timetables, and industrial time discipline, not to mention Einstein's reformulation of the passage of time as relative to one's speed of motion, fundamentally reshaped temporal habits and understandings in the West.[7] During the Modern period, the practice of associating clock time with socially dominant groups comes with an important corollary: subalterns—such as women, enslaved persons, members of

2 On the social history clocks and hourly timekeeping in this period, see, e.g., Remijsen 2007; Hannah 2009; Wolkenhauer 2011; Bonnin 2015; Jones 2016; Talbert 2017; Miller and Symons 2020; Talbert 2020; Remijsen 2021.

3 Suet. *Vit. Aug.* 49.3: *et quo celerius ac sub manum adnuntiari cognoscique posset, quid in prouincia quaque gereretur . . . .*

4 Suet. *Vit. Aug.* 50.1: *ad epistulas omnis horarum quoque momenta nec diei modo sed et noctis, quibus datae significarentur, addebat.*

5 Bonnin has demonstrated that many Roman magistrates, particularly in the West, erected sundials in public spaces as a display of *romanitas* (2015: 247–250).

6 Miller 2023: 87–114.

7 On the effects of these developments in the 19th century, see Glennie and Thrift 2009.

colonized communities, lower-class individuals, etc.—were, in contrast, depicted in various ways as “bad at”, “outside of”, or otherwise out of sync with clock time. Jimena Canales, in her analysis of Einstein’s and Bergson’s debates about the nature of time, outlines the dynamic this way:[8]

> Clock time and lived time were often associated with other binary oppositions such as machine-human, matter-mind, objective-subjective, physical-psychological, public-private, outer-inner. [. . .] At different moments in history, these oppositions obtained specifically *gendered and hierarchical* valances, as they were applied to different referents.

Canales goes on to describe the mechanical clocks of this era as “agonistic machines” that “measured the temporal distance between modernity and the dark ages . . ., denigrating the ‘Other’ in colonialized territories”.[9] In short, during this period, clocks were fashioned as tools not only for telling time but also for articulating and reinforcing social hierarchies of gender, class, race, and other forms of identity.[10] But, as noted by scholars like Mark Smith (in the context of the American plantation South) and On Barak (in the context of early Modern Egypt), there is a tension here: in order for members of these dominant groups to adhere to time-disciplined schedules, they had to rely on subalterns, such as enslaved people and free women and children of the household, in order to keep careful track of the time and maintain the ‘clockwork’ of domestic, agricultural, and professional life.[11] Thus, in the Modern period, the rhetorical trope of clock time as “powerful men’s time” is revealed to be a social construct that obfuscates realities of clock usage and know-how among subalterns.

These Modern-era examples should provoke our curiosity about the extent to which these dynamics also applied under the Roman Empire.[12] To what extent

8 Canales 2016: 117; emphasis added.

9 Canales 2016: 121. On temporal othering, a seminal work is Fabian 2014.

10 Patricia Murphy, discussing the proliferation of clock technology in Victorian England, homes in on the gendered nature of this dynamic. She demonstrates how watches and clocks of that time tended to be associated specifically with men, in conjunction with a constellation of other grand ideas, like progress, history, science, and power. Women, along with other subaltern groups, were denied affiliation with this suite of ideas and actively discouraged from owning or operating clocks (Murphy 2001: 23). In the United States, at about the same time, we find searing examples of how clock time could be associated not just with men but also with “free, white” time, while stereotypes of laziness and the derogatorily named “CPT” or “Colored People’s Time” were associated with black people, whether enslaved or freed. On clocks and “white” time, see Smith 1996; Hanchard 1999; Mills 2014; Huber 2021.

11 Smith 1996: 164–165; Barak 2014.

12 While acknowledging, of course, that the cultures, technologies, and overall *habitus* of the Roman Imperial period also differed in significant ways from those of “Western Modernity”.

did elite male Romans also conscript "clock time" as a tool for reinforcing social hierarchies of gender and class? The present chapter approaches this subject by asking the following questions: in their writings, how did elite male authors portray female clock users of various demographics? How, by reading these sources against the grain and by integrating material from non-literary sources, can we problematize their portrayals? And where might we catch glimpses of women's agency in efforts to synchronize or desynchronize their bodies with temporal norms?

As is often the case with investigations into ancient women's lived experiences, evidence pertinent to these questions is sparse, lacunose, and scattered across time, geography, and literary genres.[13] Therefore, this chapter will focus on a handful of case studies from three Imperial-era texts that differ from one another in many ways but have the shared distinction of presenting female clock users in comparatively rich detail. These include a passage from Athenaeus' *The Philosophers at Supper*, which discusses a Middle Comic play that derives its name from a hetaira nicknamed "Water Clock"; two passages from Juvenal's *Sixth Satire*, in which he lampoons, first, a dinner hostess and then female astrologers and astrology enthusiasts for their use and abuse of clock time; and, finally, a short passage from Galen's medical treatise *On Health*, in which he discusses hourly timekeeping among wetnurses. We will see that these authors present women sometimes as insufficiently precise in their clock usage and sometimes as overly precise, and that they bring up daily timekeeping to support a variety of specific points about these women's ethics and capabilities. These passages are united, however, in treating clock-using women with disparagement, while, for the most part, also hinting at ways in which such women might use or resist clock time to advance their own purposes. Before concluding, this chapter also considers evidence for female clock usage in the papyrological corpus of Roman-period Egypt and proposes that, in certain contexts, female clock usage might even have been considered an unremarkable norm.

13 On the methodological challenges of writing ancient women's history and how to mitigate those challenges, see, e.g., Richlin 2014.

2 Case Study 1: Athenaeus’ *The Philosophers at Supper* (Presenting Eubulus’ *Clepsydra*)

Our first passage comes from Athenaeus’ *The Philosophers at Supper*, written around 200 CE, a symposiastic work that recounts the learned conversations of well-known thinkers dining together at a fictional supper.[14] The characters are imaginative portrayals of historical and fictitious figures who, as part of their display of erudition, frequently cite other historical sources across a variety of genres including, as in the case of our passage here, Athenian Middle Comedy. Thus, Athenaeus’ text contains many intertwined threads of historical, literary, and cultural context that can be challenging to disentangle. As Laura McClure puts it, “[t]o grapple with Athenaeus is to confront problems of quotation and collection, authenticity and origin, cultural identity and dislocation”.[15] Therefore, we will see that, while this passage is valuable to our inquiry insofar as it suggests the presence of gendered stereotypes surrounding clock use, this passage, unlike the ones to follow, does not yield decipherable clues about how real women may have engaged with these timekeeping tools.

Within *The Philosophers at Supper*, Athenaeus reports a joke about a woman and a clock. This joke appears in the work’s thirteenth book, which claims to be “on women” in general (περὶ γυναικῶν) but is really about hetairas and the literary genres in which they appear.[16] Book 13 is structured around a debate between two dinner guests, the cynic philosopher Cynulcus and the grammarian Myrtilus, the former inveighing against hetairas—on account of their high costs, deceptive practices, and associations with elite *paideia*—and the latter delivering a paradoxical encomium of their virtues.[17] As part of his invective, Cynulcus derides Myrtilus for his encyclopedic knowledge of courtesan prosopography and, in the process, makes the following comment:[18]

> . . . many other plays took their names from hetairas: the *Thalatta* of Diocles, the *Corianno* of Pherecrates, the *Anteia* of Eunicus or Philyllius, the *Thais* and the *Phanium* of Menander, the *Opora* of Alexis, and the *Klepsydra* of Eubulus. That hetaira was so called because she used to have sex according to a water clock, until it was emptied, as Asclepiades, the son of

14 On this text, see especially Braund and Wilkins 2000. For the Greek text and commentary, see Hunter 1983. An excellent Loeb edition is also available: Olson 2007.

15 McClure 2003: 37.

16 For a nuanced discussion of the term” hetaira” and its wide semantic range, see McClure 2003: 1–17.

17 McClure (2003: 47–57) provides a detailed analysis of this debate.

18 Athenaeus, *The Philosophers at Supper* 13.21.37–46 Kaibel. All translations are my own unless otherwise indicated.

Areius, said in his treatise *On Demetrius Phalereus*.[19] And he relates that her real name was Mētichē.

. . . ἄλλα δὲ πολλά . . . δράματα ἀπὸ ἑταιρῶν ἔσχε τὰς ἐπιγραφάς, Θάλαττα Διοκλέους, Φερεκράτους Κοριαννώ, Εὐνίκου ἢ Φιλυλλίου Ἄντεια, Μενάνδρου δὲ Θαὶς καὶ Φάνιον, Ἀλέξιδος Ὀπώρα, Εὐβούλου Κλεψύδρα. οὕτω δ' ἐκλήθη αὕτη ἡ ἑταίρα, ἐπειδὴ πρὸς κλεψύδραν συνουσίαζεν ἕως κενωθῇ, ὡς Ἀσκληπιάδης εἴρηκεν ὁ τοῦ Ἀρείου ἐν τῷ περὶ Δημητρίου τοῦ Φαληρέως συγγράμματι, τὸ κύριον αὐτῆς ὄνομα φάσκων εἶναι Μητίχην.

In this list of comedies named after hetairas, Cynulcus makes reference to one composed by the Middle Comic playwright Eubulus, in which a female courtesan seems to have used a water clock to time her clients' visits precisely and thereby to control the amount of time during which they had access to her body. While the courtesan's given name, according to this Asclepiades,[20] was Mētichē, her professional nickname (and the title of the comedy itself) derives from the Greek term for 'water clock': clepsydra.[21] The specific kind of clepsydra referred to here seems to be the small, outflow water clock. This was a spouted vessel, often used to time speeches in Athenian and, later, Roman courtrooms, from which water drained to measure out short normative units of time [Fig. 1].[22] In the original Hellenistic setting of the comedy, these may simply have been units of water volume, and the clocks themselves would have acted more like egg-timers.[23] In Athenaeus' time, the term clepsydra retained this referent but could also denote a continuous timekeeper that indicated numbered hours.[24]

By having Cynulcus pause to explain the title of this play (instead of simply rattle it off along with the others in his list), Athenaeus can accomplish several things. First, of course, he can acquaint readers with a play which, this explanation implies, might not have been in frequent circulation among Athenaeus' readership. Second, he can pull laughs from his audience by having Cynulcus himself do the very thing he is accusing Myrtilus of doing—namely, citing high-brow literature on a low-brow topic. But, third and finally, Athenaeus can provoke laughs

19 FGrH 157 F 1 = Dem. Phal. fr. 40 Wehrli = fr. 3 Fortenbaugh and Schütrumpf. On Athenaeus' engagement with his sources, see, for example, Paulas 2012 and bibliography at p. 404 n. 1. On his use of comic fragments specifically, see Wilkins 2000.

20 Nothing is known of this Asclepiades (Fortenbaugh and Schütrumpf 2000: 35).

21 On names in Greek New Comedy, see Apostolakis 2024. On the relationships between hetaira names and the names of enslaved persons, see McClure 2003: 74–76.

22 On this "egg-timer" kind of clepsydra, particularly as used in courtroom settings, see Allen 1996; Ker 2009; Riggsby 2009. On the terminology of Greek and Roman water clocks more generally, see Bonnin 2015: 87–98.

23 E.g., "two χόες", as on the example discovered in the Athenian agora (Young 1939).

24 On this development, see Miller 2023: 15–31.

Fig. 1: 3D illustration of a Greek clepsydra. Javier Jaime/Shutterstock.com.

on the basis of the content itself: this explanation of Clepsydra's name was likely included, at least in part, because Athenaeus thought members of his audience would find it funny. After all, as Katherine Clarke has noted, this hetaira's use of a clepsydra in the bedroom seems intended to "strike a note of comic incongruity".[25] But why? On what, exactly, did this joke ride?

While Eubulus' comedy is not extant, the title, along with Athenaeus' brief description of it in Cynulcus' voice, raises several possible interpretations that are not mutually exclusive. McClure, for instance, suggests that this scenario might have provoked laughs because it "play[s] up the commercial aspects of the hetaera", a figure who is often presented as an expensive commodity, and indeed, Cynulcus specifies that his invective is directed against hetairas of the particularly high-end (μεγαλόμισθος) variety.[26] The presence of the root κλεψ- (from κλέπτω, "to steal") within Clepsydra's name might also have helped to activate

25 Clarke 2008: 32.

26 McClure 2003: 73. Cynulcus uses this term at 13.24.29 and 13.26.1.

this connection, calling up the image of a hetaira who fleeces her clients. Other potential sources of humor here include the implicit comparison between the courtroom and the bedroom, and the authoritative role that this sex worker takes on, kicking her clients out abruptly the moment the clock runs dry.

Underlying these interpretations, however, is the fundamental idea that someone like Clepsydra—a woman, a sex worker, and probably, within the setting of the play, a foreigner—should not be using a clock in this way, if at all. In order for the joke to land, we must assume Eubulus' and Athenaeus' audience to understand clock time to have no place in the bedroom and that, therefore, Clepsydra is doing "time" wrong: she has introduced to this private, "female" setting a temporal framework that is overly precise and better suited to spheres of public, "male" activity. The passage in *The Philosophers at Supper* does not allow us to clearly differentiate the effects of Clepsydra's multi-faceted identity. Does the joke trade primarily on her gender? Her profession? Her social or civic status? Or the particular ways in which all of these identities intersect? We can only speculate. Nor does this passage allow us to draw conclusions about how real hetairas might have kept time while working, particularly in Athenaeus' later, Roman Imperial context. After all, the character of Eubulus' Clepsydra was fictional, undoubtedly exaggerated for comic effect, and created hundreds of years before Athenaeus' audience would have encountered this passage. Nonetheless, Cynulcus' description of Eubulus' play seems to reinforce the idea that, among both sets of readerships, the correct use of "clock time" was coded as elite and/ or male.

3 Case Study 2: Juvenal's *Sixth Satire*

We will now shift genres to consider two passages from Juvenal's *Sixth Satire*, which was composed in the late first or early second century CE and has, of course, very different aims from Athenaeus' *The Philosophers at Supper*, although it, too, endeavored to provoke laughs. This goal, as we have seen, can make it challenging to uncover the precise nature of the reality to which Juvenal's text is responding, because humorous portrayals are typically meant to be read as outrageous in certain ways and hence as exceptional. However, scholars have been turning increasingly to ancient comedic writing as a valuable source of social history, on the principle that, in order for a scenario to earn a laugh, it must be anchored to familiar, legible experiences or perceptions.[27] In reading these passages

27 On the value of comedy to social historians of the Greek and Roman worlds, see, e.g., Lape and Moreno 2014.

of Juvenal, we will explore not only what tropes and conventions may have made these references to clock-using women read as "funny", but also what kinds of realities might have undergirded that humor.

Juvenal's *Sixth Satire*, carrying on the tradition of Semonides 7, is a lengthy catalogue of negative female stereotypes. A noteworthy feature of this text, however, in contrast to its seventh-century BCE predecessor, is its interest in how the women it caricatures interact with time. There are two passages where this concern really comes to the fore, the first of which is as follows:[28]

> But that fault is no more intolerable than the one where
> the woman is accustomed, while cursing, to seize her humble neighbors
> and lash them with whips. For if her deep sleep is disrupted
> by barking, "Bring the cudgels here—quickly!" she says
> and orders the dog's owner to be thrashed with them first,
> and then the dog. Oppressive to encounter, with a repulsive face,
> she goes to the baths at night, she orders her makeup jars and camp
> to be moved at night, and she delights in great sweat amid tumult.
> When her arms fall, fatigued by heavy weights,
> the experienced wrestling master presses his fingers into her tuft
> and compels the top of his mistress' thigh to cry out.
> The whole while, her miserable dinner guests are burdened with sleepiness
> and hunger. At length, she arrives flushed, thirsty for an entire jug of wine . . . .

> *nec tamen id uitium magis intolerabile quam quod*
> *uicinos humiles rapere et concidere loris*
> *†exortata† solet. nam si latratibus alti*
> *rumpuntur somni, 'fustes huc ocius' inquit*
> *'adferte' atque illis dominum iubet ante feriri,*
> *deinde canem. grauis occursu, taeterrima uultu*
> *balnea nocte subit, conchas et castra moueri*
> *nocte iubet, magno gaudet sudare tumultu,*
> *cum lassata graui ceciderunt bracchia massa,*
> *callidus et cristae digitos inpressit aliptes*
> *ac summum dominae femur exclamare coegit.*
> *conuiuae miseri interea somnoque fameque*
> *urguentur. tandem illa uenit rubicundula, totum*
> *oenophorum sitiens . . .*

The comedy here seems largely based on Juvenal's inversion of the trope with which this chapter opened, namely, of recounting a man's daily schedule in order to highlight his self-discipline and other virtues. The woman depicted here, in contrast, is hasty and impatient, ordering her slaves to exact punishment upon an

28 Juvenal VI.413–426 Braund.

offending dog and its owner right away, even though it is the middle of the night. And speaking of night, it is at this time that such a woman prefers to engage in activities, like visiting the baths or attending social gatherings, that, Juvenal implies, a more modest woman would only perform during the day, if at all. Finally, such a woman is wont to arrive late to her own dinner parties, forcing her guests to wait without food until she appears.

In developing his image of this woman, Juvenal makes frequent reference to elements of what Galen, the next author we will consider, would call the "art of hygiene", or health maintenance. This woman exercises and receives massages—but in an inappropriate manner; she drinks wine—but to grotesque excess;[29] she bathes and dines—but at the wrong times. All of this creates a cumulative impression, not of virtuous self-discipline, but of its opposite: intemperance, untimeliness, and dysregulation. With this picture, Juvenal also calls into question this woman's femininity in so far as her exercise is with heavy weights, her alcohol consumption is excessive, her behavior is both physically and sexually aggressive, and aesthetically, she is described as oppressive, repulsive, and cosmetically made-up rather than possessed of natural feminine beauty.[30] It is therefore also possible to view this woman's temporal characteristics through the lens of a critique on her femininity. Instead of being staid, punctual, and diurnal, as an "ideal woman" presumably would be, such a woman challenges gender norms by being impetuous, tardy, and unnervingly nocturnal. There is, however, some ambiguity here. Would this woman's orientation to daily timekeeping have inspired laughs because it was so unfeminine—or because it was viewed as an exaggeration of something all too feminine, at least among certain demographics of women? As Ian Goh has said of this passage, in specific relation to this woman's drunken vomiting, "there is a tentative adumbration of another diagnosis [than alcoholism alone]: conduct inappropriate to one's gender, or conversely all too appropriate to it. Women, in Juvenal's persona's eyes (or better, his myopia), are the disease".[31]

Leaving the question of gender transgression aside for the moment (we will return to it later), we might say that, overall, Juvenal presents this caricatured woman as insufficiently attuned to the clock. In another passage, however, Juve-

29 Ultimately, this woman drinks so much, she spews her guts out. For an analysis of the literary and moralizing roles that vomiting plays here, see Goh 2018: 446–448.

30 On the tropes of female drunkenness and laziness in Classical Greek literary and visual culture, see, e.g., Bowie 1995; Mitchell 2015. Clare Kelly-Blazeby (2011) offers important words of caution against assuming that all literary and iconographic portrayals of women drinking wine must necessarily be of prostitutes or hetairas in symposiastic settings.

31 Goh 2018: 449. We might extend this question, also, to the behavior of Eubulus' Clepsydra.

nal also attacks two kinds of women who are overly precise in their hourly and calendrical timekeeping. Both kinds of women share a passion for astrology, a science which promises its users increased knowledge of and control over the timing of events in their lives.[32] While one kind of woman Juvenal dismisses as ignorant of the complex principles and calculations that underlie astrological predictions, he criticizes the other for understanding these things too well:[33]

> Your Tanaquil seeks advice about the slow death of her jaundiced mother
> (though first about you), when she will bury
> her sister and her uncles, or whether her lover will live on
> after her [. . .].
> Nonetheless, she is ignorant about these things: what the
> sad star of Saturn threatens, in what sign Venus presents herself
> favorably, in what months losses and at what times gains will be given.
> But remember to avoid ever running into that sort of woman,
> in whose hands, like a fat piece of amber, you discern
> a well-worn ephemeris,[34] a woman who does not consult anyone else but
> is now herself consulted, and who will not go with her husband when he seeks
> the army camp or homeland insofar as she is called back by the numbers
> of Thrasyllus. When it pleases her to be driven to the first milestone,
> the hour is determined from a book. If the corner of her eye itches
> when rubbed, she requests cream only once her horoscope has been examined.
> Even if she lies sick, no hour seems more suitable for taking food than
> the one Petosiris has given. If she should be of moderate means,
> she will traverse the space between the goal posts . . . To wealthy women,
> a Phrygian augur will give responses [. . .].
> The fates of plebeian women are decided in the Circus and the Embankment.
>
> *consulit ictericae lento de funere matris,*
> *ante tamen de te Tanaquil tua, quando sororem*
> *efferat et patruos, an sit uicturus adulter*
> *post ipsam;* [. . .]
> *haec tamen ignorat quid sidus triste minetur*
> *Saturni, quo laeta Venus se proferat astro,*
> *quis mensis damnis, quae dentur tempora lucro:*
> *illius occursus etiam uitare memento,*
> *in cuius manibus ceu pinguia sucina tritas*
> *cernis ephemeridas, quae nullum consulit et iam*

---

32 On Greco-Roman astrology (including its medical uses), see Greenbaum 2015; 2022; 2020a; 2020b; Heilen 2018; 2019; 2020.

33 Juvenal VI.565–588.

34 An ephemeris charts the positions of various celestial bodies and asterisms at intervals throughout the day. In antiquity, ephemerides were used in what we would now call both "astronomical" and "astrological" contexts, though the two were not clearly differentiated at the time.

consulitur, quae castra uiro patriamque petente
non ibit pariter numeris reuocata Thrasylli.
ad primum lapidem uectari cum placet, hora
sumitur ex libro; si prurit frictus ocelli
angulus, inspecta genesi collyria poscit;
aegra licet iaceat, capiendo nulla uidetur
aptior hora cibo nisi quam dederit Petosiris.
si mediocris erit, spatium lustrabit utrimque
metarum et sortes ducet frontemque manumque
praebebit uati crebrum poppysma roganti.
diuitibus responsa dabit Phryx augur [. . .].
plebeium in circo positum est et in aggere fatum.

The astrological enthusiasts Juvenal describes here use precise clock and calendrical timekeeping to determine the right moment to engage in a wide variety of activities, including medical interventions like applying eye cream or taking food when sick. Such women can be found in all socioeconomic brackets: women of “moderate means” seek astrological services “between the goal posts”, while “wealthy women” consult “Phrygian augurs” and “plebeian women” go to “the Circus and the Embankment”. These women also vary in their understandings of the science itself. Some women stick to consulting supposed “experts” (whom Juvenal considers to be quacks), while others claim to be experts themselves, carrying around ephemerides and other astrological reference works and making their own calculations about which day, and which hour within the day, would be most propitious for a given medical or social action.[35] Juvenal implies that, while all of these women might *seem* quite knowledgeable and in command of their time, their temporal rigor is misplaced since astrology, in his persona’s view, is only for the blindly superstitious.

Ultimately, Juvenal presents astrology as an irrational perversion of rational clock and calendrical time, associating it with women who happen to be (or who, simply by virtue of being women, are) gullible and misguided. Yet, Juvenal also gives us a glimpse of women endeavoring to make clock time work for them. For his female astrologers, the clock is an important professional tool that allows them to make predictions and claim expert knowledge of the most propitious times to perform various actions. The women who consult astrologers are seeking this expert knowledge in order to make informed decisions for themselves about how best to situate their activities in time. Here, too, this kind of clock use is pre-

35 This kind of astrology—often termed katarchic—differs from horoscopic astrology. The former is interested in determining propitious times for action while the latter is interested in using the natal horoscope to determine the shape of a person’s life and fortunes.

sented by the author as inferior—laughably so—but nevertheless, this portrayal suggests a context in which a form of clock time could be reframed as a form of "women's time". We will see a similar dynamic in Galen's *On Health*.

4 Case Study 3: Galen's *On Health*

Galen of Pergamon was a renowned physician who traveled widely during his studies but eventually found his way to the city of Rome and into the role of court physician to two emperors.[36] His work *On Health* (in six books) was composed around 180 CE and laid out principles for maintaining health at different stages of life by adjusting one's hygienic regimen. In Book I, after introducing his methodology, Galen turns to strategies for maintaining the health of an ideally constituted body (which he presents as able, well-resourced, leisured, and male) during infancy and early childhood. In this context, he has a lot to say regarding the women who—at least in upper-class households—were most often charged with caring for such bodies: namely, wet nurses. As Antonio Ricciardetto and Danielle Gourevitch have demonstrated, based on the evidence from wet-nursing contracts preserved from Roman Egypt, wet nurses tended to belong to the lower classes and were sometimes free, often enslaved.[37]

In the passage relevant to our investigation, Galen cautions his readers that infants should not nurse shortly before a bath or massage, lest the milk come right back up again. Galen then warns:[38]

> Do not, as some nurses do now, set aside one specific time of the day, nor, like some others, provide for it when they themselves find they have some free time; because then it follows that the children will unavoidably often be harmed rather than benefited. The appropriate time specified by us will, on different occasions, turn out to fall at different times of day or night.
>
> οὐδ', ὥσπερ νῦν ποιοῦσι ἔνιαι μὲν τῶν τροφῶν, ἕνα τινὰ χρόνον ἀφορίσασαι τῆς ἡμέρας, ἔνιαι δ', ὅταν αὐταὶ σχολάσωσι, [τοῦ] τηνικαῦτα προνοούμεναι· διότι πολλάκις ἀναγκαῖόν ἐστι βλάπτεσθαι τὰ παιδία ἤπερ ὠφελεῖσθαι. ὁ γὰρ ὑφ' ἡμῶν ἀφοριζόμενος καιρὸς ἄλλοτε εἰς ἄλλον ἐμπίπτει χρόνον ἤτοι τῆς ἡμέρας ἢ τῆς νυκτός.

36 For biographies of Galen, see Mattern 2013; Nutton 2020. On how this passage relates to Galen's broader approach to hourly timekeeping, see Miller 2023: 166.
37 Ricciardetto and Gourevitch 2020.
38 Galen *On Health* IV 49.4–9 K.; trans. Singer 2023 with modification.

Galen here, like Juvenal, criticizes wet nurses of two types. While each establishes her breastfeeding schedule in a different way, he believes both approaches to be wrong-headed. One type of wet nurse Galen accuses of only making her breast accessible to the infant whenever she finds the time, which is to say unsystematically and at her own whim. The other type of woman he chastises for following the dictates of the clock too rigorously and blindly, instead of using her powers of reason. Galen presents these women as foils to himself and to the kind of expertise that he, a highly educated professional physician, can bring to the subject of daily regimen. While Galen has expert knowledge of how and when to apply clock time within health and wellness contexts, these wet nurses appear as ill-informed users of clock technology, often employing either capricious and unreasoned or overly precise and quantitative modes of timekeeping when more thoughtful, personalized methods would be more fitting.

This portrayal reinforces the idea that clock time is "rational men's time", but it also assumes that many women in the role of wet nurse *were* using clocks to structure their activities (as many breastfeeding people do to this day). Therefore, this passage, akin to the ones we examined from Juvenal's *Sixth Satire*, also tacitly acknowledges that, at some level, a form of clock time is also a form of "women's time"—specifically, wet nurses' time—while simultaneously presenting that kind of time as inferior.

5 A Counterpoint: Papyrological Evidence from Roman Egypt

We have thus far seen that three elite, male literary authors (Athenaeus, Juvenal, and Galen) all present examples of female clock users who, in various ways and for various reasons, interact with clocks "inappropriately" and are disparaged for doing so. These portrayals articulate the idea that, in the Roman period, clock time was "men's time"—in particular, "educated elite men's time"—but they also expose the contingency and constructed nature of that idea by referring to contexts in which some women may, in reality, have been quite comfortable using clocks. Before closing, I would like to explore this latter point further by examining papyrological evidence from Roman Egypt, first compiled and analyzed by Sofie Remijsen, that sheds light on clock use by women.[39] The private letters and government petitions within this corpus, dating from the third century BCE to the

39 Remijsen 2023.

fourth century CE, give the impression that, outside of the world of male-authored literature, a woman’s use of clock time might often be determined less by gender norms per se than by the relevant “chronotope”, which is to say, the set of temporal norms and expectations operational within a given place or genre.[40] Remijsen notes that, while identifiable female authors are deeply under-represented within the papyrological corpus, there are, nevertheless, numerous instances in which they refer to numbered hours, the units measured by sundials and water clocks. These references occur most commonly in the context of social invitations (e.g., to a dinner, wedding, or ritual event) and are meant to facilitate the coordination of group activities. Here is an example from a wedding invitation:[41]

> Herais invites you to dine in honor of the marriage of her children at her house tomorrow, which is the 5th [of the month], at the eighth hour [of the day].
>
> ἐρωτᾷ σε Ἡραὶς δειπνῆσαι εἰς γάμους τέκνων αὐτῆς ἐν τῇ οἰκίᾳ αὔριον, ἥτις ἐστὶν πέμπτη, ἀπὸ ὥρας θ.

In these papyri, women also use numbered hours to provide temporal detail within petitions to local government. In this text, for example, one Aurelia Ataris states in a petition that:[42]

> On the third of the intercalary days, at the tenth hour [of the day], while I was demanding payment of a debt owed to me, Poleion, together with Apeion, the son of Horion the *eirēnarch*, and Kyriakē, Poleion’s daughter, having employed I don’t know what kind of language and bandit-like manner, locked me up in his house and assaulted me with blows.
>
> κατὰ τὴν τρίτην τῶν ἐπαγωμένων, οὐκ ὖδα τίνι λόγῳ ̣καὶ λιστ[ρ]ικῷ̣ τρώπῳ χρησάμενοι, πρὸς ὥραν δεκάτην, ἐμοῦ ἀ̣πετοῦντός μου τω χρεως τῶν χρεωστῖ μοι, ἀπεκ̣λ̣ισεν με ἐν τῇ οἰκίᾳ αὐτοῦ Πολείον ἅ̣μα τοῦ υἱοῦ Ὡρίωνος τ̣ο̣ῦ ἡρηνάρχου Ἀπειόν καὶ τῆς ἀδελφης τοῦ Πολ (είονος) Κυριακῆς καὶ ἀπέκτινάν με τε͂ς πληγε͂ς·

Here, the specification “at the tenth hour” lends authority to Aurelia’s account and may nod to her status as someone sufficiently disciplined to keep track of daily time by the clock.

Ultimately, Remijsen asserts that “in business transactions, in the communication of elite lifestyles and in certain ritual contexts . . . we do find women in

---

40 The term “chronotope”, which combines the Greek words for time (*chronos*) and space (*topos*) was introduced by Mikhail Bakhtin (2014). On chronotopes in the Roman world, see Wolkenhauer 2020; Miller 2023: 33–34.

41 *P.Oxy.*1.111.

42 *P.Abinn.* 51.

sovereign control of the schedules of the calendar and the clock. In these contexts, they seem *not* to have felt inhibited by gender expectations in communicating their control of time".[43] It strikes me as significant that the contexts in which these women use numbered hours are ones in which they are interacting with men and/or intersecting with more public spheres, such as the courtroom. Perhaps, then, their use of clock time in these situations was unremarkable because these women were simply employing the temporal frameworks most appropriate to the given chronotopes. This papyrological evidence, in conjunction with our earlier close readings, should caution us against extending the trope of clock time as "men's time" too far, and assuming that women could be neither capable nor normative users of this technology.

6 Conclusion

This study explored some of the ways in which gender may have affected both representational and actual clock use in the Roman Imperial period. While powerful, educated men of this time often bragged of their disciplined schedules and sought to imitate the emperor as a master (or even instantiation) of clock time, our records preserve no encomia praising women for their daily schedules. This prompted us to ask: how, then, *were* female clock users portrayed by male authors? To what extent were Roman clocks, like early Modern ones, conscripted to reinforce hierarchies of gender and status? And what can we glean about how actual Roman-era women may have used clocks, perhaps even to push back against or carve out space for choice-making within those hierarchies? To answer the first question, we examined, as case studies, passages drawn from Athenaeus' symposiastic text *The Philosophers at Supper* as well as a satire by Juvenal and a medical treatise of Galen's. While each of these texts has its own themes, goals, and generic conventions, they all share an interest in representing women as "bad at" clock time, using it with either too great or too little precision and in inappropriate contexts. From these portrayals, clocks emerge as "male" technologies associated with a suite of other qualities like rationality, personal discipline, and temperance, while women who try to engage with these technologies are stereotypically portrayed as doing so incorrectly—irrationally, intemperately, and without discipline. Yet, in order for most of the jokes and critiques to ring true, we must assume that, behind them, were actual women who bent the rules and expectations of Roman clock time by choosing to synchronize or desynchronize

43 Remijsen 2023: 171.

their actions with its rhythms. The papyrological evidence from Roman Egypt, moreover, testifies to the fact that women, in some contexts and chronotopes, might engage with clock time both regularly and unremarkably. It would seem, then, that these temporal stereotypes, like so many others, were exploited to reinforce existing hierarchies of gender and class, but can simultaneously reveal how some women used or pointedly ignored clock time in order to exert agency over their own bodies and schedules. This they did by entering "men's" temporal zones, by learning for themselves the astrologically propitious times to take action, and by making the other people in their lives hurry up or wait.

Bibliography

Primary Sources

Braund, S. M. (ed./trans.) *Juvenal and Persius*. Loeb Classical Library 91. Cambridge, MA: Harvard University Press, 2004.

Fortenbaugh, W. W. and E. Schütrumpf (eds.) *Demetrius of Phalerum: Text, Translation and Discussion*. Rutgers University Studies in Classical Humanities 9. New Brunswick, NJ/ London: Transaction Publishers, 2000.

Hunter, R. L. (ed./comm.) *Eubulus: The Fragments*. Cambridge Classical Texts and Commentaries 24. Cambridge/ London/ New Rochelle, NJ/ Melbourne: Cambridge University Press, 1983.

Kaibel, G. (ed.) *Athenaei Naucratitae Dipnosophistarum libri XV*. Leipzig: Teubner, 1923.

Olson, S. D. (ed./trans.) *Athenaeus: The Learned Banqueters*. 8 vols. Loeb Classical Library 204. Cambridge, MA: Harvard University Press, 2007.

Singer, P. N. (ed./trans.) *Galen: Writings on Health: Thrasybulus and Health (De sanitate tuenda)*. Cambridge: Cambridge University Press, 2023.

Secondary Literature

Allen, D. "A Schedule of Boundaries: An Exploration, Launched from the Water-Clock, of Athenian Time". *Greece & Rome* 43.2, 1996: 157–168.

Apostolakis, K. E. "Proper Names, Nicknames, Epithets: Aspects of Comic Language in Middle Comedy". In *The Play of Language in Ancient Greek Comedy: Comic Discourse and Linguistic Artifices of Humour, from Aristophanes to Menander*, Trends in Classics—Supplementary Volumes, ed. K. E. Apostolakis and I. M. Konstantakos. Berlin: De Gruyter, 2024: 311–345.

Bakhtin, M. M. *Chronotopos. Aus dem Russischen von M. Dewey, mit einem Nachwort v. M. C. Frank und K. Mahlke*. Frankfurt am Main: Suhrkamp, 2014.

Barak, O. "Times of Tamaddun: Gender, Urbanity, and Temporality in Colonial Egypt". In *Women and the City, Women in the City: A Gendered Perspective on Ottoman Urban History*, ed. N. Maksudyan. New York, NY/ Oxford: Berghahn Books, 2014: 15–35.

Bonnin, J. *La mesure du temps dans l'Antiquité*. Paris: Les Belles Lettres: 2015.

Bowie, E. L. "Wine in Old Comedy". In *In Vino Veritas*, ed. O. Murray and M. Tecusan. London: British School at Rome, 1995: 113–125.

Braund, D. and J. Wilkins (eds.) *Athenaeus and His World: Reading Greek Culture in the Roman Empire*. Exeter: University of Exeter Press, 2000.

Canales, J. *The Physicist and the Philosopher: Einstein, Bergson, and the Debate That Changed Our Understanding of Time*. Princeton, NJ/ Oxford: Princeton University Press, 2016.

Clarke, K. *Making Time for the Past: Local History and the Polis*. Oxford/New York, NY: Oxford University Press, 2008.

Fabian, J. *Time and the Other: How Anthropology Makes Its Object, With a New Postscript by the Author*. New York, NY: Columbia University Press, 2014.

Glennie, P. and N. Thrift. *Shaping the Day: A History of Timekeeping in England and Wales 1300–1800*. Oxford: Oxford University Press, 2009.

Goh, I. "It All Comes Out: Vomit as a Source of Comedy in Roman Moralizing Texts". *Illinois Classical Studies* 43.2, 2018: 438–458.

Greenbaum, D.G. "Astronomy, Astrology, and Medicine". In *Handbook of Archaeoastronomy and Ethnoastronomy*, ed. C. L. N. Ruggles. New York, NY: Springer Science and Business Media, 2015: 117–132.

Greenbaum, D. G. "Hellenistic Astronomy in Medicine". In *Hellenistic Astronomy: The Science in Its Contexts*, Brill's Companions in Classical Studies, ed. A. C. Bowen and F. Rochberg. Leiden: Brill, 2020a: 350–380.

Greenbaum, D. G. "The Hellenistic Horoscope". In *Hellenistic Astronomy: The Science in Its Contexts*, Brill's Companions in Classical Studies, ed. A. C. Bowen and F. Rochberg. Leiden: Brill, 2020b: 443–471.

Greenbaum, D. G. "Divination and Decumbiture: Katarchic Astrology and Greek Medicine". In Divination and Knowledge in Greco-Roman Antiquity, ed. C. Addey. London/New York, NY: Routledge, 2022: 109–137.

Hanchard, M. "Afro-Modernity: Temporality, Politics, and the African Diaspora". *Public Culture* 11.1, 1999: 245–268.

Hannah, R. *Time in Antiquity*. London/ New York, NY: Routledge, 2009.

Heilen, S. "Galen's Computation of Medical Weeks: Textual Emendations, Interpretation History, Rhetorical and Mathematical Examinations". *SCIAMVS* 19, 2018: 201–279.

Heilen, S. "Hellenistic Horoscopes in Greek and Latin: Contexts and Uses". In *Hellenistic Astronomy. The Science in Its Contexts*, ed. A. C. Bowman and F. Rochberg. Leiden: Brill, 2019: 490–508.

Heilen, S. "Short Time in Greco-Roman Astrology". In *Down to the Hour: Short Time in the Ancient Mediterranean and Near East*, Time, Astronomy, and Calendars 8, ed. K. J. Miller and S. Symons. Leiden: Brill, 2020: 239–270.

Huber, H. "Charles Chestnutt's 'Uncle Julius' Tales: Sleepy Subversions of Scientific Racism and the Master Clock". *Studies in American Fiction* 48.1, 2021: 1–26.

Jones, A. (ed.) *Time and Cosmos in Greco-Roman Antiquity*. Institute for the Study of the Ancient World Exhibition Catalogs. Princeton, NJ: Princeton University Press, 2016.

Kelly-Blazeby, C. F. "Woman + Wine = Prostitute in Classical Athens?" In *Greek Prostitutes in the Ancient Mediterranean, 800 BCE–200 CE*, Wisconsin Studies in Classics, ed. A. Glazebrook and M. M. Henry. Madison, WI: University of Wisconsin Press, 2011: 86–105.

Ker, J. "Drinking from the Water-Clock: Time and Speech in Imperial Rome". *Arethusa* 42.3, 2009: 279–302.

Ker, J. *The Ordered Day: Quotidian Time and Forms of Life in Ancient Rome*. Baltimore, MD: Johns Hopkins University Press, 2023.

Lape, S. and A. Moreno. "Comedy and the Social Historian". In *The Cambridge Companion to Greek Comedy*, ed. M. Revermann. Cambridge: Cambridge University Press, 2014: 336–369.

Mattern, S. P. *The Prince of Medicine: Galen in the Roman Empire*. New York, NY: Oxford University Press, 2013.

McClure, L. K. *Courtesans at Table: Gender and Greek Literary Culture in Athenaeus*. New York, NY/ London: Routledge, 2003.

Miller, K. J. *Time and Ancient Medicine: How Sundials and Water Clocks Changed Medical Science*. Oxford: Oxford University Press, 2023.

Miller, K. J. and S. L. Symons (eds.) *Down to the Hour: Short Time in the Ancient Mediterranean and Near East*. Time, Astronomy, and Calendars 8. Leiden: Brill, 2020.

Mills, C. W. "White Time: The Chronic Injustice of Ideal Theory". *Du Bois Review: Social Science Research on Race* 11.1, 2014: 27–42.

Mitchell, A. G. "Humor, Women, and Male Anxieties in Ancient Greek Visual Culture". In *Laughter, Humor, and the (Un)Making of Gender: Historical and Cultural Perspectives*, ed. A. Foka and J. Liliequist. New York, NY: Palgrave Macmillan, 2015: 163–189.

Murphy, P. *Time is of the Essence: Temporality, Gender, and the New Woman*. Albany, NY: SUNY Press, 2001.

Nutton, V. *Galen: A Thinking Doctor in Imperial Rome*. Routledge Ancient Biographies. Abingdon, Oxon/ New York, NY: Routledge, 2020.

Paulas, J. "How to Read Athenaeus' *Deipnosophists*". *American Journal of Philology* 133.3, 2012: 403–439.

Remijsen, S. "The Postal Service and the Hour as a Unit of Time in Antiquity". *Historia: Zeitschrift für Alte Geschichte* 56.2, 2007: 127–140.

Remijsen, S. "Living by the Clock: The Introduction of Clock Time in the Greek World". *Klio* 103.1, 2021: 1–29.

Remijsen, S. "Women on Time: Gendered Temporalities in Greco-Roman Egypt". In *The Public Lives of Ancient Women (500 BCE–650 CE)*, Mnemosyne, Suppl. 468, ed. L. Dirven, M. Icks and S. Remijsen. Leiden: Brill, 2023: 158–172.

Ricciardetto, A. and D. Gourevitch. "The Cost of a Baby: How Much Did It Cost to Hire a Wet-Nurse in Roman Egypt?" In *Medicine and Markets in the Graeco-Roman World and Beyond: Essays on Ancient Medicine in Honour of Vivian Nutton*, ed. L. M. V. Totelin and R. Flemming. Swansea: Classical Press of Wales, 2020: 41–70.

Richlin, A. *Arguments with Silence: Writing the History of Roman Women*. Ann Arbor, MI: University of Michigan Press, 2014.

Riggsby, A. M. "For Whom the Clock Drips". *Arethusa* 42.3, 2009: 271–278.

Smith, M. M. "Time, Slavery and Plantation Capitalism in the Ante-Bellum American South". *Past & Present* 150, 1996: 142–168.

Talbert, R. J. A. *Roman Portable Sundials: The Empire in Your Hand*. Oxford/ New York, NY: Oxford University Press, 2017.

Talbert, R. J. A. "Roman Concern to Know the Hour in Broader Historical Context". In *Homo Omnium Horarum: Symbolae Ad Anniversarium Septuagesimum Professoris Alexandri Podosinov Dedicatae*, ed. A. Belousov and C. J. Ilyushechkina. Moscow: Academia Pozharskiana, 2020: 534–555.

Wilkins, J. "Dialogue and Comedy: The Structure of the Jovial Setting of the *Deipnosophistae*". In *Athenaeus and His World: Reading Greek Culture in the Roman Empire*, ed. D. Braund and J. Wilkins. Exeter: University of Exeter, 2000: 23–37.

Wolkenhauer, A. *Sonne und Mond, Kalender und Uhr: Studien zur Darstellung und poetischen Reflexion der Zeitordnung in der römischen Literatur*. Untersuchungen zur antiken Literatur und Geschichte 103. Berlin: De Gruyter, 2011.

Wolkenhauer, A. "Time, Punctuality, and Chronotopes: Concepts and Attitudes Concerning Short Time in Ancient Rome". In *Down to the Hour: Short Time in the Ancient Mediterranean and Near East*, Time, Astronomy, and Calendars 8, ed. K. J. Miller and S. L. Symons. Leiden: Brill, 2020: 214–238.

Young, S. "An Athenian Clepsydra". *Hesperia* 8.3, 1939: 274–284.

Dorian Gieseler Greenbaum

Time, Timing and Synchronicity: The Uses of Astrology in Ancient Medical Practice

Abstract: This chapter focuses on relationships of various facets of time to the astrological practices associated with medicine in the ancient Mediterranean world. It begins with a discussion of the meanings of *chronos*, *kairos* and *krisis* and their use in timing in ancient medicine, as well as how they synchronize with one another in determining the course of an illness or injury and its outcome. Also considered in this section are the topics of *chronos* as quantitative and *kairos* as qualitative, along with the synchronous or asynchronous modes in which these forms of time operate. The second part of the chapter explores these concepts within two commonly used timing methods of medical astrology: decumbiture and critical days. After defining and describing these techniques, they are then illustrated with numerous examples from astro-medical works from the late second-first century BCE to the sixth century CE, including Hippocratic writers, pseudepigraphical authors such as Petosiris, Dorotheus of Sidon, Vettius Valens, Hephaestio of Thebes, Galen and pseudo-Galen. Also included is a brief Nachleben outlining the use of these methods up to the seventeenth century. Throughout the essay, the topics investigated will show evidence of synchrony and synchronicity in astrological practices related to medicine.

Keywords: astrological medicine, medical astrology, iatromathematics, decumbiture, critical days, *kairos*, Galen, Dorotheus of Sidon, Vettius Valens, Hephaestio of Thebes

1 Introduction

Timing in ancient medicine, as today, is a crucial component of the discipline, essential in diagnosis, prognosis and therapy. Astrology, as well, heavily depends on timing in its practice. Claudius Ptolemy compared the two disciplines in his astro-

Note: I am deeply grateful to Stephan Heilen for his comments on a late draft of this chapter. I also warmly thank Graeme Tobyn for discussing finer points of decumbiture with me, and Levente László for advice on Dorotheus manuscripts. Finally, my thanks and deep appreciation for the useful and thought-provoking comments by the editors of this volume, whose suggestions made this a much better paper.

https://doi.org/10.1515/9783112235690-007

logical work *Tetrabiblos*:[1] both rely on natural astronomical cycles and phenomena; both utilise *chronos, kairos* and *krisis* as forms of time and timing; and furthermore, their paths align in the employment of astronomical/astrological practices to determine the medical timing and severity of the course of an illness.

This focus on time and timing involves synchrony as well: first, because astrology is a *technē* seeking to correlate the workings of the human body (and soul) to the cosmos (the microcosm/macrocosm analogy),[2] medical astrology aims to demonstrate synchronicity between the human body and the heavens during times of illness and disease through the timing of symptoms, crises and outcomes linked to heavenly patterns and movements, resulting in better diagnosis and prognosis. Secondly, *chronos* and *kairos,* two ways of understanding time for the Greeks, are involved in finding the right time (*kairos*) for treatment within the chronological course of the illness, which also may lead to synchrony in an astro-medical milieu.

In investigating this material, the chapter has several objectives. It will introduce two timing practices of medical astrology, decumbiture and critical days, giving examples of each and explaining how medical astrologers or doctors (they could also be the same) used them and why they found them useful. It will consider and elucidate the different kinds of time (*chronos, kairos* and *krisis*) involved in these practices and, throughout, it will explore evidence of synchrony and synchronicity in these astrological practices as they relate to medicine.

The art of medical astrology, called "iatromathematics", developed ways of determining times of crisis, remedy and recovery in disease and injury based on the positions of the Sun, Moon and planets. Decumbiture is the practice of casting an astrological chart for the moment someone felt ill enough to go to bed (from the Latin *decumbo,* lie down). The doctrine of critical days as used in astrology relates to the lunar cycle that predicts the course of an illness and its crisis points. Galen makes a fuller correlation between the lunar cycle and critical days in *On Critical Days* (*De diebus decretoriis*), as will be seen later in this chapter.

1 Ptol. *Tetr.* I 3.13 in Robbins 1940: 26–27.

2 The idea of a microcosm (the human world below the moon) and macrocosm (the cosmos beyond the human world) is mentioned as early as the 5th c. BCE: Democritus (c. 460 BCE–c. 370 BCE) says 'the human is a little cosmos' (Diels and Kranz 1966[6], II: 153.8–9, Demokritos B34: ". . . ἐν τῶι ἀνθρώπωι μικρῶι κόσμωι ὄντι . . .," cited by David the philosopher, *Prolegomena philosophiae* [*Introduction to Philosophy*], ch. 12 [Busse 1904: 38.18]); Plato develops the idea that the microcosm is part of, and is correlated to, the macrocosm in *Timaeus* 30b–d).

2 A Short History of Decumbiture

The practice of decumbiture appears in references to the earliest writers on astrology in the extant Greek texts (roughly between the 1st century BCE and the 1st century CE),[3] and continues to appear throughout antiquity in the works of writers from the 2nd to 6th centuries CE. It was subsequently practised continuously up to the end of the 17th and into the early 18th centuries. The use of decumbiture in the practice of astrological medicine was, therefore, an important tool in describing and assessing the illness and its course.

As noted above, a decumbiture chart (known as *kataklisis* in Greek, *decubitus* in Latin and decumbiture in English) was cast for the moment of falling ill, literally when someone has to lie down. The difficulties of how that moment is decided will be addressed shortly, but it will be useful at this point to understand where decumbiture fits into the astrological scheme. Astrology is made up of three different branches that each address particular concerns. Natal astrology is perhaps the most well-known, i.e. interpretation of a life based on the time and place of birth. General or universal astrology looks at the astrology of countries, populations and what affects whole groups, such as weather, war, famine, etc. These two branches use actual moments in time (the birth time) and chronological cycles (such as equinox and solstice cycles) in their interpretations. They are, therefore, based on *chronos*, in that the time of birth or the equinox is part of a series of events that *chronos* "chronicles", each event having a fixed starting point.[4] However the third branch, katarchic astrology, moves into a different territory that considers not only the time of *chronos*, but the timing of *kairos*.[5] One practice associated with this branch is for astrologers to choose the best time for beginning something (called an election), where there is an expectation of finding the "right time" in the clock time (astrologically, when the patterns in the heavens chronologically conform with the right conditions for success). In the selection of the right time, *kairos* is situated in this framework of *chronos*.[6] Other forms of katarchic astrology also consider both *chronos* and *kairos*, including decumbiture.

---

3 "Petosiris" and Critodemus appear to be the earliest ones (the latter's *terminus ante quem* is Varro, who knew Critodemus's work, and died 27 BCE: see Tolsa 2024: 10).

4 Smith 1969: 3, interpreting Aristotle's view of *chronos*, cites its "feature of serial order or direction expressed in the terms 'before' and 'after'".

5 It should be noted that, in this discussion, I mainly analyse the roles of *chronos* and *kairos* as a commentator. Decumbiture texts do not usually explicitly address the issues explored here, although we do find 'kairos' designated as the time for beginning an action, and some astrologers do acknowledge its importance in this milieu, as will be seen below.

6 Smith 1969: 3 (for *chronos* as a frame), 4–5.

2.1 Katarchic Astrology

Katarchē (καταρχή) is often translated as "inception" or "initiative". Included within katarchic astrology are four different, but related, practices:

1) elections, finding the best time to begin an action;
2) events, examining the time when an event took place to find its outcome;
3) interrogations, the time when someone asks a question of an astrologer and seeks an answer to it;
4) decumbitures, the moment considered to be when an illness begins.

Katarchē is an interesting word in Greek. It comes from the verb κατάρχω [LSJ s.v.], which in its middle form can mean begin the sacrifice or begin the rite, and becomes associated with *kairos* (καιρός), the right and proper time to begin a sacred process.[7] Examples of this association can be found in Iamblichus (the 3rd century CE Neoplatonist), who mentions it in an astrological context when determining the "opportune moment" to begin a theurgical rite.[8] *Kairos* and *katarchē* are also associated in strictly astrological texts, such as the *Anthologies* (*Anth.*) of Vettius Valens (b. 120 CE), where he stresses that a *katarchē*, here meaning an election, the moment chosen by the astrologer to begin something, must be aligned with the right and proper time, the *kairos*; if the time is not right, the enterprise will be subject to punishment and delay.[9] When the astrologer chooses a time to begin an action for a client, it must fit with the positions of planets and stars favorable for that action, and favorable with the client's natal chart: this time is the *kairos*, the right and proper time to begin it. These moments could be

7 Greenbaum 2026: 17.

8 Iamblichus, *De Mysteriis* VIII 4, 267.9–10 (Clarke, Dillon and Hershbell 2003: 316–317). For katarchic astrology in Iamblichus, see Shaw 1995: 201; Addey 2014: 105–106; Greenbaum 2022: 112; Greenbaum 2026: 18–19.

9 Valens, *Anth.* V 2.22 (Pingree 1986: 202.17–23): "I myself, since I keep a watch out for such days according to what is possible, and make my *katarchai* for actions or friendships according to the time-notation (*chronographia*) of the opportune moments (*kairoi*), used to think of the *katarchē* as unchangeable and easily brought to completion; but when I was wandering and, through the untimely (*akairos*) presence or alliance of a friend, or by necessity, I made a beginning of something, I received a result that was liable to punishment and painful or causing delay". My translation, using Heilen 2019: 240's word for *chronographia*. καὶ αὐτὸς μὲν οὖν τὰς τοιαύτας ἡμέρας φυλαττόμενος κατὰ τὸ δυνατὸν καὶ ποιούμενος τὰς καταρχὰς τῶν πράξεων ἢ τῶν φιλιῶν κατὰ τὴν τῶν καιρῶν χρονογραφίαν ἀμετανόητον ἡγούμην τὴν καταρχὴν καὶ εὐσυντέλεστον, ἔσθ' ὅτε δ' ἐπλανήθην καὶ διὰ φίλου ἄκαιρον παρουσίαν ἢ σύστασιν ἢ μετὰ ἀνάγκης καταρξάμενός τινος ἐπιζήμιον καὶ ἐπίλυπον ἢ ὑπερθετικὴν ἔκβασιν κατελαβόμην. See also the discussion in Greenbaum 2016: 40–42, Greenbaum 2022: 112–113, Addey 2022: 144–148.

a coronation, a wedding, or the founding of a city. The action or matter will begin at this specific time (*chronos*) and place, and at the moment chosen to produce a favourable outcome (*kairos*). As used in medicine, *kairos* can also have this meaning, the opportunity that must be seized before it's gone, where the right time can make all the difference in the medical outcome.[10] The time of the decumbiture, as well, must be the correctly determined moment whose heavenly patterns enable the iatromathematician (medical astrologer) to guide the prognosis. John E. Smith's observation is apt for this situation:

> [. . .] there will always be a subject-situation correlation where *kairos* is concerned, since someone will have to know or believe that he knows the right 'when' but this insight does not create that 'when' out of itself. That time belongs to the ontological structure of the order of happening.[11]

2.2 Different Ontological Times

A katarchic chart uses time in two different modes, synchronous or asynchronous: it can be cast not only for a physical time (*chronos*) and place linked directly to an action—just as the birth moment creates the natal chart—but can also be cast for times that have no such physical connection to the occasion or topic it represents, such as an interrogation, that is, making the astrological chart and interpretation based on the time when, e.g., a client asks the astrologer 'Where is my lost cat?'—a time that has no relationship to when the cat was actually lost. The moment in time considered relevant, therefore, can coincide with the actual beginning of the action or event, or be unconnected with it. The synchronous mode of the former could be considered as a "seed moment", where time, space and place are physically connected with a planted seed that will grow based on the physical conditions surrounding it.[12] But the asynchronous mode of the latter cannot claim that time connection.

---

10 Note its use in the Hippocratic aphorism: "ὁ δὲ καιρὸς ὀξὺς" ("the opportune moment fleeting"), *Aphorisms* I.1, in IV.458 Littré.

11 Smith 1986: 5–6 (= Smith 2002: 48).

12 The "seed moment" concept comes from Ptolemy, *Tetr.* I 2.4 (Robbins 1940: 8–9; = Ptol. *Tetr.* I 2.6–7 in Hübner 1998: 7.100–108), who connects the outcome of the moment a seed is planted to the quality of the heavens at that time.

An event chart can be considered as synchronous when the time of the event is known, and its circumstances and outcome can be interpreted by the astrologer based on that time. Sometimes, though, an event occurs at a time unknown to the client (such as a burglary), and a chart is cast for the time it was *discovered.* This time, then, is asynchronous from the actual event and bears no physical relationship or connection to it.[13] It is not a 'seed moment' because it is not the time when the event took place. An interrogation, in which a client asks a question of the astrologer, and a chart is drawn for the moment the question is asked, also does not have a time and space connection to the topic of the question. A question arises in the client's mind unconnected to a physical event, and may not even pertain to anything physical or material. These two asynchronous kinds of chart, then, are ontologically different from the first, synchronous, kind. Because the chart is cast for a time unconnected to a physical reality, the circumstances of its existence are more like those that occur when someone consults an oracle, showing the divinatory roots of astrology.[14] The client, by asking the question at that time, is originating a time physically unconnected to the event, yet it still is taken as valid by the astrologer as a right time, an astrologically appropriate time for casting a chart and making an interpretation (the legitimacy of the questioner's agency in this situation is assumed). Both modes involve *kairos*, but in the asynchronous mode *kairos* shows its metaphysical dimension, going beyond the usual boundaries of time and space.[15] It is a qualitative time that reflects the situation, including the agency of the person who asks the question or discovers the burglary, as the instigator of the examination. A decumbiture can have this same quality, which we will now examine along with the parameters of *kairos* in relation to *chronos*.

2.3 The Time of the Decumbiture: When Does Illness Begin?

Where does the decumbiture chart fit into this scheme? It includes both of the ontological modes described above: it may be cast both for the physical seed moment when an illness begins (the beginning of fever), *and* the conceptually different moment that happens when a patient realises she is ill. The circumstance of the former is synchronous, the latter asynchronous. We could, therefore, say a

13 See László 2022: 30–32, esp. 31, where he describes this practice as "substitution".

14 See Addey 2022: 147–148; Greenbaum in press. On divination and oracles, see also Addey 2022: 153–154. For more on the topic of divination and astrology, see also Cornelius 2003[2], Cornelius 2007, Willis and Curry 2004, cf. 61–63, Curry 2006, Greenbaum 2010 and Greenbaum in press.

15 See discussions of *kairos*, metaphysics and divination in Addey 2022: 141–147.

decumbiture can be based on *either chronos* or *kairos*. But it may be more fruitful to consider the entire concept of decumbiture as partaking of *both* kinds of time. At this point it will be useful to look, first, at the relationship between *chronos* as quantitative and *kairos* as qualitative and, second, how the two may connect. *Chronos* as quantitative is associated with duration and measure; it is "the uniform time of the cosmic system [. . .]".[16] *Kairos*, by contrast, "points to a qualitative character of time, to the special position an event or action occupies in a series [. . .]".[17] It has purpose and significance.[18] The two kinds of time are not distinct from each other, as Smith explains (my emphasis):

> *we must relate the two features of time to each other*, for it has been assumed that they are utterly distinct, time as measure being confined wholly to the subject matters of the physical sciences while qualitative time alone is appropriate for historical events and their interpretation.[19]

Smith's focus is on historical events here, but what he says can apply to the use of *kairos* in katarchic astrology, including decumbiture, where *kairos* too can have a relationship with *chronos*. Regarding the connection between them, in a later article Smith brings in the "metaphysical" along with historical aspects, observing that:

> [. . .] *kairos* presupposes *chronos* which is thus a necessary condition underlying qualitative times, but that by itself the *chronos* aspect does not suffice for understanding either specifically historical interpretations or those processes of nature and human experience where the chronos aspect reaches certain *critical points* at which a qualitative character begins to emerge, and when there are junctures of opportunity calling for human ingenuity in apprehending when the time is "right".[20]

In casting a decumbiture, the doctor and/or medical astrologer (with input from the patient) or the patient herself are aiming, consciously or not, for that propitious (*kairos*) moment that will lead to correct chronological timing for the illness and provide a sound prognosis.[21] This illustrates the synchrony of the heavens with the disease, the patient and what will transpire between them.

---

16 Smith 1986: 4 (= Smith 2002: 47).

17 Smith 1969: 1.

18 Smith 1969: 2, 7.

19 Smith 1969: 2.

20 Smith 1986: 6 (= Smith 2002: 48). In an earlier part of the paragraph he refers to "the features of time denoted by *chronos* and *kairos* with special attention to the metaphysical and historical dimensions of reality [. . .]".

21 I use the word 'aiming' here deliberately. The connection between *kairos* and stochastic arts has been examined by Allen 1994: 88, in discussing medicine as a stochastic art. Astrology was

A decumbiture based on the beginning time of fever and one based on the time of the patient's certainty that she is ill relate to the illness in two ways—perhaps we could say the former is objective and the latter subjective. But both kinds of beginning are accepted as valid by the medical astrologer as the right time (essentially the *kairos*, though that word may or may not be used) to cast a chart that will properly show the course of the disease and its timing, just as the general katarchic astrologer accepts the asynchronous time the burglary was discovered or the question was asked.

When do you know you're sick? This is the great question, and one that has concerned astro-medicine practitioners from the beginning of the practice of decumbiture. For a doctor, it may unambiguously be the moment of a physical symptom, such as fever.This was, for example, Galen's preference.[22] But Galen also realised the various possibilities of timing from the patient's perspective. He recognised that different kinds of people will have different reactions to the signs of approaching illness; some will ignore trivial signs at first, until realising they add up to being sick.[23] Others, of a robust, or stubborn, disposition may ignore symptoms until they become too obvious.[24] Still others, more sensitive, will lie down at the first hint of illness.[25] For the patient, the time is subjective, dependent on the ill person's realization that an illness has begun. Both times are astrologically significant, and so are the two forms of the decumbiture, one based on a specific physical symptom and the other on the patient's mindful realisation that she is indeed ill and needs help. Despite their different origins, both types of decumbiture are interpreted in the same way. As we have seen above, this is true for all katarchic types that have these ontological differences. Both types show valid synchronicity between the illness and the astrological positions.

An illustration of how to interpret decumbiture seen from these two different perspectives, the patient's and the doctor's (Fig. 1a–b), exists in some Greek evidence, transmitted in texts related to the work of Dorotheus of Sidon, a first century CE astrologer.

---

considered a stochastic art by both Ptolemy and Hephaestio of Thebes: for more on this, see Greenbaum 2010, Komorowska 2009; also Addey 2022: 148.

22 Galen, *De diebus decretoriis* I, 6 (IX: 797.11–13 K.). Galen follows the Hippocratics in this: *De diebus decretoriis* I, 6 (IX: 799.6–9 K.).

23 Galen, *De diebus decretoriis* I, 6 (IX: 795.13–17 K.).

24 Galen, *De diebus decretoriis* I, 6 (IX: 796.2–7 K.).

25 Galen, *De diebus decretoriis* I, 6 (IX: 796.7–9 K.). Equivalents for this and nn. 22–24 in Cooper 2011a: 142–146.

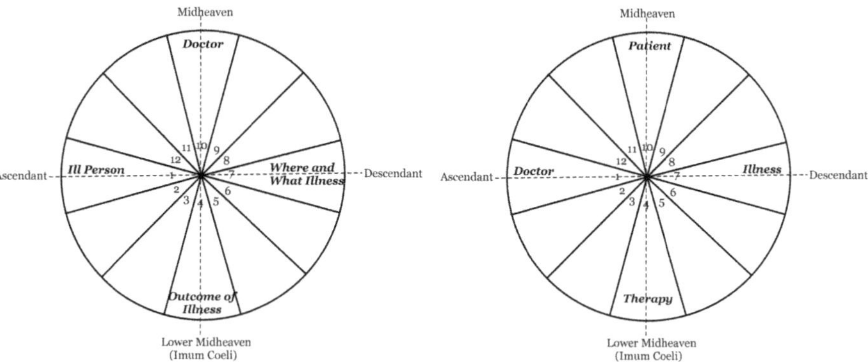

Fig. 1a-b: Interpreting patient and doctor in decumbiture.

Left side. In "Dorotheus on Sick People"[26] Set the Ascendant as the ill person, the setting place as the place where the ill person is lying sick and what kind of illness it will be, the Midheaven the doctor, the Underground the outcome of the illness. In the same way the Moon signifies what the illness is and what its cause is. And so whenever the Ascendant is beheld by the malefics, but the Descendant by the benefics (καλοποιῶν),[27] it signifies the person is

Right side. In "Another View (On those who are ill)" Let the Ascendant be the doctor, the Midheaven the patient, the Descendant the illness, the Underground the treatment. So if a malefic is in the Ascendant, the doctor will not aid the patient at all, but the patient will be harmed by him; but if a benefic is in the Ascendant, the doctor will aid the patient,[28] or even without the doctor the illness will resolve

---

26 All translations are mine unless otherwise noted.

27 This is an unusual term for a benefic ("ἀγαθοποιός" is the normal locution), but it appears in all manuscripts and Stegemann (unpublished): no. 83. Its use here, however, can be traced back to the 8th century CE astrologer Theophilus of Edessa, who employs it commonly, and his texts, as here, often rely on Dorotheus. A version of this passage can be found in his "Περὶ καταρχῶν διαφόρων" ("On Various Inceptions"), ch. 6.1 (translation in Gramaglia and Dykes 2017: 261–262; see also Pingree 2001: 16). It seems odd that benefics are involved in this rather severe prognosis, but it may be that they prevent the person from dying outright. No Arabic version exists for this section where the patient is represented by the Ascendant. My thanks to Levente László for tracing the use of "καλοποιός" to Theophilus of Edessa, and its use in all manuscripts.

28 Here Pingree includes "If a benefic is in the setting place", "ἐὰν δὲ ἀγαθοποιὸς" from L, Laur. plut. 28.34, f. 18r, and adds "δύνῃ . . ." (unaccountably without angle brackets, since the word does not appear either in L or L′ [Laur. plut. 28.13, f. 235r]). The addition seems unnecessary: L's inclusion is omitted in L′, and the sentence makes good sense. (*CCAG* I: 124, Olivieri's (1898) note to line 6, mistakenly says: "ἢ καὶ δίχα τοῦ ἰατροῦ om. L′," but it is actually omitted in L.) Stegemann's emendation (see n. 27 above), "ἐὰν δὲ ἀγαθοποιὸς <ῇ ἐν τῷ μεσουρανήματι, ὠφελήσει ὁ ἰατρὸς τὸν κάμνοντα> ἢ καὶ δίχα τοῦ ἰατροῦ αὐτομάτως ἡ νόσος ῥαΐσει", is reasonable but unneeded. Again I thank László for his advice on these paragraphs (personal communication 21 Feb 2025).

(continued)

seriously ill and the sickness will linger. But if the Midheaven is afflicted, it signifies the ill person has fallen in with a bad doctor and has grounds for complaint against the doctor. But when the Underground is beheld by malefics, it signifies unambiguous danger for the ill person, but if by benefics, it signifies recovery.[29]	on its own. If a malefic is in the Ascendant, but a benefic is in the underground centrepin, it shows that the first doctor, even if he may be quite knowledgeable, will not be able to aid the patient, but later another doctor coming in will aid him.[30]

In analyzing these passages, we should first note, in addition to the prognosis, the use of the "Hippocratic Triangle" of doctor, patient and illness.[31] The interpretations show the relationships between the players from the two perspectives. For the one who is sick (represented in the Ascendant), the doctor in the Midheaven, which represents ruling and eminence, has authority over him, and he is opposed by the illness and the place where he got sick. The Underground shows the outcome of the illness, but unlike the chart from the doctor's perspective, not the particular treatment that the doctor may give (that would be more relevant for the doctor prescribing such remedies). The descriptions of the outcomes seem more dire for the sick person, possibly because, burdened by the illness, he may not be looking on the bright side. There is even the implication of an accusation against an incompetent doctor. The doctor's perspective (when the doctor is rep-

29 "Dorotheus on Sick People", *CCAG* II: 157.11–25 = Dor. gr. Pingree 1976: 420.16–25, 421.1–5: Τοῦ Δωροθέου περὶ ἀρρώστων [1] Ὑπόθου τὸν ὡροσκόπον τὸν νοσοῦντα, τὸ δὲ δῦνον τὸν τόπον οὗ ὁ νοσῶν κατάκειται καὶ αὐτὴν τὴν νόσον ὁποία τις ἔσται, τὸ μεσουράνημα τὸν ἰατρόν, τὸ ὑπὸ γῆν τὴν ἀπόβασιν τῆς νόσου· ὡσαύτως καὶ ἡ Σελήνη σημαίνει τίς ἡ νόσος καὶ ποία καὶ τίς ἡ αἰτία αὐτῆς. [2] ὅταν οὖν ὁ ὡροσκόπος ὑπὸ τῶν κακοποιῶν θεωρῆται, τὸ δὲ δῦνον ὑπὸ τῶν καλοποιῶν, σημαίνει τὸν νοσοῦντα βαρέως ἔχειν καὶ χρονίζειν ἐν τῇ ἀρρωστίᾳ. [3] ἐὰν δὲ τὸ μεσουράνημα κακωθῇ, σημαίνει τὸν νοσοῦντα κακῷ περιτυχεῖν ἰατρῷ καὶ τοῦ ἰατροῦ εἶναι τὸ ἔγκλημα. [4] τὸ δὲ ὑπὸ γῆν ὑπὸ τῶν κακοποιῶν θεωρούμενον κίνδυνον σημαίνει τοῦ νοσοῦντος (p. 421) ἀναμφίβολον, ἐὰν δὲ ὑπὸ ἀγαθοποιῶν, σωτηρίαν σημαίνει.

30 "Another View (On those who are ill)", *CCAG* I: 124 (bottom) 2–10 = Dor. gr. Pingree 1976: 425.12–20 = Dor. arab. V, 41.36–38, 41: Ἄλλη σκέψις (in mg. περὶ νοσούντων) [1] Ἔστω μὲν ὡροσκόπος ὁ ἰατρός, τὸ δὲ μεσουράνημα ὁ κάμνων, τὸ δὲ δῦνον ἡ νόσος, τὸ δὲ ὑπόγειον ἡ θεραπεία. [2] ἐὰν οὖν κακοποιὸς ὡροσκοπῇ, οὐδὲν ὠφελήσει ὁ ἰατρὸς τὸν κάμνοντα, ἀλλὰ καὶ βλαβήσεται ὁ κάμνων ὑπ' αὐτοῦ· ἐὰν δὲ ἀγαθοποιὸς ὡροσκοπῇ, ὠφελήσει τὸν κάμνοντα ὁ ἰατρός, ἢ καὶ δίχα τοῦ ἰατροῦ αὐτομάτως ἡ νόσος ῥαΐσει. [3] ἐὰν δὲ κακοποιὸς μὲν ὡροσκοπῇ, ἀγαθοποιὸς δὲ εἴη ἐν τῷ ὑπογείῳ κέντρῳ, δηλοῖ ὅτι ὁ μὲν πρῶτος ἰατρὸς κἂν μάλιστα εἴη ἐπιστήμων, οὐδὲν δύναται ὠφελῆσαι τὸν κάμνοντα, ἄλλος δέ τις ὕστερον ἐλθὼν ἰατρὸς ὠφελήσει.

31 Hübner 2003: 186. For more on the Hippocratic Triangle, see Gourevitch 1984, Mudry 1997: 320–321, Greenbaum 2022: 121 and n. 45. For more on this specific example, Greenbaum 2022: 121–124.

resented in the Ascendant), by contrast, is much more optimistic and shows faith in both her own skills and in medicine generally, even if she doesn't end up being the final therapist. However, the patient is now in the ruling Midheaven, demonstrating that the patient in some way authorises the process (after all, it was that patient who called the doctor in the first place), and that doctor and patient must work together to defeat the illness.

Why would a medical astrologer, or a doctor (they could also be the same), find a decumbiture useful? And how was it deployed? Let us now take a look at the evidence provided in astrological texts.

3 Astrological Authors on Decumbiture

3.1 The Decumbiture as Substitution ("Hermes", "Petosiris", Protagoras)

A portion of a text on decumbiture and illness is ascribed (in a later text) to the earliest pseudepigraphical authors "Hermes", "Petosiris", and Protagoras (possibly Protagoras of Nicaea).[32] This text specifies using a decumbiture as a substitute if no time of birth is known. From the perspective of synchrony between the chart and the person's illness, the time of the decumbiture will be critical for determining the timing of the illness—with the concomitant movements of Moon and Sun—and assessing its progress. Note in this passage the use of the word *kairos* for the inception time, combined with the stochastic phrase 'in a well-aimed way' (εὐστόχως) (cf. n. 21).

> (5) Furthermore, one must speak about the same things from the "Iatromathematica" of Hermes and Petosiris and from the collections of Protagoras, and these say one must understand the inceptions on decumbiture from both the Moon and from her associations with the stars and the Sun; one must especially consider such inceptions when, if the circumstances of childbirth (10) may be lacking or unknown, at least through the transitory movements at the moment (κατὰ καιρὸν) [of the inception] and the figurations of the stars, the methods of the prognosis may proceed in a well-aimed way (εὐστόχως).[33]

32 For Protagoras, see László 2022: 249.

33 *CCAG* I: 126.5–12: (5) ἔτι δὲ περὶ τῶν αὐτῶν ῥητέον ἔκ τε τῶν ἰατρομαθηματικῶν (6) Ἑρμοῦ καὶ Πετοσίρεως καὶ ἐκ τῶν συναγωγῶν Πρωταγό- (7) ρου· φασὶ δὲ καὶ οὗτοι· τὰς περὶ κατακλίσεων καταρχὰς λαμβάνειν χρὴ (8) ἀπό τε τῆς Σελήνης καὶ τῆς πρὸς τοὺς ἀστέρας καὶ τὸν Ἥλιον αὐτῆς (9) κοινωνίας· προσεκτέον δὲ μάλιστα ταῖς τοιαύταις καταρχαῖς ὅπως, κἂν (10) ἐλλείπῃ ἢ καὶ ἄγνωστα ᾖ τὰ τῆς ἐκτέξεως, διὰ γοῦν τῶν κατὰ καιρὸν (11) παροδικῶν κινήσεών τε καὶ σχηματισμῶν τῶν ἀστέρων εὐστόχως τὰ (12) τῆς προγνώσεως προβῇ.

The decumbiture supplies a prognosis based on the moon and her relationships with the other planets ('stars') and the Sun, celestial bodies that are important in Hippocratic texts as well. Using a decumbiture as a substitute for an absent birth-chart may show a reason why the decumbiture's development and practice became useful in a medical context. While doctors and astrologers would have time-keeping devices for their work, laboring women in antiquity may not have noted the child's birthtime, or remember it, so some people would not have known exactly when they were born.[34] The decumbiture should not be considered as interchangeable with the birthchart, but it was a means for the iatromathematician to still help the patient with medical advice during an illness (though using both charts was desirable). In general astrological practice, a nativity can be used not only for interpreting the condition of the physical body, mind, soul and character from the qualities of the arrangement of the heavens at the birth moment, but can also project future results using a combination of various techniques. The decumbiture chart interprets past, present and future for medical issues.

As for "Petosiris", a common name in Egyptian, collections of fragments from later writers mention him and a "King Nechepsos".[35] These probably date from the 2nd to 1st centuries BCE. In connection with decumbiture, Juvenal mentions Petosiris in his *Satire 6*: "If she's ill and lying in bed, no moment seems/more right for eating than the one prescribed by Petosiris" (trans. S. Morton Braund).[36] The same satire contains another mention of katarchic practice and well-known astrologers like Thrasyllus (lines 575–576).[37]

Astrologers interpret the decumbiture using several methods that can be combined for a final verdict. As we saw above, the decumbiture can be assessed on its own if no birthchart is available, but often the practice was to use *both* the natal chart and the decumbiture, thus personalising even more the circumstances of the illness, aiming for better accuracy and synchrony between the person's condition and the configurations of the stars at that time. The Moon, Sun and places where the benefic planets Venus and Jupiter, and malefic planets Mars and Saturn, fall, are the main players. These feature in a number of different techniques to assess the condition of the illness or injury as well as timing its severity

34 On the topic of time-precision in Greco-Roman astrology, see Heilen 2019.

35 For Petosiris as a common name in Egyptian see Quack 2018: 112; for Petosiris and astrology, Ryholt 2011; Quack 2018: 110–118; Heilen 2015: II, 539–544; László 2022: 248–249. Ernst Riess (1892) was the first to collect the astrological fragments of Petosiris. Heilen 2011 and 2015: I, 39–52 has augmented these. It is unlikely that all texts under this name are the work of one person.

36 Juvenal, *Satire 6*, 580–581: *aegra licet iaceat, capiendo nulla uidetur / aptior hora cibo nisi quam dederit Petosiris*. In Morton Braund 2004: 288–289; Watson and Watson 2014: 74.

37 See also Kassandra Miller's reference to this in her contribution in this volume, pp. 131–132.

and duration. In all of these examinations, the Moon plays a vital and critical role, especially in acute illness, while the Sun is examined in cases of chronic illness. The reasons for this are that the Moon moves the most swiftly of the visible heavenly bodies (it travels between 12 and 14 degrees per day, changing its zodiacal sign every 2 ½ days), and parts of its cycle happen to coincide with critical times of acute illness, a circumstance particularly noted by astrologers and doctors in the Greco-Roman era and later. The Sun, by contrast, is the steady luminary, rising and setting in the same orientation without fail over a 24-hour period, and taking a whole year (approximately one zodiacal sign per month) to go through the zodiac in its annual cycle. Both luminaries, though, were seen as essential in predicting the course of disease, whether acute or chronic.

3.2 Interpreting the Decumbiture by Itself (Dorotheus of Sidon)

Without a doubt, the most prolific ancient astrologer on decumbitures is Dorotheus of Sidon in the first century CE. His work of unknown title, now called the *Carmen Astrologicum* or *Pentateuch*, written in verse, is extant in Greek fragments and prose paraphrasing by Hephaestio of Thebes (fl. 415 CE);[38] there is also an Arabic prose translation. Book V is devoted entirely to katarchic astrology, and six chapters deal with illnesses, other medical conditions such as surgery, and decumbiture. We have already seen two of his fragments showing the decumbiture's interpretation from the two perspectives of patient and doctor.

Dorotheus looks at the decumbiture on its own as well as in combination with the natal chart. This first example shows how to gather information from the decumbiture as a stand-alone chart. The Ascendant and Moon, representing the ill person's mind and body, provide the means by which the benefic and malefic planets interact by making connections to them (called aspects). In examining benefics and malefics as they affect the illness, Dorotheus demonstrates the synchronization of their positions with the improving or declining progress of the disease.

38 It is important to acknowledge here the role of Hephaestio of Thebes in spreading the work of Dorotheus on astrological medicine generally and decumbiture specifically. Because his *Apotelesmatica* provides many examples (both in prose paraphrase and poetry) of Dorotheus's work, it was critical in expanding knowledge of these practices from the Greco-Roman period.

On decumbitures and illnesses

[1] When examining diseases look at the Ascendant of the decumbiture, and the position of the Moon, and the housemaster of these, and furthermore their applications, and the twelfth-part of the Moon. [2] For if these happen to be allotted as benefics, there will be no harm, but the illness will resolve quickly, and health will follow; but if they are malefics, harm will manifest and distress generally. Particularly if Ares is allotted [with] these, the illness will be acute and dangerous; but if Kronos, the illness becomes both chronic and difficult. [3] Again, if the Moon alone appears afflicted by Kronos and Ares, the harm will only be to the body of the human; if the Ascendant alone harms, there will be delirium, harm to the mind and frenzy. If both the places of the Moon and the Ascendant are being harmed by malefics and no benefic regards them, the indication is poor, dangerous and warns of death.[39]

The first chart component Dorotheus mentions in this passage is the Ascendant (*hōroskopos*, lit. "hour-marker"), the sign and degree on the eastern horizon at the moment the decumbiture is cast. This place represents the ill person, her body and mind, and life itself (it is called "ζωή" in ancient texts). (Fig. 1 above shows the places of the chart, with the Ascendant middle left.) We can also see the overall importance of the Moon in charting the course of the disease. The techniques he mentions, finding the "house-master" (*oikodespotēs*), the planet that has the most amount of power in a particular sign and degree); and "applications" (meaning the aspects, i.e. geometrical relationships, by planets and luminaries to the Ascendant and the Moon); and the *dodekatēmorion* ("twelfth-part", meaning here the 2½ degree portion of a sign in which the Ascendant and Moon fall, which is ruled by a particular planet) are all indications of the strength, resilience and quality of the Moon and Ascendant.[40] He then assesses the ability of these planets to affect the progress of the disease for good or ill. In this, what are called the malefic planets, Mars and Saturn, are often stressed, as you can see here; but the benefic planets, Venus and Jupiter, are also essential. The passage

39 Dor. gr. Pingree 1976: 422.9–423.3 = *CCAG* I: (bottom) 122.1–15: Περὶ κατακλίσεων καὶ νόσων. [1] Σκεπτόμενος περὶ νοσημάτων βλέπε τόν τε ὡροσκόπον τῆς κατακλίσεως καὶ τὴν τῆς Σελήνης ἐποχήν, καὶ τοὺς τούτων οἰκοδεσπότας, καὶ ἔτι τὰς συναφὰς αὐτῶν, καὶ τὸ τῆς Σελήνης δωδεκατημόριον. [2] ἐὰν μὲν γὰρ ταῦτα ἀγαθοποιοὶ τύχωσι κληρωσάμενοι, οὐδεμία ἔσται βλάβη, ἀλλὰ ταχέως ἡ νόσος ῥαΐσει, καὶ ὑγίεια ἐπακολουθήσει· ἐὰν δὲ κακοποιοί, βλάβη δηλοῦται καὶ κάκωσις κοινῶς, ἰδίως δὲ, εἰ μὲν Ἄρης ταῦτα κληρώσεται, ὀξεῖα ἔσται ἡ νόσος καὶ ἐπικίνδυνος· εἰ δὲ Κρόνος, χρονία τε ἅμα καὶ χαλεπὴ γίνεται ἡ νόσος. [3] ἐὰν δὲ πάλιν ἡ Σελήνη μόνη φαίνηται κεκακωμένη ὑπὸ Κρόνου ἢ Ἄρεως, ἡ βλάβη περὶ τὸ σῶμα ἔσται μόνον τοῦ ἀνθρώπου· ἐὰν δὲ μόνος ὁ ὡροσκόπος βλαβῇ, παραφροσύνη ἔσται καὶ τῆς διανοίας βλάβη καὶ παρακοπή· εἰ δὲ ἀμφότεροι οἱ τόποι τῆς τε Σελήνης καὶ τοῦ ὡροσκόπου ὦσιν βεβλαμμένοι ὑπὸ τῶν κακοποιῶν καὶ μηδεὶς ἀγαθοποιὸς ἐπιθεωρήσῃ, φαῦλον τὸ σημεῖον καὶ κινδυνῶδες καὶ θανάτου προοίμιον.

40 These are not uncommon techniques for astrologers; see, e.g., an ancient chart that calculates them in Greenbaum and Jones 2017.

goes on to supply other means of interpretation, but this is sufficient to give the general idea. Later he stresses that many factors need to be considered to understand fully how the astrological conditions are operating; the more a planet shows a connection to the decumbiture, the more its presence is felt in the prognosis.

3.3 Interpreting the Natal Chart and Decumbiture Together (Dorotheus)

We mentioned previously (p. 153) that a decumbiture could be interpreted in conjuction with a nativity, providing an interpretation even more personally tailored to an individual. This second example is in Dorotheus, *Carmen Astrologicum* V, 31. (Hephaestio's *Apotelesmatica* III, 31.12–15 reproduces it.) The natal chart here is called the "radix" or root chart, πῆξις in Greek). This example shows that information from the birthchart co-ordinates with what the decumbiture displays in producing a diagnosis and prognosis to synchronize the astrology of the moment (combined with the astrological positions at birth) with the type, onset and development of the illness.

> [12] So examine which of the 12 zodiacal signs in the radix of the nativity was afflicted by one of the malefic stars. [13] And if it happened that the inception of the disease came to be when the Moon was in a sign that was afflicted from the beginning [i.e., in the nativity], and the times cast out from the Ascendant arrived at such a sign in which Kronos or Ares was according to the radix; or the releasings of the luminaries, the centrepins or the lots being cast out fell onto the destructive rays of the malefics, the illness comes to be most difficult. [14] For if it [the Moon] should separate from Ares or Kronos, there will be discharges or nerve pains. [15] But if the malefics in the nativity are in signs with two bodies, especially in Gemini and Pisces on account of these signs being split apart from one another[41]—and with this being so from the beginning, if [in the decumbiture] the malefics surround the Moon in their midst, in Gemini they bring on gout in the hand, but in Pisces, gout in the foot.[42]

---

41 There are four "double-bodied" signs, but only two, Gemini (the twins) and Pisces (the fishes) are separated from each other (Virgo, often depicted with wings, and Sagittarius, the centaur, are the others).

42 Dor. gr. Pingree 1976, fragment V 31, 1–5, 404.1–14, sentences 12–15 = Dor. arab. V, 31.1–5 = Hephaestio, *Apotelesmatica* III, 31.12–15 (Pingree 1973: 291.17–33): [12] σκέπτου οὖν ποῖον τῶν ιβ ζῳδίων κατὰτὴν πῆξιν τῆς γενέσεως ἐκακοῦτο ὑπό τινος τῶν κακοποιῶν ἀστέρων. [13] καὶ ἐὰν συμβῇ γενέσθαι καὶ τὴν καταρχὴν τοῦ νοσήματος ἐν τῷ κεκακωμένῳ ἐξ ἀρχῆς ζῳδίῳ τῆς Σελήνης οὔσης, οἱ δὲ χρόνοι οἱ ἀπὸ τοῦ ὡροσκόπου ἐκβαλλόμενοι καταντήσωσιν εἴς τι ζῴδιον τοιοῦτον ὁποίῳ ἦν κατὰ τὴν πῆξιν ὁ Κρό-(5)νος ἢ ὁ Ἄρης ἢ αἱ τῶν φωστήρων ἢ τῶν κέντρων ἢ τῶν κλήρων ἀφέσεις ἐκβαλλόμεναι εἰς τὰς φθαρτικὰς τῶν κακοποιῶν ἀκτῖνας ἐμπέσωσιν, χαλεπωτάτη γίνεται

Therefore, look first for the zodiac signs that are afflicted (meaning, containing the planets Saturn or Mars) in the nativity. If the Moon is in that same sign in the decumbiture, and the Ascendant comes to that sign when moving in current time, or other things in the chart connect with malefics, it predicts a very difficult illness. Aspects with Mars or Saturn will make discharges or neuralgias, and when they are in double-bodied (also called mutable) signs,[43] on both sides of the Moon,[44] they will produce gout, in the hands if Gemini and in the feet if Pisces. In zodiacal melothesia, the assigning of body parts to zodiacal signs, Gemini—ruled by Mercury—rules hands and arms, and Pisces rules the feet.[45]

3.4 The Moon in Unfortunate Places (Dorotheus)

We have seen unfortunate aspects to the Moon and Ascendant predict kinds of illness and how difficult it can be, but also how benefics can ameliorate the situation. Now we shall find that just being in what are called unfortunate places in the chart, both birthchart and decumbiture, will be enough to affect how the illness progresses and its severity. This is not necessarily an issue of timing, but rather the patient's condition and ability to withstand the illness, although the Moon's position will, naturally, depend on the time of the decumbiture to show synchrony with the symptoms. Dorotheus says

> that when the Moon in the decumbiture is in the zodiacal sign of a malefic, if that sign happens to contain a benefic in the radix, it proclaims that the sick person will suffer severely, yet in time will be pulled out of danger. It again signifies the worst when the Moon in the decumbiture happens to be in the 6th, 12th, 8th or 4th place, or in a place in the radix where it might be harmed by a malefic.[46]

ἡ νόσος. [14] εἰ μὲν γὰρ ἀπὸ Ἄρεως ἀπορρέοι ἢ ἀπὸ Κρόνου ῥευματισμοὶ ἔσονται ἢ νεύρων ἀλγηδών. [15] ἐὰν δὲ οἱ κατὰ τὴν γένεσιν κακοποιοὶ ἐν δισώμοις ὄντες ζῳδίοις, καὶ μάλιστα ἐν Διδύ-(10)μοις καὶ Ἰχθύσι διὰ τὸ ταῦτα τὰ ζῴδια τετμῆσθαι ἀπ' ἀλλήλων – ἐὰν οὖν οὕτως ἔχοντες οἱ κακοποιοὶ ὡς εἴρηται ἐξ ἀρχῆς μέσην περιέχωσι τὴν Σελήνην ἐν μὲν Διδύμοις ὄντες χειράγραν ἐπιφέρουσιν, ἐν δὲ Ἰχθύσι ποδάγραν.

43 These signs, Gemini, Virgo, Sagittarius and Pisces, come at the times when one season is ending and another beginning, thus "mutable" (changeable).

44 This is called "ἐμπερίσχεσις" in ancient Greek texts (see Heilen 2015: 807–809); it is "besiegement" in medieval astrology.

45 For more on the doctrine of melothesia, see Hübner 2013; Greenbaum 2020: 369–370, 372–374.

46 In Burnett and Pingree 1997 (*Liber Aristotilis* of Hugo of Santalla), Appendix 2, 210, no. XLV (≈ Dor. arab. V, 31.2, = Dor. arab. V, 41.57): [1] Ὅτι ἡ Σελήνη ἐν τῇ κατακλίσει ἐν ζῳδίῳ κακοποιοῦ οὖσα, εἰ τύχῃ τὸ ζῴδιον ἐκεῖνο ἀγαθοποιὸν ἔχον κατὰ πῆξιν, δυσπαθήσει<ν> μὲν ἐπαγγέλλεται τὸν νοσοῦντα, ὅμως δέ ποτε ῥυσθήσεται τοῦτον τοῦ κινδύνου. [2] κάκιστον δὲ πάλιν σημαίνει [f.

A similar example mentions the decumbiture Moon in the 4th, 6th and 8th places of the radix:

> But he [i.e. Dorotheus] also says otherwise: examine the Moon of the decumbiture; for if she happens to be either in the 4th place of the nativity, in the 6th or in the 8th, or the Moon herself was there in the radix, these things also suggest the illness is dangerous.[47]

These two passages indicate three of the worst places in the chart as dangerous, namely the 6th, 8th and 12th. They are known respectively as "Bad Fortune", "Death" or "Hades", and "Bad Daimon", because those places make no accepted geometrical aspect, thus connection, to the Ascendant, which represents the person's life and body, and are unable to provide anything good.[48] The unfortunate places are both chronologically and/or locationally badly placed. The 6th and 12th make transitions between day and night, rising and setting, and darkness and light.[49] Such temporal and spatial conditions can be dangerous. For example, the 12th, the place right before birth (the Ascendant is the moment of birth), represents labor and the dangers associated with childbirth. The 4th place, though an angle with inherent power, is nevertheless called the "Underground" (τὸ ὑπόγειον) and often represesents the end of the matter in katarchic astrology. So, for instance, when the Moon in the decumbiture is in the same place or sign as a malefic, and was likewise in one of those places in the nativity, it does not bode well for the outcome of the illness. However, as in the first passage, the ill person can recover if the sign in the decumbiture contains a benefic in the birthchart. The prognosis here is attained by weaving together the Moon's location both natally and in the decumbiture.

3.5 Sun, Moon and Timing (Dorotheus)

We also find arithmetical methods in this same text from the *CCAG*: "Another view" is a compilation of techniques on decumbiture from various astrologers, including, as here, Dorotheus.[50] These two methods involve the distance between

---

241] ὅταν τύχῃ ἐν τῇ κατακλίσει ἡ Σελήνη ἐν τῷ ς′ ἢ τῷ ιβ′ ἢ τῷ δ′ τόπῳ ἢ ἐν ᾧ τόπῳ κατὰ πῆξιν ἦν καὶ βλάπτοιτο ὑπὸ κακοποιοῦ.

47 *CCAG* I: 125.16–19 = Dor. gr. Pingree 1976: 426.17–19 = Dor. arab.V, 41.57: καὶ ἄλλως δέ φησι· σκόπει τὴν τῆς κατακλίσεως Σελήνην· ἐὰν γὰρ τύχῃ ἢ ἐν τῷ δ′ τόπῳ τῆς γενέσεως ἢ ἐν τῷ ς ἢ ἐν τῷ η′, ἢ ἔνθα ἦν ἡ Σελήνη αὐτὴ κατὰ πῆξιν, κινδυνώδη τὴν νόσον καὶ ταῦτα ὑποφαίνει.

48 For further explanation see Greenbaum 2016: 404–405.

49 Greenbaum 2016: 145, discussing Rhetorius's description of cadent places.

50 For this compilation as the work of Julian of Laodicea (fl. late 5th–early 6th c.) see László 2020: 8, 13–16.

the Sun and the Moon compared with the days from the birthdate to the time of the decumbiture (relevant phrases italicized), thus correlating the latter with the birthchart to find proper synchrony between the luminaries at birth and at the time of illness as reflected in the patterns of the decumbiture. The arithmetical format, however, puts these methods into the asynchronous mode examined earlier in this chapter in regard to katarchic charts, but here it is the method *applied* to the chart, not necessarily the chart itself. It is interesting to see that Dorotheus accepts this procedure as valid, suggesting he has no problem with asychronous practice.

5a First method: Sun, Moon and Timing from Birth to Decumbiture

> [. . .] taking the number of *the interval of* the zodiacal *signs from the Sun in the nativity to the Moon in the nativity*, and including in the enumeration the signs themselves in which the two luminaries are from the beginning, and having, as has been said, such a quantity of the signs, also take *the days from the beginning of the nativity to the decumbiture*, and *divide these by the quantity of the signs*, as has been said; and if this number is equal to the amount of the days, the one who has taken to bed will be dangerously ill.[51] (my emphasis)

5b Second method: The Two Suns: Birth and Decumbiture

> And one must *examine*, he says, *the 2 suns, that of the radix and that at the transit* [i.e. decumbiture], *and* furthermore *the transiting Moon of the decumbiture*; and if the Moon herself, before coming to her own square, applies to one of the suns, it shows the illness as milder; but if she squares herself before the application to one of the suns, the indication [i.e. prognosis] is poor.[52]

---

51 *CCAG* I: 125.9–16, from "Another view" = Dor. gr. Pingree 1976: 426.9–16 (sentence 9) = Dor. arab. V, 41.53–56: [. . .] λαβὼν ἀπὸ τοῦ κατὰ γένεσιν Ἡλίου (10) ἐπὶ τὴν κατὰ γένεσιν Σελήνην τὸν τῶν ζῳδίων αὐτῶν τοῦ διαστήματος ἀριθμόν, συναριθμῶν καὶ αὐτὰ τὰ ζῴδια ἐν οἷς εἰσιν ἐξ ἀρχῆς οἱ δύο φωστῆρες, ἔχων οὖν, ὡς εἴρηται, τὴν τοιαύτην, τῶν ζῳδίων ποσότητα, λάβε καὶ τὰς ἀπὸ τῆς ἀρχῆς τῆς γενέσεως ἕως τῆς κατακλίσεως ἡμέρας, καὶ ταύτας μέρισον παρὰ τὴν ποσότητα τῶν ζῳδίων, ὡς εἴρηται· (15) καὶ ἐὰν ἀπαρτίζῃ ὁ ἀριθμὸς οὗτος τῷ πλήθει τῶν ἡμερῶν, ὁ κατακλιθεὶς ἐπικινδύνως νοσήσει.

52 *CCAG* I: 125.19–23 ("Another view") = Dor. gr. Pingree 1976: 426.20–24 = Dor. arab. V, 41.66–68: σκοπεῖν δὲ δεῖ, φησί, τούς τε β' ἡλίους, τόν τε κατὰ πῆξιν καὶ τὸν κατὰ πάροδον, καὶ ἔτι τὴν παροδικὴν Σελήνην τῆς κατακλίσεως· καὶ ἐὰν αὐτὴ ἡ Σελήνη πρὶν ἑαυτὴν τετραγωνίσαι συνάψῃ τινὶ τῶν ἡλίων, ἐλαφροτέραν τὴν νόσον δηλοῖ· ἐὰν δὲ πρὸ τοῦ συνάψαι τινὶ τῶν ἡλίων ἑαυτὴν τετραγωνίσῃ, φαῦλον τὸ σημεῖον. The authorship of Dorotheus in these Greek excerpts is not in doubt, although they have been questioned as spurious. The section begins with "Φησὶ δὲ ὁ Δωρόθεος." Pingree 1976 has correlated them with the material in the Arabic Dorotheus. Though in

The use of the sun and moon in these two passages shows the importance of the two luminaries in assessing the length and prognosis of the illness, precisely because of their ability to show timing through their relationship in the lunar cycle. In the second method, an important phase of the Moon, the first quarter, which is equivalent to the first square the Moon makes to the Sun in the lunar cycle, shows how critical this is to the development of the illness. If she applies to either the decumbiture Sun or the natal Sun in an aspect (it would have to be a sextile in this case) before she squares herself, it will ameliorate the illness, but if she reaches her own square before making an aspect to the Sun, the effect of that square worsens the prognosis. There will be more detailed consideration of the Moon's phases and cycle in the section on critical days (Fig. 2).

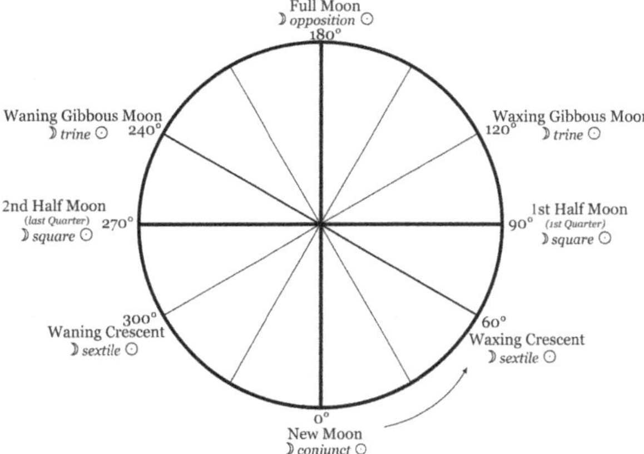

Fig. 2: Moon phases in relationship to the sun.

the Arabic version of Dorotheus they are ascribed to "Qitrinus the Sadhwali", this may be an Arabic corruption of the name of the early astrological author Critodemus. Recently, Cristian Tolsa (2024: 171–176) has proposed that this "Qitrinus" could be the early astrologer Critodemus, the author of a book called "Vision" (*Horasis*) who was often mentioned by Vettius Valens. A technique ascribed to him by Valens is similar to the arithmetical methods here, so there may be something to this hypothesis.

3.6 Strong Moon Phases ("Hermes", "Petosiris" and Protagoras")

The importance of certain moon phases in illness are outlined as well in this same *CCAG* text:[53]

> [1] So we will watch for the strong phases of the Moon. [2] They are concurrence (new moon), 1st half-moon [first quarter], full moon, 2nd half-moon [last quarter], and the bonds [contacts with the lunar nodes] as well; [3] we will pay attention to its numbers in longitude and latitude, and whether it is subtracting or adding to these numbers [i.e. fast or slow in motion]; and one must see to it that the house-master of the phase not be in superior position or opposing it, for it will produce changes and diverse diseases. [4] One must guard against the squares of the luminaries with one another or squares of the bonds, for the activity of these is strong, and the decumbiture from them precarious. [5] But figures [i.e. aspects] that are harmonious, the trines and sextiles, are less dangerous.[54]

This excerpt states clearly the timing relationship between the Moon, Sun and crisis points in an illness. This synchronicity between Moon phase and turning points in the illness emphasises even more strongly the vital role played by the luminaries. Note here the emphasis on potential peril when the luminaries square each other or the Moon squares the nodes ("squares of the bonds"). Vettius Valens similarly warns, for katarchic astrology, that if the Moon passes through the ascending node, squares or opposes it, 'especially at the same degree', '*do not . . . do anything*' (my emphasis).[55] This applies to disease treatment, too: "men will be disease-ridden and incurable."[56]

53 On Protagoras and fragments attributed to him, see László 2022: 249.

54 *CCAG* I: 126.12–21 ("Another view"): [1] ἐπιτηρήσομεν οὖν τὰς ἰσχυρὰς φάσεις τῆς Σελήνης· [2] αὗται δέ εἰσι· σύνοδος, διχότομος α', πανσέληνος, διχότομος β', ἔτι μὴν καὶ οἱ σύνδεσμοι· [3] προσέξομεν δὲ τοῖς ἀριθμοῖς αὐτῆς τοῦ τε μήκους καὶ τοῦ πλάτους, καὶ πότερον ἀφαιρεῖ ἢ προστίθησι τοῖς ἀριθμοῖς τούτοις· καὶ τὸν οἰκοδεσπότην δὲ τῆς φάσεως ὁρατέον μὴ καθυπερτερῶν αὐτὴν τύχῃ ἢ διαμετρῶν, μεταβολὰς γὰρ καὶ ποικίλα τὰ νοσήματα ἀπεργάζεται. [4] παραφυλακτέον δὲ τὰ τετράγωνα πρὸς ἄλληλα τῶν φώτων ἢ καὶ τῶν συνδέσμων, ἰσχυρὰ γὰρ ἡ τούτων) ἐνέργεια, καὶ σφαλερὰ ἡ ἐξ αὐτῶν κατάκλισις· [5] ἀκινδυνώτερα δὲ σχήματα τὰ σύμφωνα, τά τε τρίγωνα καὶ τὰ ἑξάγωνα.

55 Pingree 1986: 202.3–7 (Valens, *Anth.*, V 2.19): τῆς Σελήνης διαπορευομένηςτον καίρικον Ἀναβιβάζοντα καὶ τὰ τούτου τετράγωνα καὶ διάμετρα, μάλιστα δὲ κατὰ τὰς αὐτὰς μοίρας . . . μήτε . . . τι πράττειν. This involves the descending node also, since the nodes' positions are exactly opposed.

56 Pingree 1986: 202.30 (Valens, *Anth.*, V 2.27): οὐδὲ μὴν αἱ σωματικαὶ θεραπεῖαι εὐίατοι, ἐπίνοσοι δὲ καὶ δυσθεράπευτοι [. . .] (trans. Riley 2010). Similar, but with the Sun, see V 2.8 (Pingree 1986: 200.32–201.3).

3.7 Significant Hours in Decumbiture ("Hermes", "Petosiris" and Protagoras)

Synchrony between the illness and heavenly movement can even come down to the hour. In this practice, specific hours of day and night are designated as significant for observation by these early authors: if the decumbiture occurs in the daytime, look at the 1st, 2nd, 3rd, 4th, 5th, 6th, 7th and 12th hours; and at night the 1st, 2nd, 6th and 8th.[57] The rationale for this may be the planetary rulers associated with each day and night hour (see 3.9 below). We see from this that although the decumbiture is cast for a moment in time, it is not a static, one and done method, but a dynamic practice that shows the evolution of the illness in weeks, days and even hours.

3.8 New Moons, Birth and Decumbiture (Vettius Valens)

This arithmetical method is asynchronous, again using the Moon cycle as in Example 3.5, but in this case new moons of various kinds help in predicting whether a disease or injury will be fatal. The times of these new moons seem to be considered as seed moments of the process which can affect the final outcome. The text is in Valens' *Anthologies*. His method differs from those given by Dorotheus in Example 3.5, but is similar in format to them.[58] In a three-step process, Valens takes the number of days from the prenatal new moon (the new moon prior to

---

57 *CCAG* I: 127.8–10 ("Another view"): αἱ δ' ἐπίσημοι ὥραι τῶν κατακλίσεων παρεφυλάχθησαν, ἡμέρας μὲν α' <καὶ> β' καὶ γ' καὶ δ' καὶ ε'καὶ ς καὶ ζ' καὶ ιβ', νυκτὸς δὲ α' β' ς η'.

58 Pingree 1986: 325.26–326.7 (Valens, *Anth.* IX 6.1–5) (trans. Riley 2010): "6. On Decumbiture and Inceptions. [1] The determination of forecasts when a patient takes to his bed must be made in the following way: [2] determine the number of days from the new moon <preceding> the nativity to the birth date; divide this by 4. Make a note of the remainder of the division by 4. [3] Now we take the days from the new moon of the current [326.1] year to the birth date, and we divide that figure by 4. Note the remainder. [4] As the third step, it is necessary to take the days from the new moon preceding the illness to the day when the patient took to his bed. Divide this by 4, and compare the remainder with the previous remainders. [5] If the three figures are the same, the time must be judged fatal. If they are different, the danger resulting from the disease, the sickness or the injury will be escaped." (ς. Περὶ κατακλίσεως καὶ καταρχῶν. [1] Συγκρίνειν δὲ δεῖ καὶ τὰς γινομένας κατακλίσεις τὸν τρόπον τοῦτον. [2] ἀπὸ τῆς γενεθλίου συνόδου ἕως τῆς γεννητικῆς ἡμέρας μαθόντες τὸ τῶν ἡμερῶν πλῆθος ἐκκρούομεν ὁσάκις δυνατὸν τετραετηρίδας, τὸ περιττὸν τῶν δ̅ ἀριθμῶν σημειωσάμενοι. [3] λαμβάνομεν ἀπὸ τῆς συνόδου τοῦ καταγο-(326.1) μένου ἔτους ἕως τῆς γενεθλιακῆς ἡμέρας, καὶ ἐκκρούσαντες τετραετηρίδας τὸ περίλοιπον σημειούμεθα. [4] τρίτῳ δὲ λόγῳ λαμβάνειν χρὴ ἀπὸ τῆς πρὸ τῆς κατακλίσεως συνόδου ἕως τῆς κατακλιτικῆς ἡμέρας, καὶ ἐκκρούσαντας τὰς τετραετηρίδας τὸν λοιπὸν ἀριθμὸν συγκρίνειν τοῖς

birth) to the Moon of the decumbiture, divides it by 4 and notes the remainder. He then does the same for the new moon in the current year to the birthdate, and finally takes the number of days from the new moon preceding the illness to the Moon of the decumbiture. If the remainders from all these calculations are the same, the prognosis is fatal, but if they are different, the patient will survive. (The odds apparently favor the patient's survival.) This method appears only in Valens.[59]

3.9 Ruling Planets and Decumbiture (Paulus of Alexandria)

Not all authors were as interested in decumbiture as the ones we have just discussed. But the practice was known and mentioned even by astrologers whose main interest was natal astrology. An example is Paulus of Alexandria (fl. 378 CE), in Chapter 21 of his *Introduction to Astrology* (*Intr.*), where he advocates examining the presiding and managing of planets at particular days and times in katarchic charts as well as in nativities, including decumbiture,[60] and adds: "For doctors, it also contributes to inquiry both in diagnoses of the sick and in considerations of surgeries or medical treatments [. . .]", interestingly giving evidence that doctors used iatromathematics.[61] Each planet "presides" over a day of the week, and "manages" certain hours of the day and night, giving them power over the day and the hour in which the events of the decumbiture are taking place (cf. Tab. 1[62]). This makes the timing even more specific (see their use above in example 3.7).

προτέροις. [5] ἐὰν δέ πως αἱ τρεῖς γραφαὶ εἰς ἕνα ἀριθμὸν καταλήξωσιν, θανατικὸς ὁ χρόνος κριθήσεται· ἐὰν δὲ διάφοροι, κίνδυνος διὰ νόσου ἢ πάθους ἢ σίνους ἐπερχόμενος.)

59 László 2022: 260. One wonders, though, if it could be related to the arithmetical methods of Critodemus (see n. 52).

60 Boer 1958: 42.10–11 (Paul. Al., *Intr.*, 21); trans. in Greenbaum 2001: 39.

61 Boer 1958: 42.11–13: συμβάλλεται δὲ καὶ ἰατροῖς πρὸς ἐπίσκεψιν καὶ ἐν ταῖς τῶν νοσούντων καὶ ἐν ταῖς τῶν χειρουργιῶν ἢ θεραπειῶν ἐπιβολαῖς [. . .]

62 Table created by the author from the method in Paul. Al., *Intr*. 21 (Boer 1958: 42.16–45.1).

Tab. 1: Presiding and managing planets, and hour rulers.

Day	Presides	Manages Day Hours											
		1	2	3	4	5	6	7	8	9	10	11	12
Sunday	☉	☉	♀	☿	☾	♄	♃	♂	☉	♀	☿	☾	♄
Monday	☾	☾	♄	♃	♂	☉	♀	☿	☾	♄	♃	♂	☉
Tuesday	♂	♂	☉	♀	☿	☾	♄	♃	♂	☉	♀	☿	☾
Wednesday	☿	☿	☾	♄	♃	♂	☉	♀	☿	☾	♄	♃	♂
Thursday	♃	♃	♂	☉	♀	☿	☾	♄	♃	♂	☉	♀	☿
Friday	♀	♀	☿	☾	♄	♃	♂	☉	♀	☿	☾	♄	♃
Saturday	♄	♄	♃	♂	☉	♀	☿	☾	♄	♃	♂	☉	♀
Day	**Presides**	**Manages Night Hours**											
		1	2	3	4	5	6	7	8	9	10	11	12
Sunday	☉	♃	♂	☉	♀	☿	☾	♄	♃	♂	☉	♀	☿
Monday	☾	♀	☿	☾	♄	♃	♂	☉	♀	☿	☾	♄	♃
Tuesday	♂	♄	♃	♂	☉	♀	☿	☾	♄	♃	♂	☉	♀
Wednesday	☿	☉	♀	☿	☾	♄	♃	♂	☉	♀	☿	☾	♄
Thursday	♃	☾	♄	♃	♂	☉	♀	☿	☾	♄	♃	♂	☉
Friday	♀	♂	☉	♀	☿	☾	♄	♃	♂	☉	♀	☿	☾
Saturday	♄	☿	☾	♄	♃	♂	☉	♀	☿	☾	♄	♃	♂

3.10 The Moon, Application and Separation in Decumbiture (Serapion)

Here, the synchronicity between heavenly activities and events happening during illness or confinement is shown by the timing of Moon aspects by either separation, showing past events, or application, showing the future course of events and their timing. Length of illness and quality of the patient's condition are also assessed by this method. Serapion's dates are contested,[63] but he certainly falls within the first three centuries CE (probably not BCE). He wrote on katarchic astrology, including the doctrine of presiding and managing planets, and planetary hour rulers (as in Paulus above).[64] In the following passage, he discusses planets that aspect the Moon, Ascendant and Hermes and the application and separation of the Moon to them:

63 See Denningmann 2009 and László 2022: 250–252 for two different analyses.

64 *CCAG* I: 99.1 (bottom)–100.2.

39. [Serapion] on confinements to bed and decumbitures

[1] It will be necessary to observe carefully by whom the Moon, the Ascendant and Hermes are witnessed, and from which ones the Moon has separated. [2] For the separation signifies what has already happened, but the application deliverance or complete recovery. [3] But always for the confinements and decumbitures you will find such a thing happening from afflictions of the Moon, the Ascendant or Hermes. [4] It has to do with the difference of the affliction: for as far as the difference of witnesses is concerned, it either destroys or might mitigate. [5] If the witnessing of the benefics appears more fulsome, or the Moon applies within three days to a benefic star, the confinement will not be dangerous, nor the illness; but if the witnessing of malefics happens to be more fulsome, the one in confinement or ill will die. [6] The quality of the confinement, the illness or the death will be known from the nature of the zodiacal sign where the Moon is and from which star it will separate or apply. [7] For if the Moon is in tropical signs, the event will come to an end quickly; if in double-bodied signs, it will end at a moderate pace; but if in fixed signs or bonds, it shows slowness. [8] And the same if it is separating from a star that is stationing. [9] When the Moon while in bond [with the nodes] is afflicted, the danger will be more perilous. [10] And one must take into account the one presiding and managing, and the lord of the hour just as I have described to you in the inception about this.[65]

This passage shows a method of timing using aspects (the word "witnessing", μαρτυρία, is used here for them).[66] Before a planet makes an exact aspect with another planet, it is said to apply to that aspect (especially within 3 degrees); when it moves past the aspect, it is said to separate from it. Application represents what will happen in the future, and separation what has happened in the past. So in regard to the course of the illness, the astrologer can tell which parts of the illness have already happened, and which parts are still to come. The qualities of the

65 *CCAG* I: 101.23–102.14: λθ'. Τοῦ αὐτοῦ περὶ συνοχῶν ἢ κατακλίσεων. [1] Τὴν Σελήνην καὶ τὸν ὡροσκόπον καὶ τὸν Ἑρμῆν παρατηρεῖν δεήσει ὑπὸ τίνων μαρτυροῦνται, ἀπὸ τίνος τε ἡ Σελήνη ἀπέρρευσεν. [2] ἡ γὰρ ἀπόρροια περὶ τοῦ ἤδη γενομένου σημαίνει, ἡ δὲ συναφὴ περὶ ἀπολύσεως ἢ ὁλοκληρώσεως· [3] πάντως δὲ εὑρήσει ἐπὶ τῶν συνοχῶν ἢ κατακλίσεων ἀπὸ κακώσεως τῆς Σελήνης ἢ καὶ τοῦ ὡροσκόπου ἢ καὶ τοῦ Ἑρμοῦ γινόμενον τὸ τοιοῦτον· [4] διαφορὰ δὲ κακώσεώς ἐστι· καὶ γὰρ (p.102) ἐπὶ μαρτύρων τὴν διαφορὰν ἢ ἐπιτρίβει ἢ ἡμεροῖ· [5] ἐὰν ἐπιρροπωτέρα φανῇ ἡ τῶν ἀγαθοποιῶν μαρτυρία, ἢ καὶ ἡ Σελήνη ἐν τοῖς τριταίοις συνάψῃ ἀγαθοποιῷ ἀστέρι, ἀκίνδυνος ἔσται ἡ συνοχὴ ἤτοι ἡ νόσος· ἐὰν δὲ ἡ τῶν κακοποιῶν μαρτυρία ἐπιρροπωτέρα τύχῃ εἶναι, ἀπολεῖται ὁ ἐν τῇ συνοχῇ ἤτοι ὁ νοσῶν. [6] ἡ δὲ ποιότης τῆς συνοχῆς ἢ τῆς νόσου ἤτοι ἡ φθορὰ γνωσθήσεται ἐκ τῆς φύσεως τοῦ ζῳδίου ὅπου ἡ Σελήνη ἐστὶ καὶ ἀφ' οὗ ἀπορρεύσει ἀστέρος ἢ τῆς συναφῆς. [7] ἐὰν μὲν γὰρ ἐν τροπικοῖς ζῳδίοις ᾖ ἡ Σελήνη, ταχέως τὸ συμβεβηκὸς ἐπὶ πέρας ἥξει· ἐὰν δὲ ἐν δισώμοις, μέσως ἀποβήσεται· ἐὰν δὲ ἐν τοῖς στερεοῖς ἢ συνδέσμοις, βραδυτῆτα δηλοῖ. [8] τὸ δ' αὐτὸ κἂν ἀπὸ στηρίζοντος ἀστέρος (10) ἀπορρεύει· [9] ἐπὰν δὲ ἐπὶ συνδέσμου οὔσης τῆς Σελήνης κακωθῇ ὁ σύνδεσμος, σφαλερώτερος ἔσται ὁ κίνδυνος. [10] συμπαραλαμβάνειν δὲ δεῖ καὶ τὸν πολεύοντα καὶ διέποντα, καὶ τὸν κύριον τῆς ὥρας καθὰ ἐν τῇ καταρχῇ περὶ τούτου σοι διέγραψα.

66 Traditional aspects are the conjunction (0° angular separation between planets), sextile (60°), square (90°), trine (120°) and opposition (180°).

signs the planets are in, and the nature of the planet itself, will also factor into this assessment. The nature of the Moon's zodiacal sign signals whether the affliction will be brief, moderate, or long. The Moon's bonds, as in the Strong Moon Phases (see 3.6), also produce peril.

This section has looked at some of the major practices and methods used by astrologers in decumbiture. We have examined methods for using a decumbiture by itself and combined with the birthchart, as well as using it in lieu of a non-existent birthchart. Also investigated were the Moon and its contacts with other planets, its condition both in the nativity and decumbiture, and timing via its cycle with the Sun. There were methods for assessing the quality of specific hours during the illness and using the planetary rulers of days and hours in decumbiture. Timing was also explored through the Moon's application and separation to planets in the decumbiture. An important throughpoint in all this material is the representation of the Moon as (human) body. The Moon's motion shows symptoms moving or changing in the body, and Moon phases map the body's crisis phases. The Moon's qualities and position as affected by benefic and malefic planets result in the body affected by good and bad conditions. The Moon's significations and cycles, in short, signify and synchronize with the body's response to illness and injury. Now we shall turn to timing using aspects of critical day theory. We've seen some examples of this kind of relationship in our examination of moon phases and aspects, but now the use of critical days in astrological medicine will be more fully explored and elaborated.

4 Critical Day Theory and Astrology

To briefly summarise the early history of of critical days, the Hippocratic writers introduced critical day theory as a way to pinpoint the crisis times of an illness and its prognosis. This, as Jones first pointed out and Grmek seconded and expanded, was based on the prevalence of malaria in the ancient world, with its emphasis on the timing of fevers in the course of that illness.[67] It is important to note that a "crisis" day need not necessarily be harmful or dangerous, but rather a day when a judgement[68] must be taken on the course of the illness, and a change occurs for good or ill. The structure of critical days doctrine is varied among the Hippocratic writers, and based on different multiples of numbers, like

---

67 Jones 1923, repr. 1957: lv; Grmek 1989: 277. I owe the latter reference to Langermann 2012: 226.
68 The word κρίσις comes from κρίνω, judge, decide (LSJ s.v.).

7 and 4, that can correlate with the week and the month.[69] These can easily relate to lunar cycles (though some critical day schemes are difficult to match to them). “Acute diseases come to a crisis in fourteen days”, a Hippocratic aphorism tells us, suggesting a quality of time like the full moon (i.e., opposition of the moon to the sun).[70] But other critical days, such as the eleventh or seventeenth, do not as clearly correspond to a moon phase, although they may compare to a lunar aspect.[71] Whatever their origin or rationale, such doctrine(s) were common in ancient medicine and taken up by one of its most famous practitioners, Claudius Galen (who also employed astrological methods for critical days on occasion).[72]

Ancient astrologers used what are called “climacterics”, taken from the medical critical days doctrine but generally applied just to certain years of human life.[73] However, they could also be used in the context of astrological medicine, as we shall now see.[74] In astrological medicine, a good configuration on a crisis day will improve the health of the patient.

4.1 Seventh and Ninth Day Crisis Points (Dorotheus/Critodemus)

Dorotheus provides a first view of how the doctrine of climacterics operates in terms of illness. He may have taken this from Critodemus, a late 2nd or early 1st c. BCE astrologer.[75] If this is the case, it adds to evidence of an early beginning for the use of iatromathematics by astrologers.

69 Jouanna 1999: 338–339. Other schemes look, for example, at even and odd numbers of days.

70 *Aphorisms* II.23, trans. Jones 1931, repr. 1998: 113. IV.476 Littré: Τὰ ὀξέα τῶν νουσημάτων κρίνεται ἐν τεσσαρεσκαίδεκα ἡμέρῃσιν.

71 For more on this topic, see Pennuto 2008: 76–79.

72 See the important recent study, Heilen 2018: 205–206, who investigates Galen’s formulation of the medical week based on astrological considerations.

73 Astrologers considered “climacteric” years, namely multiples of seven (7, 14, 21, 28, 35, etc.), as critical and dangerous years in human life. See, e.g., Valens, *Anth.*, V, 2. The 63rd year was especially significant, since it was the multiplication of 7 x 9. That this concept was well-known in the ancient world is clear from its mention by the Emperor Augustus, who refers to passing his sixty-third year in a letter to his grandson Gaius (mentioned in Aulus Gellius’ *Attic Nights*, 15.7): see Harlow and Laurence 2017: 115.

74 See Nutton 2013^2: 275 and Heilen 2012. Tolsa 2024: 158–175 discusses them in relation to Critodemus’s work.

75 See Tolsa 2024: 10: “late second/early first century BC.” Tolsa (2024: 171–175) analyzes the possible attribution to Critodemus.

> (From "Another view")
>
> Dorotheus also says these figures at the crisis points (κλιμακτήρων), such as the seventh and ninth days, are dangerous; for if the days, he says, are totaled from the nativity of the one who is sick up to the time of the decumbiture and are divided by 7 evenly, or are divided by 9 evenly, there will be a crisis for that nativity: in which, if he has begun to be ill, he will be dangerously ill.[76]

Here again we see an asynchronous arithmetical method applied to the decumbiture, this time in a crisis setting. Nevertheless, it shows synchrony between the Moon phase and a crisis for the patient, using, symbolically, the day numbers of the Moon phases that correspond to the climacterically dangerous numbers of 7 and 9. It is not uncommon to see this sort of symbolism applied in astrology. What Dorotheus means here is that when the Moon comes to its first square (at seven days), and then its first trine to itself (at nine days), these crisis points will indicate a dangerous situation if one adds up the number of days from the nativity to the time of the decumbiture, divides them by 7 or 9 and finds that there is no remainder. This will exacerbate the crisis (a remainder would mean a less critical time for the illness in terms of danger).

4.2 Opposing Planets Cause Death (Vettius Valens/ Critodemus)

This excerpt is the last sentence of part of a section in the *Anthologies* also based on Critodemus, in which Valens discusses length of life, and which planets will cause death based on their position opposite to a vulnerable planet. He includes a chart example illustrating the principle of crisis and death when transits to "inimical places" occur in the birthchart.[77] As a kind of afterthought for the use of this technique, he adds this last sentence:

---

76 *CCAG* I: 125.2–8 = Dor. gr. Pingree 1976: 426.3–8 ≈ Dor. arab. V, 41.47–56: (Ἄλλη σκέψις) φησὶ δὲ ὁ Δωρόθεος καὶ ταῦτα τὰ σχήματα ἐπικίνδυνα εἶναι, οἷον τά τε ἑβδομαδικὰ καὶ ἐννεαδικὰ τῶν κλιμακτήρων· εἰ γὰρ αἱ συναγόμεναι, φησίν, ἡμέραι ἀπὸ τῆς γενέσεως αὐτῆς τοῦ νοσοῦντος ἕως τῆς κατακλίσεως καὶ μεριζόμεναι παρὰ τὸν ζʹ καταλήξωσιν εἰς τὸν ζʹ ἢ μεριζόμεναι παρὰ τὸν θʹ καταλήξωσιν εἰς τὸν θʹ, κλιμακτὴρ ἔσται τῇ γενέσει ἐκείνῃ· ᾗ ἐὰν κατάρξηται νοσεῖν, ἐπικινδύνως νοσήσει.

77 This birthchart, with death transits, is dated 7 Oct 61 in Pingree 1986: xviii, no. 5; and Neugebauer and van Hoesen 1959: 82–83. In his analysis of this section, Tolsa 2024: 219, relying on the arguments of Peter 2001: 148–149, amends the date to 7 Oct 2 CE, and calculates the date of death as 27 Oct 36 CE, based on the positions of the transiting planets in Pingree.

> One must also examine the *decumbitures* in regard to the opposite [place], the [planets] that are in the inimical places and those producing the monthly, daily and hourly critical times (κλιμακτῆρας) in regard to the thirty [degrees] of the Moon, from which the opposite star is found.[78] (my emphasis)

This could thus be understood as an adaptation of a technique of natal astrology applied to a decumbiture. It is slightly unusual that techniques of natal astrology would transfer to katarchic practice, but because climaterics can be used as death indicators, Valens may have thought of applying the technique to crisis times in decumbitures as an "off label" use of a natal technique for decumbiture.

4.3 On Aspects of the Moon with Benefics and Malefics at Critical Times, and the Importance of Light (Dorotheus and Hephaestio)

Both Dorotheus and Hephaestio provide illumination on these topics. First, in yet another example from Dorotheus, we see the importance of timing by the Moon cycle itself to chart the course of an illness and its connection with benefic or malefic planets, then relating this to crisis days. These techniques complement some of the previous information we saw concerning Moon phases and relationships to planets, such as Example 3.5b (Two Suns), p. 158 and Example 3.10 (Serapion), p. 163.

> [8] And one must examine these too: [9] taking the position of the Moon in the moment of the decumbiture, see from the ephemerides after 7 days the Moon coming into its figure with itself, that is to the square; after 9 days it comes into the trine figure of the inception [i.e. decumbiture]; after 14 days, its own diameter; after 19 days it comes into the right trine; after 21 days it will come into its right square figure. [10] And so one must examine these, the 5 figures of the Moon, precisely, and to which of the stars it is about to apply after the configuration of the inception [i.e. the decumbiture]. [11] For if it applies to benefics, well-being will happen, but if to malefics, distress and harm. [12] The diseases that have their beginning in the day come to a crisis in 7 or 14 days; the ones that begin at night, in 10 or 20 days. [13] So in examining these, you may know not only the day of the well-being or distress, but also the hour; [14] for the benefics encountering the Moon in the critical times produce well-being, according to which hour they regard it by degree; but the malefics pro-

78 Valens, *Anth.*, III 6.23 (Pingree 1986: 136.11–13) = VIII 9.23 (Pingree 1986: 306.11–14): Σκοπεῖν δὲ δεῖ καὶ τὰς κατακλίσεις πρὸς τὸν ἐναντίον [τόπον] καὶ τοὺς ἐπὶ τοὺς ἐχθρους τόπους* ὄντας καὶ τοὺς μηνιαίους καὶ τοὺς ἡμερησίους καὶ ὡριαίους κλιμκτῆρας ποιοῦντας πρὸς τὴν τῆς Σελήνης τριακοντάδα, ἐξ ἧς ὁ ἐναντίος ἀστὴρ εὑρίκεται.

*VIII.9, 23 = ἐπὶ τοῖς ἐχθροῖς τόποις. Riley 2010 and Tolsa 2024: 217 have omitted translating καὶ, 'also', in the first line. But the section from which this extract comes begins with "Σκοπεῖν δὲ δεῖ", while this sentence at the end adds καὶ, suggesting an afterthought.

duce distress and pain. [15] Kronos comes to be more damaging in the illnesses beginning at night, but Ares in the day. [16] When the Moon and the Ascendant are in tropical zodiacal signs, they make the illnesses recur.[79]

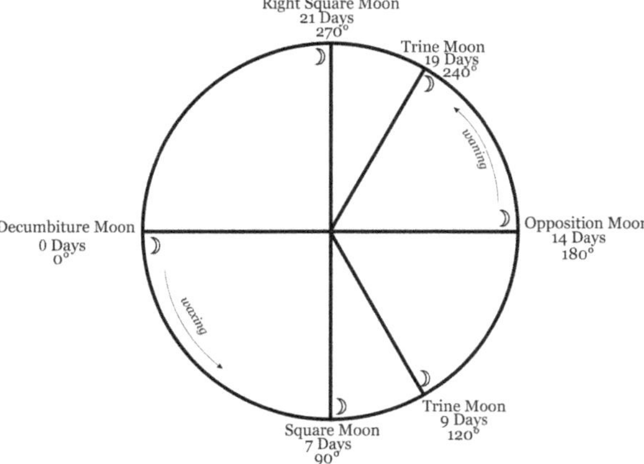

Fig. 3: The moon cycle in decumbiture.

As shown in Fig. 3, the Moon comes to square herself in about seven days, to her waxing trine in nine days, opposes herself (full moon) in 14 days, then comes to the waning trine at 19 days and the right square at 21 days. These day numbers have some similarity with those used as critical days. What this and the previous examples demonstrate is a combination of the Moon cycle and critical days in medical astrology to aid in the prognosis of an illness. In this passage Dorotheus also distinguishes between day and night decumbiture charts in terms of their

79 "Dorotheus, On Decumbitures and Illnesses" *CCAG* I: 123.9–27 = Dor. gr. Pingree 1976: 423.16–424.13; = Dor. arab.V, 41.15–18, 23–25. ≈ Hephaestio, *Apotelesmatica* III, 31.8: [8] δεῖ δὲ σκοπεῖν καὶ ταῦτα· [9] λαβὼν τὴν τῆς Σελήνης ἐποχὴν ἐν τῷ καιρῷ τῆς κατακλίσεως, βλέπε ἐκ τῶν ἐφημερίδων μετὰ ζ′ ἡμέρας τὴν Σελήνην ἐρχομένην ἐν τῷ ἑαυτῆς σχήματι, τουτέστι τῷ τετραγώνῳ· μετὰ δὲ ἡμέρας θ′ ἐν τῷ τῆς καταρχῆς ἔρχεται τριγώνῳ σχήματι· μετὰ δὲ ἡμέρας ιδ′ ἑαυτὴν διαμετρήσει δηλονότι· μετὰ δὲ ἡμέρας ιθ′ ἐν τῷ δεξιῷ τριγώνῳ ἔρχεται· μετὰ δὲ ἡμέρας κα′ ἐλεύσεται ἐν τῷ δεξιῷ τετραγώνῳ αὐτῆς σχήματι. [10] ταῦτα οὖν ἀκριβῶς δεῖ σκοπεῖν τὰ ε′ σχήματα τῆς Σελήνης, καὶ τίνι τῶν ἀστέρων μετὰ τὸ τῆς καταρχῆς σχῆμα συνάπτειν μέλλει·[11] εἰ μὲν γὰρ ἀγαθοποιοῖς συνάπτῃ, εὐφορία γίνεται, εἰ δὲ κακοποιοῖς δυσφορία καὶ βλάβη· [12] αἱ δὲ καταρχόμεναι νόσοι ἐν ἡμέρᾳ, διὰ ζ′ ἢ διὰ ιδ′ ἡμέρας κρίνονται· αἱ δὲ ἐν νυκτί, δι᾿ ἡμέρας ι′ ἢ κ′. [13] ταῦτα οὖν σκοπῶν, οὐ μόνον τὴν ἡμέραν τῆς εὐφορίας ἢ δυσφορίας προγνώσῃ, ἀλλὰ καὶ τὴν ὥραν· [14] οἱ μὲν γὰρ ἀγαθοποιοὶ ἐν ταῖς κρίσεσιν ὑπαντῶντες τὴν Σελήνην, εὐφορίαν ποιοῦσιν, καθ᾿ ἣν ὥραν μοιρικῶς αὐτὴν ἐπιθεωρήσουσιν· οἱ δὲ κακοποιοὶ δυσφορίαν καὶ ἄλγος. [15] ὁ Κρόνος βλαβερώτερος γίνεται τοῖς ἐν νυκτὶ καταρχομένοις νοσεῖν, ὁ δὲ Ἄρης τοῖς ἐν ἡμέρᾳ. [16] ἡ Σελήνη καὶ ὁ ὡροσκόπος ἐν τοῖς τροπικοῖς ζῳδίοις ὄντες, τὰς νόσους ὑποτροπιάζειν ποιοῦσιν.

timing. In those that begin at night, it takes longer for the illness to come to a crisis point, perhaps because of the slower pace of the night as opposed to day when the Sun shines and there is more activity. It seems that physical light also has a physical effect on timing.[80] In addition to distinguishing between day and night decumbiture charts, Dorotheus uses hour rulers for even more precision. The reason that Saturn is more damaging for illness beginning at night is because it is a diurnal planet according to the astrological doctrine of sect; Mars damages in the day because it is a nocturnal planet.[81] These all seem to be methods of arriving at synchronicity between a crisis happening for the patient and the exact point of the Moon cycle, even to the hour.

In regard to the importance of light where the Moon is concerned in assessing the course of an illness, we must also note a passage in Hephaestio that relates to this Dorothean example, which additionally describes timing for crisis points based on the Moon cycle:

> [7] One must look out for the decumbiture happening when the Moon is one zodiacal sign away from the concurrence [the new moon, i.e. conjunction with the Sun], that the one who has taken to bed will not stop being ill, but when she is *beginning to shine and waxing*, the illness receives an increase in intensity. [8] Such illnesses are either fatal or hard to treat, and symptoms and remissions happen according to the figurations of the Moon; for they alone are judged every three days, as she changes from sign to sign; on the fourth day they [are judged] in the sextile, on the ninth day in the triangle, on the fourteenth day in the diameter, and on the twenty-first when she comes to be in the right-hand square, as the critical times [κρίσεις] happen to come about through such figures. [9] And increases in intensity of harm occur from the destructive planets aspecting [the Moon], but remissions from benefics.[82] (my emphasis)

---

80 I thank Stephan Heilen, personal communication, 2–5 February 2025, for advice on issues of light and dark in the two passages under examination here.

81 Malefics signify more positive outcomes when their sect (diurnal or nocturnal) aligns with the chart time (day or night). 'Sect' (αἵρεσις) refers, in this context/case, to the practice of dividing the planets into two groups based on whether they are considered diurnal or nocturnal. The diurnal planets are Sun, Jupiter and Saturn; Moon, Venus and Mars are nocturnal; Mercury is diurnal ahead of the Sun, nocturnal behind it. Astrological charts also are classified as diurnal or nocturnal based on the Sun's position above or below the horizon. Astrological doctrine prefers planets to be in a chart of the same sect. For more, see Greenbaum 2016: 403–404.

82 Hephaestio, *Apotelesmatica* III, 31.7–9 (Pingree 1973: 290.24–291.3): [7] Παραφυλακτέον δ' <ὅτι> ὁπόταν κατακλίσεως γενομένης Σελήνη ἀπέχῃ ἓν ζῴδιον ἀπὸ τῆς συνόδου ὁ κατακλιθεὶς οὐ παύσεται τῆς νόσου, ἀλλ' ἀρξαμένης αὐτῆς φωτίζεσθαι καὶ αὐξανομένης ἐπίτασιν καὶ ἡ νόσος λαμβάνει. [8] αἱ τοιαῦται οὖν νόσοι ἢ θανάσιμοί εἰσιν ἢ δυσθεράπευτοι, καὶ ἐπισημασίαι δὲ γίνονται καὶ ἀνέσεις κατὰ τοὺς τῆς Σελήνης σχηματισμούς· μόνοι μὲν γὰρ τριταῖοι κρίνονται ἐκ ζῳδίου εἰς ζῴδιον μεθισταμένης αὐτῆς, οἱ δὲ τεταρταῖοι κατὰ ἑξάγωνον, ἐναταῖοι δὲ εἰς τὸ τρίγωνον, τεσσαρεσκαιδεκαταῖοι δὲ εἰς τὸ διάμετρον, μιᾶς δὲ καὶ κʹ ἐν τῷ δεξιῷ τετραγώνῳ γενομένης αὐτῆς

Here, Hephaestio also notices the effect of light; in this case, the Moon's light. The Moon gains power when visible and waxing. He emphasizes that the waxing cycle of the Moon increases the intensity of the illness. He also emphasizes the harms caused by malefics, though adding that benefics allow relief. We will see some interesting parallels for these points in Galen, Pseudo-Galen and others, to whom we shall turn now for the use of astrology in critical day doctrine.

4.4 Galen, Critical Days and Astrology

Galen's relationship with astrology has been explored before.[83] His use of astrology within critical day doctrine, from his treatise *De diebus decretoriis*, yields a well-known passage relevant to this discussion. I have explored this passage in other contexts, but it is worth repeating here because it correlates a decumbiture with the natal chart, as well as mentioning techniques previously examined in the present study.

From Galen, "On Critical Days" (*De diebus decretoriis*) (my emphasis):

> We must again take up that topic which we, having made careful observations, find always to be most true. It is what the Egyptian astronomers discovered, namely that *the moon is disposed by nature to indicate what kinds of qualities the days will have*, not only in disease, but also in health. For if it is *placed with the well-tempered planets, which they also call benefics*, it will cause the days to be good; but if *with the ill-tempered [malefic planets], they will turn out wretched*. For example, let it be, when someone is born, that the benefics are in Aries, but the malefics in Taurus; this person absolutely, whenever the moon comes to be in Aries, Cancer, Libra and Capricorn, will fare well. But whenever it occupies Taurus, one of its squares or its opposing zodiacal sign, his life at that time will be spent badly and wretchedly. And furthermore, beginnings of illnesses will be most pernicious when the moon is in Taurus, Leo, Scorpio and Aquarius, but not dangerous and delivering recovery when it is passing through Aries, Cancer, Libra and Capricorn. And in regard to the great *alterations which* we said *occur at the squares and oppositions every seven days*, in the destructive illnesses they [the alterations] are also destructive, but again, in good circumstances, good outcomes necessarily occur.[84]

ὡς συμβαίνειν διὰ (p. 291) τοσούτων σχημάτων τὰς κρίσεις γίνεσθαι. [9] καὶ τῶν μὲν φθοροποιῶν ἐπιθεωρούντων ἐπιτάσεις γίνονται τοῦ κακοῦ, τῶν δὲ ἀγαθοποιῶν ἀνέσεις.

83 E.g., Toomer 1985, Nutton 2008; Cooper 2011b, Greenbaum 2015, Heilen 2018, Greenbaum 2020, Greenbaum 2022.

84 Galen, *De diebus decretoriis* III, 6 (IX: 911.14–912.16 K.): [1] Ἐκεῖνο δ' αὖθις ἀναληπτέον, ὅπερ καὶ ἡμεῖς παραφυλάξαντες ἀληθέστατον εὕρομεν ἀεὶ τὸ πρὸς τῶν Αἰγυπτίων ἀστρονόμων εὑρημένον, ὡς ἡ σελήνη τὰς ἡμέρας ὁποῖαί τινες ἔσονται δηλοῦν πέφυκεν οὐ τοῖς νοσοῦσι μόνον, ἀλλὰ καὶ τοῖς ὑγιαίνουσιν. [2] εἰ μὲν γὰρ πρὸς τοὺς εὐκράτους (912) ἵσταιτο τῶν πλανητῶν, οὓς δὴ καὶ ἀγαθοποιοὺς ὀνομάζουσιν, ἀγαθὰς ἀπεργάζεσθαι τὰς ἡμέρας· εἰ δὲ πρὸς τοὺς δυσκράτους, ἀνιαράς.

Methods of lucky and unlucky days are attested from the New Kingdom in Egypt onwards.[85] That these could be connected to katarchic astrology is not that far-fetched.[86] As we have seen, the Moon is arguably *the* major player in charting an illness; and furthermore, astrology was well-established in an Egyptian milieu, certainly, at least, from the Ptolemaic period.[87] So Galen's reference to Egyptian astronomers—the words *astronomia* and *astrologia* were interchangeable in antiquity—is quite reasonable. Next, he imagines a hypothetical situation in which someone is born with the benefics in Aries and malefics in Taurus. The words he uses to describe them, εὔκρατος and δύσκρατος, are not those typically used by astrologers, but he certainly knows what terms the astrologers use because he mentions those, too—ἀγαθοποιός and κακοποιός. A person with such a configuration will generally have good days when the Moon is in Aries or any of the cardinal signs, but unfortunate ones when it is in Taurus or other fixed signs. Thus the Moon's position in a fortunate or unfortunate sign synchronizes with a good or bad day for the person.

Furthermore, we see in this passage exactly what Dorotheus, and Hephaestio, have said: that benefics aid the Moon, and thus the patient, at the crisis day, while malefics harm her. Because of the arrangement Galen describes, when such a person "begins" an illness—a reference to a decumbiture?—those benefics and malefics will supply their qualities to the Moon at the beginning and, as the illness progresses, through the Moon's squares and oppositions to herself either in signs that are improving or those that are worsening the ailment. We have already seen the Moon's relationships to other planets and herself in the passages on the Two Suns (Example 3.5) from Dorotheus, and the Moon's aspects with planets in Serapion (Example 3.10), as well as the recently discussed examples from Dorotheus and Hephaestio. So Galen's observations have a correlation in medical astrological practice.[88]

---

[3] ἔστω γὰρ ἀποκυϊσκομένου τινὸς ἐν μὲν τῷ κριῷ τοὺς ἀγαθοποιοὺς, ἐν δὲ τῷ ταύρῳ τοὺς κακοποιοὺς εἶναι, πάντως οὗτος ὁ ἄνθρωπος, ἐπειδὰν μὲν ἐν κριῷ καὶ καρκίνῳ καὶ ζυγῷ καὶ αἰγοκέρωτι γένηται ἡ σελήνη, καλῶς ἀπαλλάσσει. [4] ἐπειδὰν δ' ἤτοι τὸν ταῦρον αὐτὸν, ἢ τι τῶν τετραγώνων, ἢ τὸ διάμετρον αὐτοῦ ζώδιον ἐπέχῃ, κακῶς τηνικαῦτα καὶ ἀνιαρῶς διάγει. [5] καὶ δὴ καὶ νοσημάτων ἀρχαὶ τῷδε κάκισται μὲν ἐν ταύρῳ καὶ λέοντι καὶ σκορπίῳ καὶ ὑδροχόῳ τῆς σελήνης οὔσης, ἀκίνδυνον δὲ καὶ σωτήριον τὸν κριὸν καὶ τὸν καρκίνον καὶ τὸν ζυγὸν καὶ τὸν αἰγόκερων διερχομένης, [6] καὶ τὰς ἀλλοιώσεις τὰς μεγάλαςἂς ἐν τοῖς τετραγώνοις τε καὶ διαμέτροις ἔφαμενγίγνεσθαι καθ' ἑβδομάδα, ἐν μὲν τοῖς ὀλεθρίοις νοσήμασιν ὀλεθρίας καὶ αὐτὰς, ἐν δ' αὖ τοῖς περιεστηκόσιν ἀγαθὰς ἀνάγκη γίνεσθαι.

85 See Theis 2016, Leitz 1994.

86 For the specifics, see Greenbaum 2026: 10.

87 See Quack 2018.

88 Given when Galen lived (129–ca. 200 CE), some knowledge of Dorotheus seems possible, as well as earlier or contemporary astrological authors.

Regarding the waxing phases of the Moon, Galen further provides a parallel to Hephaestio's statement on this topic. In Book III of *On Critical Days*, Galen gives a new method for determining the length of the medical week.[89] The method itself is not germane here, but a remark Galen makes about the Moon's visibility is: "So, since the time the Moon is *visible and (thus astrologically) efficacious* is twenty-six days and a half [. . .]"[90] He ties the efficacy of the Moon to its visibility, and therefore its light, as a means of astrological effect on the course of illness. In enhancing precision of the Moon's visibility, Galen enhances the doctor's ability to arrive at synchrony between the visible Moon and its effect on the patient.

In short, in the genuine Galen we find examples of astrological doctrines that can be applied to his own system of medical practice. And from these we can see indications of why the Pseudo-Galenic treatise *Prognostica de decubitu* was considered to be a genuine Galenic work. Other pseudepigraphical texts, the *Iatromathematika* ascribed to "Hermes", and an *Epitome* of Pancharius, have similarities with the *Prognostica* in dealing with astrological medicine, decumbiture and methods of critical days.

4.5 The *Iatromathematica* ("Hermes") and *Prognostica de decubitu* (Pseudo-Galen)

These two texts (along with the Pancharius *Epitome*) have similarities and overlaps that have been previously explored.[91] Here, two examples will demonstrate some of their affinities with practices in iatromathematical material from ancient astrologers that show synchronistic conditions. The first, from the *Iatromathematica* of "Hermes", correlates the Moon's waxing and waning to the illness, and shows a noticeable similarity of content to the passages we have seen from Dorotheus and Hephaestio:

> **(1) From *The Iatromathematica of Hermes to Ammon the Egyptian***
> If the Moon in the decumbiture happens to be configured with both benefics and malefics, the suffering will be persistent and periodic, but the ill person will recover—though unevenly. But one must keep these things in mind, that as the Moon waxes, so does the illness. When she begins to wane the illness will begin to progress toward the better. And it is clear

89 See Heilen 2018.

90 III, 9 (IX: 932.5–7 K.): ἐπεὶ τοίνυν (5) ὁ μὲν τῆς φάσεώς ἐστι τῆς ἐναργοῦς καὶ δραστηρίου χρόνος εἴκοσιν ἓξ ἡμερῶν καὶ ἡμισείας [. . .], trans. Heilen 2018: 211 (my emphasis).

91 Heeg 1911; Cumont 1935; Wilson and George 2006; Heilen 2015: vol. 2, 1305–1307; Rovati 2018: 25–34.

> that if she is waxing, the illness as well will increase up to the time when she looses the bond [that is, goes past a conjunction, waxing square or opposition with the Sun or lunar node]. In this way things will turn out for the better. Let such an examination be made for every inception that has to do with the body.[92]

The second passage appears both in the *Prognostica* and the *Iatromathematica*. Each text details all of the zodiacal signs that the Moon can be in, giving possible aspects it can make, especially to malefic and benefic planets. It further suggests what illnesses will arise in a particular sign, and the critical times, particularly the squares and oppositions (first quarter, full moon and last quarter) that may occur and their effects. Thus they are distilling doctrines of medical astrology into a simplified form. This example, for the Moon in Leo, includes outcomes when it encounters Mars, some crisis times and outcomes linked to the phases of the Moon in that zodiacal sign. The texts in Rovati's edition are printed side by side and are almost identical.

> **(2) Pseudo-Galen, *Prognostica*, Moon in Leo = *Iatromathematica*, Moon in Leo**
> If someone lies down when the Moon is in Leo, and Mars conjoins, opposes or squares, the origin of the illness will be from an excess of blood. And there will be fevers with diarrhoea, weak pulse, fainting spells, loss of appetite and weight, lethargy and enervation of the whole body, and a heart condition. For these symptoms, things that are astringent and cooling will be suitable. If no benefic regards the Moon, he will die around the 9th day. When benefics are regarding the Moon, the one in peril from the opposition will be saved.[93]

Note that the lack of a benefic aspecting the Moon will result in the death of the person around day 9, which is the waxing trine of the Moon. However, if benefics do aspect her, the sick person, although in a perilous condition from the Moon's opposition to herself at the full moon, will recover.

92 Ἑρμοῦ τοῦ Τρισμεγίστου Ἰατρομαθηματικὰ πρὸς Ἄμμωνα Αἰγύπτιον, I, 7 (Rovati 2018: 86): ἐὰν δὲ ἡ Σελήνη τύχῃ ἐπὶ τῇ κατακλίσει καὶ αγαθοποιοῖς καὶ κακοποιοῖς / σχηματιζομένη, περιστήσεται τὰ πάθη καὶ ἔσται περιοδικά, ἀνωμαλίσας δὲ ὁ / νοσῶν σωθήσεται. δεῖ δὲ ἐπὶ τούτων νοεῖν, ὅτι ἐφ' ὅσον ἡ Σελήνη προστίθησι τοῖς / ἀριθμοῖς, ἐπὶ τοσοῦτον ἡ νόσος ἐπαύξεται. ὅταν δὲ ἄρξηται ἀφαιρεῖσθαι τοῖς / [5] ἀριθμοῖς, ἐπὶ τὸ βελτίον ἄρξεται καὶ ἡ νόσος προϊέναι καὶ φανερόν, ὡς ἐὰν τοῖς / ἀριθμοίς προστιθῇ, ἡ νόσος αὐξηθήσεται, ἕστ' ἂν σύνδεσμον λύσῃ. οὕτω γὰρ ἐπὶ / τὸ κρεῖττον τραπήσεται. ἡ δὲ τοιαύτη ἐπίσκεψις καὶ ἐπὶ πάσης ἔστω σωματικῆς / καταρχῆς.

93 Rovati 2018: 102, PD 5B 1–17 (sim. *Iatromathematica* II5B, 102.1–16) ≈ XIX: 549.6–15 K.: [1] ἐὰν δὲ τῆς Σελήνης οὔσης ἐν Λέοντι κατακλιθῇ τις, Πυρόεντος συνόντος ἢ διαμετροῦντος ἢ τετραγονίζοντος, ἔσται ἡ καταρχὴ τῆς νόσου, ἀπὸ πλήθους αἵματος. [2] καὶ ἔσονται πυρετοὶ ῥοώδεις καὶ σφυγμοὶ ἄτονοι καὶ ἐνδεδυκότες καὶ λειποθυμίαι καὶ ἀνορεξίαι καὶ βάρος καὶ καταφορὰ καὶ πάρεσις παντὸς τοῦ σώματος καὶ καρδιακὴ διάθεσις. [3] τούτοις οὖν ἁρμόσει πάντα τὰ στεγνοῦντα καὶ ψύχοντα. [4] ἐὰν οὖν μηδεὶς ἀγαθοποιὸς ἐπιθεωρῇ τὴν Σελήνην, μέχρι τῆς θ' <ἡμέρας> τελευτήσει. [5] ἀγαθοποιῶν δὲ ἐπιθεωρούντων τὴν Σελήνην, ἀπὸ τῆς διαμέτρου κινδυνεύσας σωθήσεται.

5 Nachleben

The importance of these practices is not limited to antiquity, but persists through the early modern period (whose practitioners continued to draw on earlier doctrines). Astrology was taught in European universities until the end of the 17th century,[94] and its use was often connected to the practice of medicine. Astrological medicine as used by doctors (including the methods examined here) was especially popular in the 16th and 17th centuries. A number of the astrological doctrines we have examined here found their way into the medieval, Renaissance, and early modern periods, in Greek, Arabic and Latin.[95] Later compilations of iatromathematical texts such as we saw in the excerpts from Dorotheus, the popularity of the *Prognostica de decubitu* and the *Iatromathematica*, and the teaching of astrology in the medical curricula of European universities into the early modern period, all combined to keep iatromathematics going.

Outside the strictly medical environment, an extremely popular astrological text even up to the 17th century was the Pseudo-Ptolemaic *Centiloquium*, a list of 100 aphorisms first appearing in the tenth century.[96] Versions are extant in Greek, Arabic, Latin and English.[97] The Latin translators included luminaries like Adelard of Bath and Plato of Tivoli. There also exist glosses on the text associated with Gerard of Cremona and others. At least twelve of the *verba* (aphorisms) are iatromathematical in nature,[98] and some can be related to ancient astro-medical texts like Dorotheus. For example, *Verbum* 57 talks about afflictions to the seventh house requiring a change of doctor, but the commentary (*expositio*) mentions what appears in Dorotheus, namely the two versions of interpreting decumbiture with the Ascendant representing either the ill person or doctor.[99] *Verbum* 42 says

94 See Vermij and Hirai 2017; Rutkin 2018.

95 Islamicate astrologers, such as Sahl ibn Bishr and Abū Maᶜshar, whose works were later translated into Latin, significantly advanced knowledge of these doctrines.

96 Emanuele Rovati, whose PhD thesis is "The Early Western Reception of Pseudo-Ptolemy's Centiloquium and Ahmad ibn Yusuf's Commentary", states that "they rank second in the list of the most widespread Latin treatises on astrology"; See https://www.iaka.uzh.ch/de/klph/research/mlat/dissertationes/er.html (last accessed on February 8, 2026), citing information in Juste 2016: 177.

97 For the English translation, see Coley 1676: 315–328.

98 I thank Rovati for alerting me to these examples.

99 *Verbum* 57 (glosses in italics): "Cum fuerit septimum et eius dominus impediti in egris, remove medicum ab egro *in alio: in egro permuta medicum eius.* Expositio. Ascendens et eius dominus secundum astrologos significant esse egroti, septimum vero et eius dominus medicum eius *hoc est contrarium ei quod dictum est in Çaele, quoniam in eo ascendens datur medico et decimum infirmo et septimum infirmitati et quartum medicine.* Qui cum infortunati fuerint, significant er-

that if the Moon is in the same sign in the decumbiture as a malefic in the natal chart, or squaring or opposing it, the illness will be difficult; its commentary refers to Galen saying the same thing in the second book of *On Critical Days*.[100]

Within a medical framework, techniques on decumbiture and critical days were used by medical practitioners like Girolamo Cardano, Thomas Bodier and Nicholas Culpeper.[101] By the sixteenth century, the use of decumbiture had matured to a fine art that continued well into the seventeenth century.

6 Conclusion

This chapter has explored concepts of time, timing, synchrony and synchronicity as used in in ancient medical astrology. Astrology is inherently concerned with time, and this chapter has investigated practices in medical astrology that show how iatromathematical methods use time, and timing, to reflect synchrony and synchronicity between heavenly events and events on earth. The practices of decumbiture and critical days were chosen to exemplify these topics.

Decumbiture, casting a chart for the time a person falls ill or is injured, is a practice within the katarchic branch of astrology, and this investigation began by explaining its position within this branch. Katarchic astrology is concerned with the moments of events, and the timing of those events, using two different kinds of time, *chronos* and *kairos*. We discussed the uses of *chronos* and *kairos* in ka-

rorem medici et turbationem eius." "When the seventh [house] and its lord are impeded in sick people, remove the doctor from the sick one; change his doctor to another." Explanation: "According to the astrologers, the Ascendant and its lord signify the state of the sick one, the seventh and its lord, his doctor; this is contrary to what was said in Sahl [Sahl b. Bishr, *De interrogationibus*, ch. 6], since in it the Ascendant is given to the doctor, the tenth to the sick one, the seventh to the sickness and the fourth to the medicine. When these have malefics, they signify the doctor's error and his confusion." My thanks to Rovati for sharing this material from his PhD research.

100 *Verbum* 42: "In egritudinibus si fuerit Luna in signo in quo fuit infortuna hora nativitatis eius vel in quarto vel in opposito, erit egritudo difficilis [. . .]" "In illnesses if the Moon is in a sign in which there was a malefic at the time of his nativity or in square or opposition, the illness will be difficult [. . .]" "Expositio: Iam patefecit nobis Galienus hoc in tractatu secundo de libro Dierum creticorum [. . .]" "Now Galen disclosed this to us in the second tractate of the book On Critical Days [. . .]"

101 For Cardano, see Grafton and Siraisi 2006 (citing Magini 1607: 82–83); for Cardano and Bodier, Cooper 2013. For Culpeper, see Culpeper 1651, repr. 1655, 1658. This is his *Astrological Judgment of Diseases from the Decumbiture of the Sick*, so popular that it went into three editions. Culpeper claimed to use methods from Hippocrates and Galen.

tarchē. Katarchic astrology can also operate within either a synchronous mode, in which a chart is cast for a physical time and place linked directly to an action; or an asynchronous mode, where the chart is cast for a time that has no physical connection to the occasion or topic (such as asking a question and using that moment as the time to cast the chart). Decumbiture contains both of these modes, and its practice includes both *chronos* and *kairos*. The time of the decumbiture may be based on the beginning of fever, or for when the person felt ill and had to lie down. Thus it can be valid in both synchronous and asynchronous modes, but in either case it must be the proper time for showing synchrony between the illness and the astrological positions.

The next sections focused on examples from ancient astrologers writing on decumbiture and critical days. These varying practices demonstrated how iatromathematicians used the time of *chronos* and the timing of *kairos* to assess a patient's medical condition and the course of the illness, and to make an accurate prognosis. Their aim was to synchronize the patterns in the heavens during the time of the illness with the parameters of the illness for that patient—all with the goal of providing the best possible therapy.

Many of these examples used the Moon, the luminary most important for timing because of the speed of its movement through the zodiac in each lunar cycle. In the decumbiture the Moon's position both in the zodiac and as placed in the decumbiture chart, as well as its cycle with the Sun, gave important timing information. Timing through critical days in astrology, as also used by Galen (who was familiar with astrological practice), showed synchrony between these days and the lunar cycle. By using decumbiture and the doctrine of critical days, astrologers were able to create a system of astrological medicine that demonstrated synchronicity between the components of an illness or injury and the timing of events within it, and the prognosis for predicting an outcome.

Astrology's very basis and reason for existence is founded on the connection between earthly and heavenly events, and synchronicity between those realms is a critical part of its practice. Central to this foundation is the microcosm/macrocosm analogy. Astrology is also a form of divination that bases its practice on a highly-developed rational knowledge system (it is called an *epistēmē*), using both metaphysics and physics, as well as philosophical concepts from Platonism, Aristotle and the Stoics. It is considered, like medicine, as a stochastic art, not an exact science. It also aims to address the random event, or the chance occurrence, that may affect timing and synchrony between humans and the superlunary world. It allows for *kairos* as well as *chronos*, as we have seen in this chapter.

Ancient medicine also relies on synchronicity in its practice. It finds it not only in earthly conditions between living beings and their environment but, like astrology, in correlations with the cosmos and the relationship between microcosm and macrocosm. This cosmic connection was long acknowledged in Hippocratic medicine by the statement that 'If someone should suppose that these things [celestial phenomena] only belong to meteorology, he might change his mind if he comes to understand that astronomy contributes not a small, but a very great part, to medicine' (astrology being included within the term *astronomia*).[102]

We have seen that medical astrology is concerned with diagnosis, prognosis and therapy, just as medicine is, and has a robust tradition to support it. Iatromathematics is thus perfectly positioned to attain the medical goal for discovering proper timing for accurate prognosis and therapy, through its ability to demonstrate both synchrony and synchronicity between the events that occur when someone becomes sick or injured, and the heavenly positions and cycles of celestial bodies. In its history, we see iatromathematical texts incorporating the work of doctors such as Galen, and Galen using astrological concepts in his work on the medical week in Book 3 of *On Critical Days*.[103] Astrological medicine thus demonstrates its worth in the practice of ancient medicine.

Abbreviations

CCAG	*Catalogus Codicum Astrologorum Graecorum*
Dor. gr.	Pingree, D. (ed./trans.) *Dorothei Sidonii* Carmen Astrologicum
Dor. arab.	Pingree, D. (ed./trans.) *Dorothei Sidonii* Carmen Astrologicum
Heph. *Apotel.*	Pingree, D. (ed.) *Hephaestionis thebani* apotelesmaticorum *libri tres*
LSJ	Liddell, Scott, Jones, *Greek-English Lexicon*, 9th edition
Paul. Al. *Intr.*	Boer, E. (ed.) *Pauli Alexandrini* Elementa Apotelesmatica
Ptol. *Tetr.*	Robbins, F. E. (trans.) *Ptolemy* Tetrabiblos; also Hübner, W. (ed.) *Claudii Ptolemaei* Ἀποτελεσματικά
Valens, *Anth.*	Pingree, D. (ed.) *Vettii Valentis Antiocheni* Anthologiarum *libri novem*

Bibliography

Manuscripts

(L) Laurentianus Pluteus, 28.34. 11th century Florence: Bibliotheca Medicea Laurenziana.
(L') Laurentianus Pluteus, 28.13. 14th century Florence: Bibliotheca Medicea Laurenziana.

102 Hipp., *De aere, aquis, locis* 2.15–18, in II.14 Littré; Diller 1999:26.18–20.
103 Heilen 2018: 205.

Primary Sources

Boer, E. (ed.) *Pauli Alexandrini* Elementa Apotelesmatica. Leipzig: B. G. Teubner, 1958.

Burnett, C. and D. Pingree (eds.) *The* Liber Aristotilis *of Hugo of Santalla*. London: The Warburg Institute, 1997.

Clarke, E. C., J. M. Dillon and J. P. Hershbell (ed./trans./comm.) *Iamblichus.* On The Mysteries. Atlanta: Society of Biblical Literature, 2003.

Coley, H. *Clavis Astrologiae Elimata or a Key to the whole Art of Astrology*. London: B. Tooke and T. Sawbridge, 1676.

Cooper, G. M. (ed./trans./comm.) *Galen*, De diebus decretoriis, *from Greek into Arabic. A Critical Edition, with Translation and Commentary, of Ḥunayn ibn Isḥāq, Kitāb ayyām al-buḥrān*. Farnham, Surrey/ Burlington, VT: Ashgate, 2011a.

Culpeper, N. *Semeiotica Urania. Or an Astrological Judgement of Diseases from the Decumbiture of the Sick*. London: Nathaniel Brooks, 1651.

Busse, A. (ed.) *Davidis* prolegomena *et in Porphyrii* Isagogen *commentarium*. (CAG 18.2) Berlin: G. Reimer, 1904.

Diels, H. and W. Kranz (eds.) *Die Fragmente der Vorsokratiker: Griechisch und Deutsch*. Vol. 2. Berlin: Weidmann, 1966[6].

Diller, H. (ed./trans.) *Corpus Medicorum Graecorum*, Vol. I 1,2: Hippocratis de aere, acquis, locis. Berlin: Akademie Verlag, 1999.

Gramaglia, E. J. (trans.) and B. N. Dykes (ed.) *Astrological Works of Theophilus of Edessa*. Minneapolis, MN: Cazimi Press, 2017.

Greenbaum, D. G. (trans.) *Late Classical Astrology: Paulus Alexandrinus and Olympiodorus with the Scholia from Later Commentators*. Reston, VA: ARHAT, 2001.

Heilen, S. (ed./trans./comm.) Hadriani genitura. *Die astrologischen Fragmente des Antigonos von Nikaia. Edition, Übersetzung und Kommentar*. 2 vols. Berlin/Boston: De Gruyter, 2015.

Hübner, W. (ed.) *Claudii Ptolemaei Opera quae exstant omnia* Vol. III, 1: Ἀποτελεσματικά. Stuttgart/ Leipzig: B. G. Teubner, 1998.

Jones, W. H. S. (trans.) *Hippocrates.* Ancient Medicine. Airs, Waters, Places. Epidemics 1 *and* 3. The Oath. Precepts. Nutriment. Cambridge, MA: Harvard University Press, 1923.

Jones, W. H. S. (trans.) Hippocrates, Heracleitus. *Nature of Man. Regimen in Health. Humours. Aphorisms. Regimen 1–3. Dreams. Heracleitus. On the Universe*. Cambridge, MA: Harvard University Press, 1931.

Jouanna, J. *Hippocrates*. Translated by M. B. DeBevoise. Baltimore, MD: The Johns Hopkins University Press, 1999.

Kroll, W. *Catalogus Codicum Astrologorum Graecorum*, Vol. II. Codices Venetos. Brussels: Henri Lamertin, 1900.

Littré, E. (ed./trans.) *Oeuvres complètes d'Hippocrate*. Paris: J. B. Baillière, 1839–1861.

Magini, G. A. *De astrologica ratione ac usu dierum criticorum seu decretoriorum*. Venice: printed by Bartholomaeus Rodellam, heir of Damianus Zenarius, 1607.

Morton Braund, S. (ed./trans.) Juvenal, Persius. *Juvenal and Persius*. Cambridge, MA: Harvard University Press, 2004.

Neugebauer, O. and H. B. van Hoesen. *Greek Horoscopes*. Philadelphia, PA: The American Philosophical Society, 1959.

Olivieri, A. (ed.) *Catalogus Codicum Astrologorum Graecorum*, Vol. I. Codices Florentinos. Brussels: Henri Lamertin, 1898.

Peter, H. "Kritodem. Testimonien- und Fragmentsammlung" Licentiate thesis, Universität Zürich, 2001.
Pingree, D. (ed.) *Hephaestionis thebani* apotelesmaticorum *libri tres*. 2 vols. Leipzig: B. G. Teubner, 1973.
Pingree, D. (ed./trans.) *Dorothei Sidonii* Carmen Astrologicum*: Interpretationem Arabicam in linguam Anglicam versam una cum Dorothei fragmentis et Graecis et Latinis*. Leipzig: B. G. Teubner, 1976.
Pingree, D. (ed.) *Vettii Valenti Antiocheni* Anthologiarum *libri novem*. Leipzig: B. G. Teubner, 1986.
Riess, E. (ed.) *Nechepsonis et Petosiridis Fragmenta Magica*. *Philologus*, Suppl. 6.1. Göttingen: Diederich, 1892.
Riley, M. (trans.) *Vettius Valens*, Anthologies, 2010. https://www.csus.edu/indiv/r/rileymt/Vettius%20Valens%20entire.pdf (last accessed on December 18, 2025).
Robbins, F. E. (trans.) *Ptolemy*, Tetrabiblos. Cambridge, MA: Harvard University Press, 1940.
Rovati, E. „Die «Iatromathematika» des Hermes Trismegistos: Einleitung, Text, Übersetzung" *Technai* 9, 2018: 9–132.
Stegemann, V. (ed./trans./comm.) *Die Fragmente des Dorotheos von Sidon*, Lieferung IV. Unpublished.
Tolsa, C. (ed./trans./comm.) *The Orphic Astrologer Critodemus: Fragments with Annotated Translation and Commentary*. Untersuchungen zur antiken Literatur und Geschichte 155. Berlin/Boston: De Gruyter, 2024.
Watson, L. and P. Watson (eds.) *Juvenal*. Satire 6. Cambridge: Cambridge University Press, 2014.

Secondary Literature

Allen, J. "Failure and Expertise in the Ancient Conception of an Art". In *Scientific Failure*, ed. T. Horowitz and A. I. Janis. Lanham, MD: Rowman and Littlefield, 1994: 81–108.
Addey, C. *Divination and Theurgy in Neoplatonism: Oracles of the Gods*. Farnham, Surrey/Burlington, VT: Ashgate, 2014.
Addey, C. "Divination and the *kairos* in Ancient Greek Philosophy and Culture". In *Divination and Knowledge in Greco-Roman Antiquity*, ed. C. Addey. London/New York: Routledge, 2022: 138–173.
Cooper, G. M. "Galen and Astrology: A Mésalliance?" *Early Science and Medicine* 16.2, 2011b: 120–146.
Cooper, G. M. "Approaches to the Critical Days in Late Medieval and Renaissance Thinkers". *Early Science and Medicine* 18.6, 2013: 536–565.
Cornelius, G. *The Moment of Astrology: Origins in Divination*. Bournemouth: The Wessex Astrologer, 2003[2].
Cornelius, G. "The Unique Case of Interpretation: Explorations in the Epistemology of Astrology". In *Seeing with Different Eyes: Essays in Astrology and Divination*, ed. P. Curry and A. Voss. Newcastle: Cambridge Scholars Publishing, 2007: 227–254.
Cumont, F. "Les 'Prognostica de decubitu' attribués à Galien". *Bulletin de l'Institut historique belge de Rome* 15, 1935: 119–131.
Curry, P. "Truth, the Body and Divinatory Astrology". Conference Paper for *Astrology and the Body, 1100–1800*. Cambridge University, 8–9 September 2006.
Denningmann, S. „Die Datierung des Astrologen Serapion". *MHNH: Revista Internacional de Investigación sobre Magia y Astrología Antiguas* 9, 2009: 159–174.
Gourevitch, D. *Le triangle hippocratique dans le monde gréco-romain: le malade, la maladie et son médecin*. Rome: École française de Rome, 1984.

Grafton, A. and N. Siraisi. "Between the Election and My Hopes: Girolamo Cardano and Medical Astrology". In *Secrets of Nature: Astrology and Alchemy in Early Modern Europe*, ed. W. R. Newman and A. Grafton. Cambridge, MA/London: MIT Press, 2006: 69–131.

Greenbaum, D. G. "Arrows, Aiming and Divination: Astrology as a Stochastic Art". In *Divination: Perspectives for a New Millennium*, ed. P. Curry. Farnham, Surrey: Ashgate, 2010: 179–209.

Greenbaum, D. G. "Astronomy, Astrology and Medicine". In *Handbook of Archaeoastronomy and Ethnoastronomy*, ed. C. L. N. Ruggles. New York/Heidelberg/Dordrecht/London: Springer Reference, 2015: 117–132.

Greenbaum, D. G. *The Daimon in Hellenistic Astrology: Origins and Influence*. Leiden/Boston: Brill, 2016.

Greenbaum, D. G. "Hellenistic Astronomy in Medicine". In *Hellenistic Astronomy: The Science in Its Contexts*, ed. A. C. Bowen and F. Rochberg. Leiden/Boston: Brill, 2020: 350–380.

Greenbaum, D. G. "Divination and Decumbiture: Katarchic Astrology and Greek Medicine". In *Divination and Knowledge in Greco-Roman Antiquity*, ed. C. Addey. London/New York: Routledge, 2022: 109–137.

Greenbaum, D. G. "The Origins of Questions in Astrology." In *Astrologers at Work: Essays in Honour of Helena Avelar*, edited by Luís Campos Ribeiro and Charles Burnett, Leiden/Boston: Brill, 2026: 1–58.

Greenbaum, D. G. "Modern Western Astrology, Prediction and Divination: An Autoethnography". In *Horoscopy Across Civilizations*, ed. S. Heilen. In press.

Greenbaum, D. and A. Jones. "P.Berl. 9825: An elaborate horoscope for 319 CE and its significance for Greek astronomical and astrological practice". *ISAW (Institute for the Study of the Ancient World) Papers* 12, 2017: http://dlib.nyu.edu/awdl/isaw/isaw-papers/12 (last accessed on December 18, 2025).

Grmek, M. D. *Diseases in the Ancient Greek World*. Translated by M. Muellner and L. Muellner. Baltimore/London: The Johns Hopkins University Press, 1989.

Harlow, M. and R. Laurence. "Augustus *Senex*: Old Age and the Remaking of the Principate". *Greece & Rome* 64.2, 2017: 115–131.

Heeg, J. „Über ein angebliches Diokleszitat". *Sitzungsberichte der Königlich Preussischen Akademie der Wissenschaften* 47, 1911: 991–1007.

Heilen, S. 2011 "Some metrical fragments from Nechepsos and Petosiris". In *La poésie astrologique dans l'Antiquité*, edited by Isabelle Boehm and Wolfgang Hübner, Paris: De Boccard, 2011: 23–29

Heilen, S. "The Doctrine of the 3rd, 7th and 40th Days of the Moon in Ancient Astrology". *MHNH: Revista Internacional de Investigación sobre Magia y Astrología Antiguas* 12, 2012: 179–198.

Heilen, S. "Galen's Computation of Medical Weeks: Textual Emendations, Interpretation History, Rhetorical and Mathematical Examination". *SCIAMVS* 10, 2018: 201–279.

Heilen, S. "Short Time in Greco-Roman Astrology". In *Down to the Hour: Short Time in the Ancient Mediterranean and Near East*, ed. K. J. Miller and S. Symons. Leiden/Boston: Brill, 2019: 239–270.

Hübner, W. *Raum, Zeit und soziales Rollenspiel der vier Kardinalpunkte in der antiken Katarchenhoroskopie*. Munich/Leipzig: K. G. Saur Verlag, 2003.

Hübner, W. *Körper und Kosmos. Untersuchungen zur Ikonographie der zodiakalen Melothesie*. Wiesbaden: Harrassowitz Verlag, 2013.

Jouanna, J. *Hippocrates*. Translated by M. B. DeBevoise. Baltimore/London: The Johns Hopkins University Press, 1999.

Juste, D. "The Impact of Arabic Sources on European Astrology: Some Facts and Numbers". In *Micrologus* 24, *The Impact of Arabic Sciences in Europe and Asia*, edited by A. Paravicini-Bagliani. Florence: SISMEL edizioni del Galluzzo, 2016: 173–194.

Komorowska, J. "Astrology, Ptolemy and *technai stochastikai*". *MHNH: Revista Internacional de Investigación sobre Magia y Astrología Antiguas* 9, 2009: 129–140.

Langermann, Y. T. "Critical Notes on a Study of Galen's On Critical Days in Arabic or A Study in Need of Critical Repairs". *Aestimatio* 9, 2012: 220–240.

László, L. "Julianus of Laodicea and his Astrological Fragments". *Mnemosyne* 2020: 1–20, https://doi.org/10.1163/1568525X-BJA10051.

László, L. "The Inceptions of the Emperor Zeno's Anonymous Astrologer". Doct. Diss., Eötvös Loránd University, 2022.

Leitz, C. *Tagewählerei. Das Buch ḥ3t nḥḥ pḥ.wy ḏt und verwandte Texte, Part 1*. Ägyptologische Abhandlungen 55. Wiesbaden: Harrassowitz, 1994.

Liddell, H. G., R. Scott and H. S. Jones. *A Greek-English Lexicon*. Oxford: Clarendon Press, 1996[9].

Mudry, P. "Éthique et médecine à Rome: La préface de Scribonius Largus ou l'affirmation d'une singularité". In *Médecine et morale dans l'Antiquité*, ed. H. Flashar and J. Jouanna. Geneva: Fondation Hardt, 1997: 297–322.

Nutton, V. "Greek Medical Astrology and the Boundaries of Medicine". In *Astro-Medicine: Astrology and Medicine, East and West*, ed. A. Akasoy, C. Burnett and R. Yoeli-Tlalim. Florence: Sismel, Edizioni del Galluzzo, 2008: 17–31.

Nutton, Vivian. *Ancient Medicine*. Abingdon, Oxon/New York, NY: Routledge, 2013[2].

Pennuto, C. "The Debate on Critical Days in Renaissance Italy". In *Astro-Medicine: Astrology and Medicine, East and West*, ed. A. Akasoy, C. Burnett and R. Yoeli-Tlalim. Florence: Sismel, Edizioni del Galluzzo, 2008: 75–98.

Pingree, D. "From Alexandria to Baghdād to Byzantium. The Transmission of Astrology". *International Journal of the Classical Tradition* 8.1, 2001: 3–37.

Quack, J. F. "Egypt as an astronomical-astrological centre between Mesopotamia, Greece, and India". In *The Interaction of Ancient Astral Science*, ed. D. Brown. Bremen: Hempen Verlag, 2018: 69–123.

Rutkin, H. D. "How to Accurately Account for Astrology's Marginalization in the History of Science and Culture: The Central Importance of an Interpretive Framework". *Early Science and Medicine* 23.3, 2018: 217–243.

Ryholt, K. "New Light on the Legendary King Nechepsos of Egypt". *The Journal of Egyptian Archaeology* 97, 2011: 61–72.

Shaw, G. *Theurgy and the Soul: The Neoplatonism of Iamblichus*. University Park, PA: The Pennsylvania State University Press, 1995.

Smith, J. E. "Time, Times and the 'Right Time': *Chronos* and *Kairos*". *The Monist* 53.1, 1969: 1–13.

Smith, J. E. "Time and Qualitative Time". *The Review of Metaphysics* 40.1, 1986: 3–16.

Smith, J. E. "Time and Qualitative Time". In *Rhetoric and* Kairos*: Essays in History, Theory and Praxis*, ed. P. Sipiora and J. S. Baumlin. Albany, NY: State University of New York Press, 2002: 46–57.

Theis, C. "Searching for a Source of the Coptic Hemerology: Diachronic and Synchronic Approaches". *Mythos* 16, 2016: 61–79.

Toomer, G. J. "Galen on the Astronomers and Astrologers". *Archive for History of Exact Sciences* 32.3/4, 1985: 193–206.

Vermij, R. and H. Hirai (eds.) "The Marginalization of Astrology". Special Issue, *Early Science and Medicine* 22.5/6, 2017: 405–520.

Willis, R. and P. Curry. *Astrology, Science and Culture: Pulling Down the Moon*. Oxford/New York: Berg, 2004.

Wilson, M. and D. George. "Anonymi, *de Decubitu*: Contexts of Rationality". *Mouseion* Series III, 6, 2006: 439–452.

Index of Passages Cited

General Index

Discussions of ancient authors' views and works can be found through the references in the Index of Passages Cited.

The following volumes have been published in this series:

Volume 2
Detel, Wolfgang. *Subjektive und objektive Zeit: Aristoteles und die moderne Zeit-Theorie*. Berlin/Boston: De Gruyter, 2021.

Volume 3
Singer, P. N. *Time for the Ancients: Measurement, Theory, Experience*. Berlin/Boston: De Gruyter, 2022.

Volume 4
Gertzen, Thomas L. *Aber die Zeit fürchtet die Pyramiden: Die Wissenschaften vom Alten Orient und die zeitliche Dimension von Kulturgeschichte*. Berlin/Boston: De Gruyter, 2022.

Volume 6
Zachhuber, Johannes. *Time and Soul: From Aristotle to St. Augustine*. Berlin/Boston: De Gruyter, 2022.

Volume 7
Golitsis, Pantelis. *Damascius' Philosophy of Time*. Berlin/Boston: De Gruyter, 2023.

Volume 8
Defaux, Olivier. *La Table des rois: Contribution à l'histoire textuelle des ›Tables faciles‹ de Ptolémée*. Berlin/Boston: De Gruyter, 2023.

Volume 9
Fischer, Julia (ed.). *Zwiegespräche über die Zeit: Dialoge in der Berlin-Brandenburgischen Akademie der Wissenschaften aus Anlass des sechzigsten Geburtstags von Christoph Markschies*. Berlin/Boston: De Gruyter, 2024.

Volume 10
Walter, Anke (ed.). *The Temporality of Festivals: Approaches to Festive Time in Ancient Babylon, Greece, Rome, and Medieval China*. Berlin/Boston: De Gruyter, 2024.

Volume 12
Sieroka, Norman. *Zeit-Hören: Erfahrungen, Taktungen, Musik*. Berlin/Boston: De Gruyter, 2024.

Volume 13
Birk, Ralph/Coulon, Laurent (eds.). *The Thebaid in Times of Crisis: Revolt and Response in Ptolemaic Egypt*. Berlin/Boston: De Gruyter, 2025.

Volume 14
Pallavidini, Marta. *(A)synchronic (Re)actions: Crises and Their Perception in Hittite History*. Berlin/Boston: De Gruyter, 2025.

Volume 15
Nosch, Marie-Louise Bech. *Time and Textiles in Ancient Greece*. Berlin/Boston: De Gruyter, 2025.

www.degruyterbrill.com

Volume 16
Klinger, Jörg. *Das Erfassen von Zeit im Kontext der Vergangenheit.* Berlin/Boston: De Gruyter, 2026.

Volume 17
Zachhuber, Johannes. *Time and History in Denis Pétau. Philosophy, Science, and Religion in Early Modern France.* Berlin/Boston: De Gruyter, 2026.

Volume 18
Ossendrijver, Mathieu. *Conceptions of Cyclicity in Babylonian and Greco-Roman Scholarship.* Berlin/Boston: De Gruyter, 2025.

Volume 19
Schumacher, Lydia. *From Eternal to Everlasting: God and Time in Franciscan Thought.* Berlin/Boston: De Gruyter, 2026.

Volume 20
Wiedemann, Felix. *The Modern Hammurapi: An Old Babylonian King in Imperial Germany.* Berlin/Boston: De Gruyter, 2026.

Volume 21
Niehoff, Maren R./Markschies, Christoph (eds.). *Aspects of Time in Jewish and Christian Exegesis.* Berlin/Boston: De Gruyter, 2026.

www.ingramcontent.com/pod-product-compliance
Lightning Source LLC
LaVergne TN
LVHW010901110826
845149LV00005B/1438